OFFICIAL SQA PAST PAPERS WITH ANSWERS

INTERMEDIATE 2

HISTORY
2009-2013

SQA

HODDER GIBSON
LEARN MORE

Hodder Gibson is grateful to the copyright holders, as credited on the final page of the Question Section, for permission to use their material. Every effort has been made to trace the copyright holders and to obtain their permission for the use of copyright material. Hodder Gibson will be happy to receive information allowing us to rectify any error or omission in future editions.

Hachette UK's policy is to use papers that are natural, renewable and recyclable products and made from wood grown in sustainable forests. The logging and manufacturing processes are expected to conform to the environmental regulations of the country of origin.

Orders: please contact Bookpoint Ltd, 130 Park Drive, Abingdon, Oxon OX14 4SE. Telephone: (44) 01235 827720. Fax: (44) 01235 400454.

Lines are open 9.00–5.00, Monday to Saturday, with a 24-hour message answering service. Visit our website at www.hoddereducation.co.uk. Hodder Gibson can be contacted direct on: Tel: 0141 848 1609; Fax: 0141 889 6315; email: hoddergibson@hodder.co.uk

This collection first published in 2013 by

Hodder Gibson, an imprint of Hodder Education,

An Hachette UK Company

2a Christie Street

Paisley PA1 1NB

{BrightRED   Hodder Gibson is grateful to Bright Red Publishing Ltd for collaborative work in preparation of this book and all SQA Past Paper and National 5 Model Paper titles 2013.

Typeset by PDQ Digital Media Solutions Ltd, Bungay, Suffolk NR35 1BY

Printed in the UK

A catalogue record for this title is available from the British Library

ISBN 978-1-4718-0255-3

3 2 1

2014 2013

Introduction

Study Skills – what you need to know to pass exams!

Pause for thought

Many students might skip quickly through a page like this. After all, we all know how to revise. Do you really though?

Think about this:

"IF YOU ALWAYS DO WHAT YOU ALWAYS DO, YOU WILL ALWAYS GET WHAT YOU HAVE ALWAYS GOT."

Do you like the grades you get? Do you want to do better? If you get full marks in your assessment, then that's great! Change nothing! This section is just to help you get that little bit better than you already are.

There are two main parts to the advice on offer here. The first part highlights fairly obvious things but which are also very important. The second part makes suggestions about revision that you might not have thought about but which WILL help you.

Part 1

DOH! It's so obvious but …

Start revising in good time

Don't leave it until the last minute – this will make you panic.

Make a revision timetable that sets out work time AND play time.

Sleep and eat!

Obvious really, and very helpful. Avoid arguments or stressful things too – even games that wind you up. You need to be fit, awake and focused!

Know your place!

Make sure you know exactly **WHEN and WHERE** your exams are.

Know your enemy!

Make sure you know what to expect in the exam.

How is the paper structured?

How much time is there for each question?

What types of question are involved?

Which topics seem to come up time and time again?

Which topics are your strongest and which are your weakest?

Are all topics compulsory or are there choices?

Learn by DOING!

There is no substitute for past papers and practice papers – they are simply essential! Tackling this collection of papers and answers is exactly the right thing to be doing as your exams approach.

Part 2

People learn in different ways. Some like low light, some bright. Some like early morning, some like evening / night. Some prefer warm, some prefer cold. But everyone uses their BRAIN and the brain works when it is active. Passive learning – sitting gazing at notes – is the most INEFFICIENT way to learn anything. Below you will find tips and ideas for making your revision more effective and maybe even more enjoyable. What follows gets your brain active, and active learning works!

Activity 1 – Stop and review

Step 1

When you have done no more than 5 minutes of revision reading STOP!

Step 2

Write a heading in your own words which sums up the topic you have been revising.

Step 3

Write a summary of what you have revised in no more than two sentences. Don't fool yourself by saying, 'I know it but I cannot put it into words'. That just means you don't know it well enough. If you cannot write your summary, revise that section again, knowing that you must write a summary at the end of it. Many of you will have notebooks full of blue/black ink writing. Many of the pages will not be especially attractive or memorable so try to liven them up a bit with colour as you are reviewing and rewriting. **This is a great memory aid, and memory is the most important thing.**

Activity 2 — Use technology!

Why should everything be written down? Have you thought about 'mental' maps, diagrams, cartoons and colour to help you learn? And rather than write down notes, why not record your revision material?

What about having a text message revision session with friends? Keep in touch with them to find out how and what they are revising and share ideas and questions.

Why not make a video diary where you tell the camera what you are doing, what you think you have learned and what you still have to do? No one has to see or hear it but the process of having to organise your thoughts in a formal way to explain something is a very important learning practice.

Be sure to make use of electronic files. You could begin to summarise your class notes. Your typing might be slow but it will get faster and the typed notes will be easier to read than the scribbles in your class notes. Try to add different fonts and colours to make your work stand out. You can easily Google relevant pictures, cartoons and diagrams which you can copy and paste to make your work more attractive and **MEMORABLE**.

Activity 3 – This is it. Do this and you will know lots!

Step 1

In this task you must be very honest with yourself! Find the SQA syllabus for your subject (www.sqa.org.uk). Look at how it is broken down into main topics called MANDATORY knowledge. That means stuff you MUST know.

Step 2

BEFORE you do ANY revision on this topic, write a list of everything that you already know about the subject. It might be quite a long list but you only need to write it once. It shows you all the information that is already in your long-term memory so you know what parts you do not need to revise!

Step 3

Pick a chapter or section from your book or revision notes. Choose a fairly large section or a whole chapter to get the most out of this activity.

With a buddy, use Skype, Facetime, Twitter or any other communication you have, to play the game "If this is the answer, what is the question?". For example, if you are revising Geography and the answer you provide is "meander", your buddy would have to make up a question like "What is the word that describes a feature of a river where it flows slowly and bends often from side to side?".

Make up 10 "answers" based on the content of the chapter or section you are using. Give this to your buddy to solve while you solve theirs.

Step 4

Construct a wordsearch of at least 10 X 10 squares. You can make it as big as you like but keep it realistic. Work together with a group of friends. Many apps allow you to make wordsearch puzzles online. The words and phrases can go in any direction and phrases can be split. Your puzzle must only contain facts linked to the topic you are revising. Your task is to find 10 bits of information to hide in your puzzle but you must not repeat information that you used in Step 3. DO NOT show where the words are. Fill up empty squares with random letters. Remember to keep a note of where your answers are hidden but do not show your friends. When you have a complete puzzle, exchange it with a friend to solve each other's puzzle.

Step 5

Now make up 10 questions (not "answers" this time) based on the same chapter used in the previous two tasks. Again, you must find NEW information that you have not yet used. Now it's getting hard to find that new information! Again, give your questions to a friend to answer.

Step 6

As you have been doing the puzzles, your brain has been actively searching for new information. Now write a NEW LIST that contains only the new information you have discovered when doing the puzzles. Your new list is the one to look at repeatedly for short bursts over the next few days. Try to remember more and more of it without looking at it. After a few days, you should be able to add words from your second list to your first list as you increase the information in your long-term memory.

FINALLY! Be inspired...

Make a list of different revision ideas and beside each one write **THINGS I HAVE** tried, **THINGS I WILL** try and **THINGS I MIGHT** try. Don't be scared of trying something new.

And remember – "FAIL TO PREPARE AND PREPARE TO FAIL!"

Intermediate 2 History

The course

The Intermediate 2 qualification in History gives you the opportunity to study the subject across a variety of time periods and places. You will be given an understanding of one or more important parts of Scottish and British history, as well as one or more parts of European and World history. You will gain skills in the understanding of key historical areas and be able to structure writing, support arguments with knowledge, analyse presented information and draw conclusions based on presented and recalled information. You will also learn how to research and present your findings, and evaluate and compare sources.

How the course is graded

The grade you finally get for Intermediate 2 History depends on three things:

- The internal assessments you do in school or college (the "NABs") – these don't count towards the final grade, but you must have passed them before you can achieve a final grade.

- Your Extended Response – this is an independent piece of research on an essay question that you have agreed with your teacher/lecturer. You will complete the essay in a one hour supervised write-up. The essay is submitted in April for marking by SQA and counts for 20 marks out of an overall total of 70.

- The exam you sit in May – that's what this book is all about!

Some things to think about...

There are a number of things that candidates should think about to produce effective answers. This section takes you through the process of the different types of questions.

The five mark 'describe' question

This question relies on your ability to recall knowledge as there is no source provided. You need to give at least five *developed* points that are relevant to the question asked. This means that you must provide specific and accurate detail in your answer, rather than being vague.

The 'explain' question

This question begins with '*Why*' you need to explain the reasons why something happened rather than describe what happened. You are provided with a source which will contain at least four points that you can identify. However, you cannot simply copy four statements from the source. You must put these into your own words –

you have to interpret what the source says. In addition, in order to obtain full marks, you need to add at least one point from your recalled knowledge. These recalled points must be relevant to the question asked.

The 'How useful' question

This question has proved to be the most difficult one for many candidates. It is based on a source and is preceded by a rubric which tells who wrote the source and when it was written, or drawn or photographed. You must use the rubric and the source, as well as recall, to obtain full marks. You will obtain one mark for commenting on key areas which evaluate the source. You should:

- comment on whether the source is a primary or secondary source, stating it was from a period when something relevant to the question was happening e.g. '*The source is useful because it is a primary source from 1902, a time of extensive poverty in Britain...*'.

- comment on the authorship of the source and why that makes the source useful, e.g. '*The source was written by Seebohm Rowntree who investigated the extent of poverty in York and published his findings...*'

- comment on the purpose of the source – why do you think it was produced?

- provide an example of the source's usefulness by stating a point of content from the source.

- try to suggest a point of omission from the source – what does it not tell you about the situation you are being asked about? This, of course, has to come from your own knowledge.

You may also comment on whether the source is biased though it is usual to link this to authorship. Remember that not every source is biased and you should therefore think carefully about the author and what the source actually says before you make a point about bias.

As you can see from the points above, there are more than enough opportunities to gain the maximum of four marks for this question.

The comparison question

The other type of source question is the comparison question, which asks you to determine agreement or disagreement between two sources. Answers to this type of question have improved greatly over the past five years or so. You should try to provide developed comparisons that state a general point of agreement / disagreement, and then support this with a statement from each of the two sources, e.g. *Sources A and B agree that the Nazis thought the Aryan race was superior to others.* This is the general point of agreement for which you would gain one mark. *Source A states that the Aryan people of northern Europe were superior in every way and Source B agrees by saying that the Aryans of Germany and Scandinavia were the Master Race.* This is the supporting statement. (This example is taken from the 2013 past paper, European and World context 12: The Road to War).

The extended response question

You should be aware that you must also do an extended response as part of the examination. This will need to be completed and sent to SQA before you sit the examination. You must choose your own question or issue from within the specified content for one of the three units you are studying.

You are allowed to take in a plan of no more than 150 words to the one-hour write-up session. You will be assessed on the quality of your introduction and conclusion, your knowledge and your argument. It is very important that you choose your issue carefully. You need to have an issue which will lead you into an argument and then a balanced conclusion. A general statement such as "The Liberal Reforms" will not do this. This will simply lead to a description of the reforms and you will be unlikely to pass. A better question would be

"Explain why the Liberal Government passed social reforms between 1906 and 1914". Better still would be "Were the reports of Booth and Rowntree the main reason why the Liberal Government passed social reforms between 1906 and 1914?" This question allows you to argue the case for this, but also to consider other possibilities, such as the need to provide fit men for the defence of the country and for industry, the need for the Liberals to ensure the new Labour Party did not take votes from them and the need for reform to help those who were desperately poor. This would lead you to evaluate the importance of each part and to summarise and provide a clear answer in your conclusion.

You are allowed support from your teacher/lecturer for your extended response and you should make sure you consult them about your chosen issue. They may be able to make suggestions about what you should read and how you can develop your plan.

Good luck!

History is an interesting and rewarding subject to study. The skills that History teaches are useful in showing us how to structure writing and be critical of evidence. In the exam, think before you put pen to paper. You will have worked hard to get to this stage. Don't Panic! Keep calm, answer the questions and do the best that you can. GOOD LUCK!

[BLANK PAGE]

X044/201

NATIONAL QUALIFICATIONS 2009	TUESDAY, 2 JUNE 9.00 AM – 10.45 AM	HISTORY INTERMEDIATE 2

The instructions for this paper are on *Page two*. Read them carefully before you begin your answers. Some sources in this examination have been adapted or translated.

XSQA

PB X044/201 6/11420

INSTRUCTIONS

Answer **one** question from Part 1, The Short Essay

Answer **one** context* from Part 2, Scottish and British

Answer **one** context* from Part 3, European and World

Answer **one** other context* from

       either   Part 2, Scottish and British

       or   Part 3, European and World

*Answer all the questions in each of your chosen contexts.

Contents

[Turn over

PART 1: THE SHORT ESSAY

Marks

Answer **one** question. For this question you should write a short essay using your own knowledge. The essay should include an introduction, development and conclusion. Each question is worth 8 marks.

SCOTTISH AND BRITISH CONTEXTS:

CONTEXT 1: MURDER IN THE CATHEDRAL: CROWN, CHURCH AND PEOPLE, 1154–1173

Question 1: Explain why knights were important in the twelfth century.   **8**

CONTEXT 2: WALLACE, BRUCE AND THE WARS OF INDEPENDENCE, 1286–1328

Question 2: Explain why John Balliol lost his position as King of Scots in 1296.   **8**

CONTEXT 3: MARY, QUEEN OF SCOTS AND THE SCOTTISH REFORMATION, 1540S–1587

Question 3: Explain why Mary, Queen of Scots, faced difficulties ruling Scotland when she returned in 1561.   **8**

CONTEXT 4: THE COMING OF THE CIVIL WAR, 1603–1642

Question 4: Explain why there were problems between Crown and Parliament during the reign of James VI and I.   **8**

CONTEXT 5: "ANE END OF ANE AULD SANG": SCOTLAND AND THE TREATY OF UNION, 1690S–1715

Question 5: Explain why there was so much opposition to a Union in Scotland before 1707.   **8**

CONTEXT 6: IMMIGRANTS AND EXILES: SCOTLAND, 1830S–1930S

Question 6: Explain why Scots emigrants made a valuable contribution in Canada and the United States.   **8**

CONTEXT 7(A): FROM THE CRADLE TO THE GRAVE? SOCIAL WELFARE IN BRITAIN, 1890S–1951

Question 7(*a*): Explain why the Liberal reforms, 1906–1914, failed to solve the problems of the poor.   **8**

Marks

CONTEXT 7(B): CAMPAIGNING FOR CHANGE: SOCIAL CHANGE IN SCOTLAND, 1900S–1979

Question 7(b): Explain why many industries in Scotland experienced problems in the years between the two world wars.

8

CONTEXT 8: A TIME OF TROUBLES: IRELAND, 1900–1923

Question 8: Explain why support for Sinn Fein increased after 1916.

8

EUROPEAN AND WORLD CONTEXTS:

CONTEXT 1: THE NORMAN CONQUEST, 1060–1153

Question 9: Explain why David I introduced feudalism to Scotland.

8

CONTEXT 2: THE CROSS AND THE CRESCENT: THE FIRST CRUSADE, 1096–1125

Question 10: Explain why Pope Urban II called the First Crusade.

8

CONTEXT 3: WAR, DEATH AND REVOLT IN MEDIEVAL EUROPE, 1328–1436

Question 11: Explain why the Hundred Years' War broke out between England and France in 1337.

8

CONTEXT 4: NEW WORLDS: EUROPE IN THE AGE OF EXPANSION, 1480S–1530S

Question 12: Explain why European countries wanted to search for new lands between the 1480s and 1530s.

8

CONTEXT 5: "TEA AND FREEDOM": THE AMERICAN REVOLUTION, 1763–1783

Question 13: Explain why the colonists won the American War of Independence.

8

CONTEXT 6: "THIS ACCURSED TRADE": THE BRITISH SLAVE TRADE AND ITS ABOLITION, 1770–1807

Question 14: Explain why there was increasing support for the campaign against the slave trade by the 1780s.

8

Marks

CONTEXT 7: CITIZENS!
THE FRENCH REVOLUTION, 1789–1794

Question 15:   Explain why few French people supported Louis XVI in 1789.

8

CONTEXT 8: CAVOUR, GARIBALDI
AND THE MAKING OF ITALY, 1815–1870

Question 16:   Explain why Cavour was important to Italian unification.

8

CONTEXT 9: IRON AND BLOOD? BISMARCK AND THE
CREATION OF THE GERMAN EMPIRE, 1815–1871

Question 17:   Explain why Bismarck's leadership was important to the unification of the German states.

8

CONTEXT 10: THE RED FLAG:
LENIN AND THE RUSSIAN REVOLUTION, 1894–1921

Question 18:   Explain why the Reds won the Civil War.

8

CONTEXT 11: FREE AT LAST?
RACE RELATIONS IN THE USA, 1918–1968

Question 19:   Explain why black people rioted in many American cities in the 1960s.

8

CONTEXT 12: THE ROAD TO WAR, 1933–1939

Question 20:   Explain why events after Munich, September 1938, led to the outbreak of war in 1939.

8

CONTEXT 13: IN THE SHADOW OF THE BOMB:
THE COLD WAR, 1945–1985

Question 21:   Explain why the USA became involved in a crisis over Cuba in 1962.

8

[END OF PART 1: THE SHORT ESSAY]

[Turn over for PART 2: SCOTTISH AND BRITISH CONTEXTS on *Page eight*

PART 2:

HISTORICAL STUDY: SCOTTISH AND BRITISH

Marks

**CONTEXT 1: MURDER IN THE
CATHEDRAL: CROWN, CHURCH
AND PEOPLE, 1154–1173**

Answer the following questions using recalled knowledge and information from the sources where appropriate.

Source A was written in 1177 by Peter of Blois, Henry II's secretary.

Source A

> Every day the king travels around his kingdom. He never rests and works tirelessly to make sure that his people are at peace. On occasion, he attacks the barons but this is only so that the law of the country can be upheld. No one is more honest, more polite and more generous to the poor than the king. He is truly loved by his people.

1. How useful is **Source A** as evidence of the character of Henry II?   **4**

2. Describe the life of a monk in medieval times.   **5**

Source B explains why Henry II and Archbishop Becket quarrelled.

Source B

> Henry II appointed Thomas Becket as Archbishop of Canterbury in 1162. Almost immediately their friendship was tested when Becket resigned as Chancellor. Until then Becket had been a loyal servant, so this action stunned the king. Becket then refused to sign the Constitutions of Clarendon and would not agree to reduce the power of the Church. When summoned to appear at the Northampton trial, Becket fled to France without the king's permission. He remained there for six years protected by the king of France.

3. Why did Henry II and Archbishop Becket quarrel? (Use **Source B** and recall.)   **5**

[END OF CONTEXT 1]

Marks

HISTORICAL STUDY: SCOTTISH AND BRITISH

CONTEXT 2: WALLACE, BRUCE
AND THE WARS OF
INDEPENDENCE, 1286–1328

Answer the following questions using recalled knowledge and information from the sources where appropriate.

Source A was written by a Scottish chronicler some time after the death of Alexander III in 1286.

Source A

> On 19th March, the king was delayed by the ferry at South Queensferry until dusk on a dark, stormy night. When advised by his companions not to go beyond Inverkeithing that night, he rejected their advice and with an escort of knights he hurried along a very steep track towards Kinghorn. To the west of that place, his horse stumbled and he was killed.

1. How useful is **Source A** as evidence about the death of King Alexander III? **4**

2. Describe what happened at the Battle of Stirling Bridge. **5**

Source B explains why the Scots sent the Declaration of Arbroath to the Pope in 1320.

Source B

> In the years after Bannockburn, although Bruce controlled Scotland, he was not accepted internationally as its king. Earlier efforts to gain recognition by invading the north of England had failed. They had only annoyed Edward. The Scots then tried to increase the pressure on Edward by invading Ireland, but this ended in disaster when Edward Bruce was killed in 1318. When they sent the declaration to the Pope in 1320, they hoped he would recognise Bruce as king.

3. Why did the Scots send the Declaration of Arbroath to the Pope in 1320? (Use **Source B** and recall.) **5**

[END OF CONTEXT 2]

Marks

HISTORICAL STUDY: SCOTTISH AND BRITISH

> ### CONTEXT 3: MARY, QUEEN OF SCOTS AND THE SCOTTISH REFORMATION, 1540s–1587

Answer the following questions using recalled knowledge and information from the sources where appropriate.

Source A explains why Protestantism spread in Scotland in the 1540s and 1550s.

Source A

> In Germany, the ideas of Martin Luther had started the Reformation movement. Some Scots began questioning the teachings of the Catholic Church. During the Rough Wooing, English invaders had encouraged this by distributing English translations of the Bible so people could study the Bible for themselves. The Catholic Church continued to use the Latin Bible. Religious pamphlets, smuggled into Scotland from Europe, also spread Protestant ideas. The "Good and Godly Ballads" made these ideas popular. Protestantism began to spread more quickly in Scotland.

1. Why did Protestantism spread in Scotland in the 1540s and 1550s? (Use **Source A** and recall.)   **5**

2. Describe the events surrounding the murder of Darnley in 1567.   **5**

Source B is part of a letter written by Mary, Queen of Scots, to Queen Elizabeth in 1582.

Source B

> While I was in Scotland, my subjects were encouraged to speak, act and finally to rebel against me by the agents, spies and secret messengers sent there in your name. I do not have any specific proof of that except for the confession of one person whom you rewarded very generously for his hard work at that time.

3. How useful is **Source B** as evidence of Mary's opinion of Queen Elizabeth?   **4**

[END OF CONTEXT 3]

Marks

HISTORICAL STUDY: SCOTTISH AND BRITISH

CONTEXT 4: THE COMING OF THE CIVIL WAR, 1603–1642

Answer the following questions using recalled knowledge and information from the sources where appropriate.

Source A is from "A Concise History of Scotland" by Fitzroy McLean, published in 1974.

Source A

> The new service book was read for the first time in St Giles on 23 July 1637 amid scenes of violence which soon developed into a riot. Tradition says the females of the congregation played a leading part, egged on by a certain Jenny Geddes. Before long, the Privy Council were forced to shut themselves in Holyroodhouse to escape the mob.

1. How useful is **Source A** as evidence of how the Scots reacted to Charles I's introduction of the Common Prayer Book in 1637?   **4**

Source B explains why Charles I became unpopular in England between 1629 and 1640.

Source B

> Since the Middle Ages, only people who lived near the coast had to pay Ship Money. In 1635 Charles I made people from inland areas pay Ship Money tax as well. There were strong objections because the king had imposed this new tax without the consent of Parliament. He also fined people who had built on common land, or in royal forests. Anyone who refused to pay was tried in special courts. The king was seen as a tyrant. People turned against him.

2. Explain why Charles I became unpopular in England between 1629 and 1640. (Use **Source B** and recall.)   **5**

3. Describe the events between 1640 and 1642 which led to the outbreak of the Civil War.   **5**

[END OF CONTEXT 4]

Marks

HISTORICAL STUDY: SCOTTISH AND BRITISH

CONTEXT 5: "ANE END OF ANE AULD SANG": SCOTLAND AND THE TREATY OF UNION, 1690s–1715

Answer the following questions using recalled knowledge and information from the sources where appropriate.

Source A is a public notice published by the Directors of the Company of Scotland in 1698.

Source A

> The Court of Directors now have ships ready and loaded with provisions and all manner of things needed for their intended expedition to settle a colony in the Indies. They give notice that to encourage people to go on this expedition, they promise to give them fifty acres of good ground to grow their crops.

1. How useful is **Source A** as evidence about Scottish preparations for the Darien Expedition? **4**

Source B explains why many Scottish nobles agreed to the Act of Union.

Source B

> The Scottish nobility has been criticised for "betraying" Scotland at the time of the Union. There was, however, a considerable effort put into convincing them of the wealth which a Union would bring to Scotland. They would prosper by having access to England's colonies and after the Union many did invest in the sugar trade of the West Indies. Besides, a Union would guarantee the Protestant Succession and its supporters would gain both royal approval and the benefits it brought.

2. Why did many Scottish nobles agree to the Act of Union? (Use **Source B** and recall.) **5**

3. In what ways did Scotland change as a result of the Act of Union? **5**

[END OF CONTEXT 5]

Marks

HISTORICAL STUDY: SCOTTISH AND BRITISH

> **CONTEXT 6: IMMIGRANTS AND EXILES: SCOTLAND, 1830s–1930s**

Answer the following questions using recalled knowledge and information from the sources where appropriate.

Source A is evidence given to a government enquiry in 1836 by a Catholic priest in Aberdeen.

Source A

> The number of cotton and linen factories in Aberdeen has continued to grow since the Irish people were encouraged to come to us. Finding work is easy and fairly good wages are offered to them in these factories. A considerable number of Irish people have come to the city and have brought their families with them.

1. How useful is **Source A** as evidence of the reasons Irish people came to Scotland after 1830?   4

2. Describe the experience of Irish immigrants in the west of Scotland.   5

Source B explains why many Scots emigrated overseas in the twentieth century.

Source B

> Mr Macdonald, the headmaster, said that he had faith in Canada. Many of his best pupils who were now living in Canada were succeeding. This was obvious from the money and letters they sent home to their parents. He then introduced the Canadian immigration agent, who spoke first in Gaelic and then in English. He said Canada was a huge country which offered great opportunities for farming. He enthusiastically praised the country as he showed view after view of scenes of Canada on the screen.

3. Why did many Scots emigrate overseas in the twentieth century? (Use **Source B** and recall.)   5

[END OF CONTEXT 6]

HISTORICAL STUDY: SCOTTISH AND BRITISH

Marks

CONTEXT 7(a): FROM THE CRADLE TO THE GRAVE? SOCIAL WELFARE IN BRITAIN, 1890s–1951

Answer the following questions using recalled knowledge and information from the sources where appropriate.

Source A comments on changing attitudes towards poverty.

Source A

> By the start of the twentieth century, attitudes towards the poor in Britain were changing. Trade unions felt the Liberals and Conservatives did not do enough for the poor. There was also a growth in Socialist thinking which felt very strongly that a high level of poverty was wrong. The Labour Party was formed in 1900. It stood for practical reforms to tackle poverty. The Labour Party threatened to take support away from the Liberals. Frightened by this, the Liberals began to think of ways to help the poor.

1. Why did attitudes towards poverty change in the early twentieth century? (Use **Source A** and recall.)   **5**

Source B is a cartoon from the Daily Herald newspaper in 1942.

Source B

2. How useful is **Source B** as evidence of the ideas in the Beveridge Report?   **4**

3. Describe the reforms introduced by Labour after 1945 to improve the lives of the British people.   **5**

[END OF CONTEXT 7(a)]

HISTORICAL STUDY: SCOTTISH AND BRITISH   *Marks*

> ### CONTEXT 7(b): CAMPAIGNING FOR CHANGE: SOCIAL CHANGE IN SCOTLAND, 1900s–1979

Answer the following questions using recalled knowledge and information from the sources where appropriate.

1. Describe the ways sport became more popular in Scotland between 1900 and 1939.   **5**

Source A explains why women had not gained the right to vote by 1914.

Source A

> In the years before the Great War, the government had a number of problems to deal with and did not regard votes for women as very important. In addition, the Prime Minister, Mr Asquith, was personally opposed to giving women the franchise. Emmeline Pankhurst founded the Women's Social and Political Union even though most men believed that women should not get involved in politics. When women began militant actions such as breaking shop windows, they were accused of being irresponsible.

2. Why had women not gained the right to vote by 1914? (Use **Source A** and recall.)   **5**

Source B is a photograph of a class being taught to wash clothes in a Dundee school in 1938.

Source B

3. How useful is **Source B** as evidence of the way Scottish children were educated in the 1930s?   **4**

[END OF CONTEXT 7(b)]

Marks

HISTORICAL STUDY: SCOTTISH AND BRITISH

CONTEXT 8: A TIME OF
TROUBLES: IRELAND, 1900–1923

Answer the following questions using recalled knowledge and information from the sources where appropriate.

Source A explains why the Ulster Unionists were against Home Rule for Ireland.

Source A

> Unionists knew that the Home Rule Bill could not be defeated in parliament. The Unionists argued that Home Rule would destroy their way of life. Ulster was far richer than the rest of Ireland and many believed that they would be forced into poverty if the law was accepted. Led by MPs such as Edward Carson, as many as 50,000 Unionists attended meetings in Belfast. They were afraid that Ulster would be isolated from the Empire and that the Protestant Church could be weakened.

1. Why were the Ulster Unionists against Home Rule for Ireland? (Use **Source A** and recall.)   **5**

Source B is a poster produced by the Irish National Party in 1915.

Source B

2. How useful is **Source B** as evidence of Irish Nationalists' attitudes towards the First World War?   **4**

3. Describe the Civil War which broke out in Ireland in 1922.   **5**

[END OF CONTEXT 8]

[END OF PART 2: SCOTTISH AND BRITISH CONTEXTS]

Marks

PART 3:

HISTORICAL STUDY: EUROPEAN AND WORLD

> ### CONTEXT 1: THE NORMAN CONQUEST, 1060–1153

Answer the following questions using recalled knowledge and information from the sources where appropriate.

Sources **A** and **B** are about Earl Harold's right to become King of England in 1066.

Source A

> King Edward died in London having reigned for twenty three years. The next day he was buried amid the bitter grieving of all present. After the burial, Harold, whom Edward had nominated as his rightful successor, was chosen as King by all the powerful lords of England and on the same day was crowned legitimately and with great ceremony by Aldred, Archbishop of York.

Source B

> Harold did not wait for public support but broke the oath he had taken to support William's rightful claim to the throne. With the help of a few of his supporters, he seized the throne on the day of Edward's funeral at the very time when all the people were mourning their loss. He was illegally crowned by Stigund of Canterbury, who had been excommunicated by the Pope.

1. How far do **Sources A** and **B** disagree about Harold's right to be King of England?   **4**

2. Describe the methods used by William to increase his royal authority.   **5**

Source C explains why there was an increase in the number of abbeys and monasteries in Scotland.

Source C

> David was the youngest son of the saintly Queen Margaret and was very religious. He began a building of abbeys and monasteries such as would never be known again in Scotland. Much of the wealth that David gained from his burghs was poured into these great new projects. David encouraged his nobles to leave land to the church. Master craftsmen were brought from England and France. The kingdom was alive with a new spirit and his work was carried on by the kings that followed.

3. Why did the number of abbeys and monasteries in Scotland increase during the reign of David I? (Use **Source C** and recall.)   **5**

[END OF CONTEXT 1]

Marks

HISTORICAL STUDY: EUROPEAN AND WORLD

> **CONTEXT 2: THE CROSS AND THE CRESCENT: THE FIRST CRUSADE, 1096–1125**

Answer the following questions using recalled knowledge and information from the sources where appropriate.

Source A explains why the Peoples' Crusade failed.

Source A

> After months of travelling, Peter the Hermit arrived at Constantinople. The journey had been difficult and many in his army had already been killed. Emperor Alexius warned the Crusaders not to attack the Muslims but to wait for the knights. The Crusaders were eager to get to Jerusalem and so ignored this advice. Soon afterwards, the Crusaders began arguing amongst themselves. They elected their own leaders and no longer listened to Peter the Hermit. In despair he left the Crusade and returned to Constantinople.

1. Why did the Peoples' Crusade fail? (Use **Source A** and recall.)   5

2. Describe the capture of Nicaea by the First Crusade.   5

Sources B and **C** describe the Crusaders' victory at Antioch.

Source B

> Kerbogha and the Muslim forces attacked the Crusaders the minute they left the city. Bohemond led the Crusaders and organised the knights. Without his leadership they would have been defeated. Although they were tired and hungry, they continued to fight. The Muslims were brave and did not give up. Eventually the Crusaders forced them to flee the battlefield and won a great victory.

Source C

> Although the Muslim forces surrounded Antioch, they did not attack the Crusaders when they left the city. Bohemond commanded the army but could not organise his knights and was nearly defeated. The Crusaders were only victorious because the Muslims did not respect Kerbogha. They refused to fight and fled the battlefield. Their cowardly behaviour meant the Muslims lost the battle.

3. How far do **Sources B** and **C** disagree about the Crusaders' victory at Antioch?   4

[END OF CONTEXT 2]

Marks

HISTORICAL STUDY: EUROPEAN AND WORLD

CONTEXT 3: WAR, DEATH AND REVOLT IN MEDIEVAL EUROPE, 1328–1436

Answer the following questions using recalled knowledge and information from the sources where appropriate.

Source A explains why the Black Death spread across Europe in the fourteenth century.

Source A

> When a rat died of plague its fleas would leave and carry the disease to humans. This happened because humans and rats lived close together. Trading ships were often infested with rats. If these rats died of plague their fleas could give it to sailors and the people in the ports. A ship would therefore carry the plague until the sailors died of it. Diseased rats could also get into merchants' wagons and be carried across the country. This explanation of the spread of the plague is called the trade route theory.

1. Why did the Black Death spread across Europe in the fourteenth century? (Use **Source A** and recall.)   5

Sources B and **C** describe the role of Henry V in the Hundred Years' War.

Source B

> Henry V was the last great Plantagenet king. He believed strongly in his right to the French throne and convinced many Frenchmen that his cause was just. His great speech to his archers before Agincourt inspired victory. He was a leader who expected discipline from others and showed great self-discipline himself. However, under the stress of war he could become cruel towards his defeated enemies.

Source C

> Henry had no right to the crown of France. He had no right to that of England either. According to the legend, the war with France showed Henry's military genius. Really, it was a story of gambler's luck. The superior French army got stuck in the mud at Agincourt. At Agincourt, he was a war criminal, massacring prisoners in defiance of the conventions of war.

2. How far do **Sources B** and **C** disagree about the role of Henry V in the Hundred Years' War?   4

3. What part did Joan of Arc play in reawakening French national pride?   5

[END OF CONTEXT 3]

Marks

HISTORICAL STUDY: EUROPEAN AND WORLD

> **CONTEXT 4: NEW WORLDS:**
> **EUROPE IN THE AGE OF**
> **EXPANSION, 1480s–1530s**

Answer the following questions using recalled knowledge and information from the sources where appropriate.

Source A is about shipbuilding and navigation.

Source A

> The Age of Exploration was possible because of new inventions. The most important of these inventions was the carrack. This ship had a lateen sail which made ships faster and far more manouverable. Longer journeys were possible which encouraged European rulers to search for new lands. Astrolabes helped sailors identify their location at sea. The development of log lines helped sailors calculate their speed and longitude. A great deal of expansion was then achieved in just fifty years.

1. Why did developments in shipbuilding and navigation make voyages of exploration easier between the 1480s and 1530s? (Use **Source A** and recall.)   **5**

Sources B and **C** describe Columbus's arrival in the New World.

Source B

> They arrived at a small island. Soon the local people came to watch them. The Admiral went on shore with Vicente Yanez, the captain of the Nina. The Admiral called to the two captains and to the others who leaped on shore, and said that they should bear faithful testimony that he had taken possession of the said island for the King and Queen. He presented the natives with red caps and strings of beads to wear upon the neck.

Source C

> After a voyage of more than two months the fleet sighted land. On 12th October Columbus set foot in the New World. Watched by naked, silent natives, he took control of the island in the name of the King and Queen of Spain and gave thanks to God. Gifts were exchanged with the natives. Columbus believed they were somewhere in the Indies, near Cipangu.

2. How far do **Sources B** and **C** agree about what happened when Christopher Columbus first arrived in the New World?   **4**

3. Describe the exploration of North America up to 1540.   **5**

[END OF CONTEXT 4]

Marks

HISTORICAL STUDY: EUROPEAN AND WORLD

> ### CONTEXT 5: "TEA AND FREEDOM": THE AMERICAN REVOLUTION, 1763–1783

Answer the following questions using recalled knowledge and information from the sources where appropriate.

Source A is about the colonists' relationship with Britain.

Source A

> Many colonists were suffering as trade was poor and they believed the British government was responsible. Despite this, the Americans hoped that the economy would soon improve. However, Granville, a British government minister, introduced tough trade policies which made things worse. Consequently, the colonists saw British naval officers and customs men as greedy and unwanted. They represented a distant and unsympathetic government. This helped push many well-to-do colonists towards opposition to Britain and increased the likelihood of armed rebellion.

1. Why were many colonists unhappy with British rule by 1776? (Use **Source A** and recall.)   **5**

Sources B and **C** are about the American forces which fought against the British army.

Source B

> The Revolutionary War was waged by small armies. The American forces were often led by inefficient, even incompetent, commanders who fought muddled campaigns. The men gathering in Boston were enthusiastic but badly armed and lacking supplies. The American commander, George Washington, could rely on no more than 5000 regular soldiers. Most men were part-time and served for only a few months. Britain's professional army was larger but not large enough to subdue the Americans.

Source C

> Many officers who led the American forces were not trained in the different types of warfare. The whole army was short of artillery, cavalry and almost all sorts of supplies. Within each state there were part-time soldiers. Many were militiamen who met and trained in their spare time and, although they did not have a uniform, they still came to fight for their country's freedom.

2. To what extent do **Sources B** and **C** agree about the condition of the American army?   **4**

3. Describe the events leading up to the British surrender at Saratoga in 1777.   **5**

[END OF CONTEXT 5]

Marks

HISTORICAL STUDY: EUROPEAN AND WORLD

> CONTEXT 6: "THIS ACCURSED
> TRADE": THE BRITISH SLAVE TRADE
> AND ITS ABOLITION, 1770–1807

Answer the following questions using recalled knowledge and information from the sources where appropriate.

1. Describe conditions for slaves during the Middle Passage.   5

Sources A and **B** describe slave auctions in the West Indies.

Source A

> Slaves were treated in most cases like cattle. A man went about the country buying up slaves and he was called a "speculator". Then he would sell them to the highest bidder. Oh! It was pitiful to see children taken from their mothers' breasts, mothers sold, husbands sold to a different owner than their wives. One woman had a baby and he wouldn't buy the baby.

Source B

> The slave master made us hold up our heads while customers felt our hands and arms and looked at our teeth, precisely as someone examines a horse which he is about to purchase. All the time the auction was going on one mother was crying aloud. She begged the man not to buy her son unless he also bought her; but the boy was sold on his own to the man who offered the most money.

2. How far do **Sources A** and **B** agree about what happened during slave auctions?   4

Source C explains why people were in favour of the slave trade.

Source C

> The slave trade continued to be defended by businessmen who made large profits from it. Evidence from Bristol and Liverpool indicated that profits of 30 per cent from slave voyages were common. The Triangular Trade linked Britain, West Africa and the Caribbean. The Triangular Trade also helped Britain's industrial development. In Manchester, for example, it was said to have helped the growth in manufacturing. Work was provided for many at the port of Liverpool.

3. Why were some people in favour of the slave trade? (Use **Source C** and recall.)   5

[END OF CONTEXT 6]

Marks

HISTORICAL STUDY: EUROPEAN AND WORLD

CONTEXT 7: CITIZENS! THE
FRENCH REVOLUTION, 1789–1794

Answer the following questions using recalled knowledge and information from the sources where appropriate.

1. Describe the changes introduced by the Legislative Assembly in 1791.   **5**

Source A describes the growth of feeling against the monarchy in France in 1792.

Source A

> Although Louis had been allowed to live comfortably in his palace he made no secret that he disliked having to share power with the Legislative Assembly. He supported war with Austria hoping that French defeat would restore his royal authority. The radicals imprisoned the king and his family after the storming of the Tuileries. Louis rejected the advice of moderate advisors to fully implement the Constitution of 1791. By then many people suspected that Louis was privately encouraging counter-revolution.

2. Why was there growing dislike of the monarchy in France in 1792? (Use **Source A** and recall.)   **5**

Sources B and **C** describe the events of September 1792 which came to be known as the September Massacres.

Source B

> On August 10th 1792, Danton's supporters seized control and set up the Commune which became the real power in Paris. Danton gave a violent speech encouraging the Paris mobs to rise up. The sans-culottes attacked the prisons which they believed were secretly sheltering enemies of the revolution. They killed about one and a half thousand people. Street fights continued and barricades were set up all over the city.

Source C

> The news of the invasion of France by the Prussian army led to panic in Paris. Working class people began rioting, believing they were defending the revolution. From the night of September 2nd, in three prisons in Paris at least fifteen hundred women, priests and soldiers were brutally murdered. Although Danton condemned the massacres, he must take the blame for having stirred up the sans-culottes.

3. How far do **Sources B** and **C** agree about the events of the September Massacres in Paris in 1792?   **4**

[END OF CONTEXT 7]

Marks

HISTORICAL STUDY: EUROPEAN AND WORLD

> **CONTEXT 8: CAVOUR, GARIBALDI AND THE MAKING OF ITALY, 1815–1870**

Answer the following questions using recalled knowledge and information from the sources where appropriate.

1. Describe the growth of nationalism in Italy between 1815 and 1847.   **5**

Sources A and **B** describe the events of the 1848 revolutions in Milan and Naples.

Source A

> Early in the year trouble broke out in Milan. The sight of Austrian soldiers smoking in the streets was an excuse for the people to show their dislike of the troops. Small-scale fights broke out, quickly followed by larger riots and eventually by a full scale revolution. The Austrian commander decided to withdraw his troops from the area. The revolutionaries set up a provisional government and prepared to continue the fight against Austria.

Source B

> There were clashes between the people and the troops in Naples. Arms were handed out to the townspeople and the next day protest grew as peasants from outside the city arrived to join the rising. The army replied by shelling the city and two days later reinforcements of 5000 troops arrived. Despite this, by April the revolutionaries had taken over. The middle and upper-class nationalists set up a provisional government.

2. How far do **Sources A** and **B** agree about the events of the 1848 revolutions in the Italian cities?   **4**

Source C describes the importance of Garibaldi.

Source C

> As a military leader Garibaldi was a good, sometimes brilliant, commander, excellent at sizing up the situation. He inspired great enthusiasm and devotion in his men. His conquest of the south was a remarkable achievement. His chance meeting with Mazzini in 1833 gave him a cause to fight for. All Garibaldi's actions can be explained by his total devotion to the idea of Italian unity. It became the driving obsession of his life.

3. Why was Garibaldi important to the unification of Italy in 1861? (Use **Source C** and recall.)   **5**

[END OF CONTEXT 8]

Marks

HISTORICAL STUDY: EUROPEAN AND WORLD

CONTEXT 9: IRON AND BLOOD? BISMARCK AND THE CREATION OF THE GERMAN EMPIRE, 1815–1871

Answer the following questions using recalled knowledge and information from the sources where appropriate.

Sources A and **B** describe actions against the student movement in Germany in the early nineteenth century.

Source A

> At a student demonstration an Austrian spy was murdered. The Austrian government was determined to prevent further incidents. At a meeting of the Confederation of Carlsbad in 1819, it was agreed to set up inspectors to oversee the universities. In addition to this, student organisations were outlawed. In most German states a strict press censorship was enforced. The effect of the decrees was the dismissal of a number of professors.

Source B

> The first sign of nationalist feeling occurred in the Students' Unions in the universities. Metternich and the Austrian government were determined to stop this. At a meeting of the Confederation at Carlsbad in 1819, decrees were passed which suppressed the student societies, causing many university teachers to be dismissed. Student societies re-emerged in the 1830s. Flags of black, red and gold came to symbolise liberal ideas.

1. How far do **Sources A** and **B** agree about the actions taken against the student movement?   **4**

Source C is about the growth of nationalism in the German states.

Source C

> The folk tales of the Brothers Grimm celebrated Germany's past and looked forward to the day when it would at last be one nation. United by language, it was felt by many that the German states should also be united by the same government. By 1836, twenty five of the thirty nine German states had joined the Zollverein. The development of the railways in the 1830s and 1840s had made the German states co-operate, ending their isolation from one another. By 1850 over 3000 miles of railways had been laid.

2. Why did nationalism grow within the German states between 1815 and 1850? (Use **Source C** and recall.)   **5**

3. Describe the events leading to Austria's defeat by Prussia in 1866.   **5**

[END OF CONTEXT 9]

HISTORICAL STUDY: EUROPEAN AND WORLD

Marks

CONTEXT 10: THE RED FLAG:
LENIN AND THE RUSSIAN
REVOLUTION, 1894–1921

Answer the following questions using recalled knowledge and information from the sources where appropriate.

Source A is about the outbreak of the 1905 Revolution.

Source A

> By 1905 there was a growing desire to overthrow the repressive government of Nicholas II. There was a great deal of poverty in the cities and the countryside. The revolutionary movement gained strength following Russia's humiliating defeat by Japan. In January an uprising to remove the Tsar began. The non-Russian areas of the empire witnessed violent disturbances. Revolutionary groups became much more organised. They formed a soviet in St Petersburg. A soviet was a type of worker's parliament.

1. Why was there a revolution in Russia in 1905? (Use **Source A** and recall.)   **5**

2. Describe the effects of the First World War on the Russian people.   **5**

In **Sources B** and **C**, Bolshevik leaders argue about the decision to call a revolution in October 1917.

Source B is from a letter by Lenin.

Source B

> The Bolsheviks can and must take state power immediately into their own hands. They can do so because revolutionary elements in Petrograd and Moscow are now very strong. We can and must overcome our opponents' resistance and gain power. By promising peace and land we will be able to form a government that no-one will be able to overthrow. The majority of the people are on our side. By seizing power in Moscow and Petrograd we shall win absolutely and unquestionably.

Source C is from a letter by two Bolsheviks, Kamenev and Zinoviev.

Source C

> We are convinced that to call an uprising now would put the party and the revolution at risk. Our party is strong but the workers and soldiers are not ready to take to the streets now. The right mood does not exist. The party must be given time to grow. An uprising now will destroy what we have already achieved. We raise a voice against this ruinous policy.

3. How far do **Sources B** and **C** disagree about the decision to call a revolution in October 1917?   **4**

[END OF CONTEXT 10]

Marks

HISTORICAL STUDY: EUROPEAN AND WORLD

> ### CONTEXT 11: FREE AT LAST? RACE RELATIONS IN THE USA, 1918–1968

Answer the following questions using recalled knowledge and information from the sources where appropriate.

1. What problems faced black Americans who moved north in the 1920s and 1930s?   **5**

Source A explains black Americans' reaction to the Civil Rights Movement.

Source A

> Between 1945 and 1959, the Civil Rights Movement made much progress. Black activists, especially the NAACP, were the moving force behind Supreme Court decisions. The Supreme Court had declared segregated schools unconstitutional in 1954. Progress in carrying out this declaration was very slow over the next ten years. Unending black pressure forced President Eisenhower to propose a Civil Rights Act in 1957. The Civil Rights Movement was gaining heroes such as Rosa Parks during this period, though there were also victims such as Emmett Till.

2. Why did black Americans feel that progress towards civil rights had been made between 1945 and 1959? (Use **Source A** and recall.)   **5**

Sources B and **C** describe the sit-ins.

Source B

> Some Civil Rights workers believed that the sit-ins showed students that they could take action themselves. Young black people realised that they could make a difference to Civil Rights by winning the support of both black and white Americans. However, sit-ins only achieved limited success in some of the towns and cities where the protests were used. Much more needed to be done to improve Civil Rights.

Source C

> The very act of protesting meant the students believed they could make a difference. When they "sat in" these young people practiced non-violence, they dressed in their best clothes and they studied books. This helped to encourage black community support and won the respect and even admiration of some white Americans. However, the sit-ins only enjoyed success in a few Southern states. In the Deep South, white Americans refused to desegregate and the protestors faced resistance from the white authorities.

3. How far do **Sources B** and **C** agree about the success of the sit-ins?   **4**

[END OF CONTEXT 11]

Mark

HISTORICAL STUDY: EUROPEAN AND WORLD

CONTEXT 12: THE ROAD TO WAR,
1933–1939

Answer the following questions using recalled knowledge and information from the sources where appropriate.

Source A is about Britain's policy of Appeasement in the 1930s.

Source A

> The Great Depression meant that money could not be found for rearmament and the government knew that the British people were totally opposed to war. Chamberlain, who had been Chancellor before becoming Prime Minister in 1937, had a reputation as a social reformer. Chamberlain was in favour of personal, face to face talks among Europe's leaders and believed he could negotiate directly with Hitler. The British Government took the view that communist Russia was the real threat to peace in the world.

1. Why did Britain follow a policy of Appeasement in the 1930s? (Use **Source A** and recall.)   5

2. Describe the aims of Hitler's foreign policy.   5

Sources B and **C** are opinions about the Anschluss between Germany and Austria in 1938.

Source B

> It is clear that Anschluss is popular among the Austrian people who are, after all, German in language and culture. Keeping Germany and Austria apart had been one of the more spiteful terms of Versailles and this wrong is now made right. Therefore Europe is likely to benefit from a period of peace and prosperity as Germany moves into a brighter future.

Source C

> Germany has taken over Austria. Any intelligent person can see that an even more powerful Germany is a threat to the peace and stability of Europe. The decision in 1919 to forbid Anschluss had been a very sensible one for limiting the war-like ambitions of Germany. We have permitted Hitler to brutally invade an independent country whose population has no love for Nazism.

3. How far do **Sources B** and **C** disagree about the Anschluss?   4

[END OF CONTEXT 12]

Marks

HISTORICAL STUDY: EUROPEAN AND WORLD

> **CONTEXT 13: IN THE SHADOW OF THE BOMB: THE COLD WAR, 1945–1985**

Answer the following questions using recalled knowledge and information from the sources where appropriate.

Source A is about the Berlin Wall.

Source A

> On 12 August 1961 a record 4000 East Germans fled to West Berlin to start a new life in the West. Those who left were often young and well educated. In the small hours of 13 August, Soviet and East German "shock workers" closed the border and put barbed wire across the streets. The East Germans claimed that enemy agents had been stationed in West Berlin. The agents were using Berlin as a centre of operations against East Germany and the Soviet Union. Berlin had become a divided city.

1. Why did the Soviet Union build the Berlin Wall in 1961? (Use **Source A** and recall.)   5

Sources B and **C** are about the tactics of the Vietcong.

Source B

> The Vietcong, or "Charlie" as the Americans called them, were the locally born guerrilla fighters of South Vietnam. The Vietcong consisted of three groups: units of regular soldiers, provincial forces, and part-time guerrillas. The Vietcong generally avoided large scale attacks on the enemy but continually harassed their troops and installations causing heavy American casualties. They travelled light, carrying basic weapons and few supplies.

Source C

> Our first real battle was in the Michelin Rubber Plantation. Thousands of Vietcong launched wave after wave of attacks on our camp. But they had all kinds of Chinese and Russian weapons, such as flamethrowers and rocket launchers. Eventually we counter-attacked and pushed them back. Fortunately, we only lost around seven guys. The Vietcong body count was reported to have been 800, but I thought it was more.

2. How far do **Sources B** and **C** disagree about the tactics used by the Vietcong?   4

3. Describe the steps taken to reduce tension between the USA and the USSR during the 1960s and 1970s.   5

[END OF CONTEXT 13]

[END OF PART 3: EUROPEAN AND WORLD CONTEXTS]

[END OF QUESTION PAPER]

[BLANK PAGE]

[BLANK PAGE]

X044/201

| NATIONAL QUALIFICATIONS 2010 | WEDNESDAY, 26 MAY 9.00 AM – 10.45 AM | HISTORY INTERMEDIATE 2 |

The instructions for this paper are on *Page two*. Read them carefully before you begin your answers. Your Invigilator will tell you which contexts to answer in Parts 2 and 3 of the examination.

XSQA

INSTRUCTIONS

Answer **one** question from Part 1, The Short Essay

Answer **one** context* from Part 2, Scottish and British

Answer **one** context* from Part 3, European and World

Answer **one** other context* from

> **either**   Part 2, Scottish and British
>
> **or**   Part 3, European and World

*Answer all the questions in each of your chosen contexts.

Contents

[Turn over

PART 1: THE SHORT ESSAY

Marks

Answer **one** question. For this question you should write a short essay using your own knowledge. The essay should include an introduction, development and conclusion. Each question is worth 8 marks.

SCOTTISH AND BRITISH CONTEXTS:

CONTEXT 1: MURDER IN THE CATHEDRAL: CROWN, CHURCH AND PEOPLE, 1154–1173

Question 1:   Explain why Henry II faced difficulties on becoming king in 1154.   8

CONTEXT 2: WALLACE, BRUCE AND THE WARS OF INDEPENDENCE, 1286–1328

Question 2:   Explain why the Scots won the battle at Bannockburn.   8

CONTEXT 3: MARY, QUEEN OF SCOTS AND THE SCOTTISH REFORMATION, 1540s–1587

Question 3:   Explain why Riccio became unpopular with Darnley and the Scottish nobles.   8

CONTEXT 4: THE COMING OF THE CIVIL WAR, 1603–1642

Question 4:   Explain why Charles I was an unpopular monarch in England by 1640.   8

CONTEXT 5: "ANE END OF ANE AULD SANG": SCOTLAND AND THE TREATY OF UNION, 1690s–1715

Question 5:   Explain why many Scots were disappointed by the Act of Union by 1715.   8

CONTEXT 6: IMMIGRANTS AND EXILES: SCOTLAND, 1830s–1930s

Question 6:   Explain why Irish immigrants were attracted to Scotland between 1830 and 1930.   8

CONTEXT 7: FROM THE CRADLE TO THE GRAVE? SOCIAL WELFARE IN BRITAIN, 1890s–1951

Question 7:   Explain why the Liberal government passed social welfare reforms between 1906 and 1914.   8

Marks

CONTEXT 8: CAMPAIGNING FOR CHANGE: SOCIAL CHANGE IN SCOTLAND, 1900s–1979

Question 8:   Explain why there was still a need to improve many women's lives after 1918.

8

CONTEXT 9: A TIME OF TROUBLES: IRELAND, 1900–1923

Question 9:   Explain why the Anglo-Irish War broke out in 1919.

8

EUROPEAN AND WORLD CONTEXTS:

CONTEXT 1: THE NORMAN CONQUEST, 1060–1153

Question 10:   Explain why knights were important in medieval society.

8

CONTEXT 2: THE CROSS AND THE CRESCENT: THE FIRST CRUSADE, 1096–1125

Question 11:   Explain why the Crusaders were able to keep control of the Holy Land after 1097.

8

CONTEXT 3: WAR, DEATH AND REVOLT IN MEDIEVAL EUROPE, 1328–1436

Question 12:   Explain why France was unsuccessful in the war against England between 1415 and 1422.

8

CONTEXT 4: NEW WORLDS: EUROPE IN THE AGE OF EXPANSION, 1480s–1530s

Question 13:   Explain why the Spaniards were able to defeat **either** the Aztecs **or** the Incas.

8

CONTEXT 5: "TEA AND FREEDOM": THE AMERICAN REVOLUTION, 1763–1783

Question 14:   Explain why the American War of Independence broke out in 1775.

8

CONTEXT 6: "THIS ACCURSED TRADE": THE BRITISH SLAVE TRADE AND ITS ABOLITION, 1770–1807

Question 15:   Explain why it took so long for Britain to abolish the slave trade.

8

Marks

CONTEXT 7: CITIZENS!
THE FRENCH REVOLUTION, 1789–1794

Question 16:   Explain why the French people were unhappy with their government by 1789.   **8**

CONTEXT 8: CAVOUR, GARIBALDI
AND THE MAKING OF ITALY, 1815–1870

Question 17:   Explain why Garibaldi's leadership was important to the unification of Italy.   **8**

CONTEXT 9: IRON AND BLOOD? BISMARCK AND THE
CREATION OF THE GERMAN EMPIRE, 1815–1871

Question 18:   Explain why the nationalist movement had failed to unite the German states by 1850.   **8**

CONTEXT 10: THE RED FLAG:
LENIN AND THE RUSSIAN REVOLUTION, 1894–1921

Question 19:   Explain why the Tsar was able to remain in power following the 1905 revolution.   **8**

CONTEXT 11: FREE AT LAST?
RACE RELATIONS IN THE USA, 1918–1968

Question 20:   Explain why the demand for civil rights continued to grow after 1945.   **8**

CONTEXT 12: THE ROAD TO WAR, 1933–1939

Question 21:   Explain why Hitler's actions created problems in Europe between 1933 and 1939.   **8**

CONTEXT 13: IN THE SHADOW OF THE BOMB:
THE COLD WAR, 1945–1985

Question 22:   Explain why America lost the war in Vietnam.   **8**

[END OF PART 1: THE SHORT ESSAY]

[Turn over for PART 2: SCOTTISH AND BRITISH CONTEXTS on *Page eight*

PART 2:

Marks

HISTORICAL STUDY: SCOTTISH AND BRITISH

> ### CONTEXT 1: MURDER IN THE CATHEDRAL: CROWN, CHURCH AND PEOPLE, 1154–1173

Answer the following questions using recalled knowledge and information from the sources where appropriate.

Source A explains why castles were important in the twelfth century.

Source A

> During Henry II's reign, castles were built of stone and with extra walls and towers. These castles became a key symbol of power. They were also the administrative centres of each town. The numerous rooms inside a castle meant that it was an ideal base for the local garrison carrying out guard duty. Although many castles had been built illegally during the civil war there was no doubt that they were useful during times of attack when food, drink and other supplies could be stored there.

1. Why were castles important in the twelfth century? (Use **Source A** and recall.)   **5**

Sources B and **C** describe the life of a monk in medieval times.

Source B

> At 2 o'clock in the morning, monks were woken for a service in the chapel. Although they were given time to sleep, monks were expected to pray at least 8 times a day. Breakfast included bread and fruit and was eaten in silence. After breakfast, monks were allowed a little free time but were expected to spend most of the day working in the fields or carrying out other duties.

Source C

> Many monks lived their lives by St Benedict's rule. During meal times talking was strictly forbidden so monks listened to prayers or to readings from holy books. Services began in the middle of the night and every monk was expected to pray in church several times a day. Isolated from the local community, monks were not allowed to leave the monastery and had to forget their previous life.

2. How far do **Sources B** and **C** agree about the lives of monks in medieval times?   **4**

3. Describe the murder of Archbishop Becket.   **5**

[END OF CONTEXT 1]

Marks

HISTORICAL STUDY: SCOTTISH AND BRITISH

> ### CONTEXT 2: WALLACE, BRUCE AND THE WARS OF INDEPENDENCE, 1286–1328

Answer the following questions using recalled knowledge and information from the sources where appropriate.

1. Describe the events between 1286 and 1292 that led to Edward I becoming overlord of Scotland.   5

Source A explains why the leadership of William Wallace was important.

Source A

> Wallace has become a folk hero in Scotland. Although he was only the second son of an unimportant knight, for a short while he became Guardian of Scotland uniting people under his leadership. He reorganised the army of Scotland and prepared for an English invasion. He also looked for foreign help. Bishop Lamberton was sent to Rome and Paris to plead Scotland's cause there. Wallace also renewed trade with Germany to obtain iron for weapons which he needed for his army.

2. Why was the leadership of William Wallace important during the Wars of Independence? (Use **Source A** and recall.)   5

Sources B and **C** are about the amount of support Robert Bruce had in 1320.

Source B

> In the Declaration of Arbroath of 1320, the Scottish nobles explained to the Pope why all the Scots thought Robert Bruce was their king. They argued that he had royal blood and that his actions had won him the support of the Scottish people. On top of that, they argued that they wanted him as king because he had saved Scotland from being taken over by the King of England.

Source C

> Even while the Declaration of Arbroath was being written, some Scottish nobles were plotting against Robert Bruce. They felt he was a ruthless thug who had murdered his main rival in a church. Other Scottish nobles claimed to be more closely related to the Scottish royal family than Bruce. They, however, had not been successful in war. These disagreements caused problems in Scotland.

3. How far do **Sources B** and **C** disagree about the amount of support Robert Bruce had in 1320?   4

[END OF CONTEXT 2]

Marks

HISTORICAL STUDY: SCOTTISH AND BRITISH

> ### CONTEXT 3: MARY, QUEEN OF SCOTS AND THE SCOTTISH REFORMATION, 1540s–1587

Answer the following questions using recalled knowledge and information from the sources where appropriate.

Source A explains why Henry VIII ordered the invasions of Scotland after 1544.

Source A

> The death of King James V after the Scottish defeat at Solway Moss gave King Henry VIII the opportunity to break the Auld Alliance between France and Scotland. He freed Scottish prisoners of war on condition they supported the marriage of Mary to his son, Edward. Within a year the Scots had agreed to this in the Treaty of Greenwich. However, when Henry then made more and more demands on them, the French encouraged the Scots to resist. Finally the Scots announced that the Treaty was broken.

1. Why did Henry VIII of England order the invasions of Scotland after 1544? (Use **Source A** and recall.)   **5**

2. Describe the events leading up to the signing of the Treaty of Edinburgh in 1560.   **5**

Sources B and **C** are about how well Mary, Queen of Scots ruled Scotland.

Source B

> Mary returned to Scotland as Queen in 1561. Mary was a Roman Catholic who believed that she should rule England instead of her Protestant cousin, Elizabeth. She neglected the government of Scotland by leaving the running of the country to a group of Protestant nobles. She did not really care about the issue of religion in Scotland.

Source C

> Until Mary allowed her heart to rule her head by marrying Darnley, she had been a successful ruler in Scotland. She had defeated the nobles who challenged her authority and had established a successful government under her half-brother Moray. As a Roman Catholic, her tolerant treatment of Scotland's new Protestant church was ahead of its time.

3. How far do **Sources B** and **C** disagree about how well Mary, Queen of Scots ruled Scotland?   **4**

[END OF CONTEXT 3]

Marks

HISTORICAL STUDY: SCOTTISH AND BRITISH

> ### CONTEXT 4: THE COMING OF
> ### THE CIVIL WAR, 1603–1642

Answer the following questions using recalled knowledge and information from the sources where appropriate.

Sources A and **B** describe James VI and I.

Source A

> James VI and I was well educated and clever. The Union of the Crowns united the monarchs of Scotland and England and James became king of both countries. He claimed that kings were appointed by God, and could do as they wished. He lost people's respect by giving money and power to favourites at court. His son, Charles I was to prove a less popular king.

Source B

> The reign of the Stuarts began in 1603. James VI and I was a highly intelligent man. From the start of his reign he spent a lot of money, not only on himself but on gifts and pensions to courtiers. Although he believed in the Divine Right of Kings he did not try to be an absolute monarch in his relations with Parliament. Charles I would use his royal prerogative to a greater extent.

1. How far do **Sources A** and **B** agree about James VI and I?   4

2. Describe the methods used by James VI and I to raise money during his reign.   5

Source C explains why Charles I faced opposition to his rule in Scotland.

Source C

> When Charles decided to enforce his religious views on the Scottish people, he met fierce resistance. Many Scots were Presbyterians who carried out their own religious services and they disliked these changes. They showed this when they signed the National Covenant in 1638, sometimes in blood. The Scots also resented Charles because he was an absentee King and he visited Scotland only once during his reign. Scotland was a poor country and many Scots thought Charles did not care. Deep resentment and suspicion grew across Scotland.

3. Why did Charles I face opposition to his rule in Scotland? (Use **Source C** and recall.)   5

[END OF CONTEXT 4]

Marks

HISTORICAL STUDY: SCOTTISH AND BRITISH

> **CONTEXT 5: "ANE END OF ANE
> AULD SANG": SCOTLAND AND
> THE TREATY OF UNION, 1690s–1715**

Answer the following questions using recalled knowledge and information from the sources where appropriate.

1. Describe what happened during the Worcester affair.　　**5**

Source A explains why Queen Anne wanted a Treaty of Union.

Source A

> Queen Anne came to the throne of Scotland and England in 1702. She wanted a complete Union of the two countries because she found it difficult to control the Scottish Parliament. She also faced complaints that her policies were harming Scotland. The Scottish Parliament was even threatening to end the Union of the Crowns. However, at first, these problems with Scotland made it more difficult for England to fight the war against France.

2. Why did Queen Anne want a Treaty of Union between England and Scotland? (Use **Source A** and recall.)　　**5**

Sources B and **C** are about Scottish attitudes to the Treaty of Union.

Source B

> The Treaty of Union was passed in 1707. Scots thought the Equivalent was money to help the country recover from the Darien Scheme. Scots felt they would have influence in a new and more powerful kingdom. They thought their traders would benefit from access to English colonies.

Source C

> Scots feared that, once they lost their independence, they would have little influence over government decisions. Others worried that businesses in Scotland would suffer from competition from English imports. They also thought the money paid to Scotland was a bribe to rich and powerful men—the only way that a Union could be passed.

3. How far do **Sources B** and **C** disagree about Scottish attitudes to the Treaty of Union?　　**4**

[END OF CONTEXT 5]

Marks

HISTORICAL STUDY: SCOTTISH AND BRITISH

> ### CONTEXT 6: IMMIGRANTS AND EXILES: SCOTLAND, 1830s–1930s

Answer the following questions using recalled knowledge and information from the sources where appropriate.

Sources **A** and **B** are about Scottish attitudes to Irish immigration.

Source A

> Irish immigrants tended to concentrate in particular areas because they were disliked by the native Scots. It was natural that the immigrants should live together but the determination to stick to their own culture was looked upon with suspicion. There were accusations that they did not wish to become "new Scots". In addition, the Irish did not receive much credit for their contribution to the Scottish economy.

Source B

> There was a reluctance to admit that Irish workers were essential to the development of industry in Scotland even though they were to be found wherever work needed doing. Many Scots criticised immigrants for keeping to their native language and religion. It became clear that there was a great deal of resentment against the immigrants in Scotland.

1. How far do **Sources A** and **B** agree about Scottish attitudes to Irish immigration?   4

Source C explains why poor Scots were able to emigrate in the nineteenth century.

Source C

> Some landlords saw it as in their own interests to encourage poor tenants to seek their fortunes elsewhere. The landlords were willing to pay the full travelling costs, especially to Canada. Landlords often wrote off rent arrears so that the tenants would have some money for their new life and some even bought their cattle which provided the emigrant with some extra help. Glasgow and Edinburgh feared a massive influx of Highlanders and the city authorities made a contribution towards their expenses in emigrating.

2. Why were many poor Scots able to emigrate during the nineteenth century? (Use **Source C** and recall.)   5

3. In what ways did Scots help to improve the lands to which they emigrated?   5

[END OF CONTEXT 6]

Mark

HISTORICAL STUDY: SCOTTISH AND BRITISH

> ### CONTEXT 7: FROM THE CRADLE TO THE GRAVE? SOCIAL WELFARE IN BRITAIN, 1890s–1951

Answer the following questions using recalled knowledge and information from the sources where appropriate.

Sources A and **B** describe the Old Age Pensions Act of 1908.

Source A

> The Liberal government passed a series of welfare reforms to help the old, the young and the sick. A pensioner with a yearly income of up to £21 received the full 25p a week. Pensions were not made available to those who had been in prison during the previous ten years. The pension was not a generous amount. The Liberals were criticised for not doing enough to tackle the real causes of poverty.

Source B

> The Pensions Act entitled people over seventy with an annual income of up to £21 to 25p a week of a pension. The government stated that these payments were not meant to be a complete solution to the problem of poverty in old age. However, the foundation stones of the welfare state had been laid. Any seventy year old was entitled to a pension provided they had avoided imprisonment in the previous ten years and they had not continually avoided work.

1. How far do **Sources A** and **B** agree about the Old Age Pensions Act of 1908?   4

2. Describe the ways the Beveridge Report of 1942 suggested tackling the social problems facing Britain.   5

Source C is about the welfare reforms passed by the Labour government between 1945 and 1951.

Source C

> Poor housing and homelessness were still serious problems by 1951. The Labour government also did little to enhance the educational opportunities for working class children, most of whom left school at fifteen with no paper qualifications. People thought the National Health Service was a great success but there was still a shortage of hospitals and health centres. There was still a long way to go before the problems of poverty and deprivation were adequately solved. The Labour Party lost the General Election of 1951.

3. Why were some people disappointed with the Labour welfare reforms by 1951? (Use **Source C** and recall.)   5

[END OF CONTEXT 7]

HISTORICAL STUDY: SCOTTISH AND BRITISH

Marks

> ### CONTEXT 8: CAMPAIGNING FOR CHANGE: SOCIAL CHANGE IN SCOTLAND, 1900s–1979

Answer the following questions using recalled knowledge and information from the sources where appropriate.

Sources A and **B** describe changes to Scots drinking habits in the early twentieth century.

Source A

> By 1900, people were drinking less alcohol. The number of public houses decreased and convictions for drunkenness fell. This was due more to the increased tax on alcohol than to the temperance movement. People also preferred to spend their money on the new consumer and household goods which were increasingly available, as well as on leisure activities.

Source B

> As the twentieth century progressed Scottish men were drinking much less than they had in the nineteenth century. The reasons for this are many. One was the development of many different things to do. The number of pubs in some areas fell where people voted for this. Alcohol became much more expensive when the government raised the tax on spirits by 34% in 1909 and then cut pub opening times to five and a half hours a day in 1914.

1. How far do **Sources A** and **B** agree about reasons why people were drinking less in Scotland in the early 20th century?   **4**

2. Describe the unrest on Red Clydeside between 1915 and 1919.   **5**

Source C describes the effects of North Sea Oil on the north of Scotland.

Source C

> Oil had a huge impact upon the north of Scotland. Aberdeen became the oil capital of Europe and the boom spread to smaller east coast towns such as Fraserburgh, Peterhead and Montrose. Giant rigs became a common sight in the Moray and Cromarty Firths because of the construction yards at Ardersier and Nigg. There were almost 3,000 new jobs created in the Shetland Islands. Dozens of companies moved to the north east to provide support and other services to the industry.

3. Why was the development of North Sea Oil so important for the economy of the north of Scotland? (Use **Source C** and recall.)   **5**

[END OF CONTEXT 8]

Mark

HISTORICAL STUDY: SCOTTISH AND BRITISH

> **CONTEXT 9: A TIME OF
> TROUBLES: IRELAND, 1900–1923**

Answer the following questions using recalled knowledge and information from the sources where appropriate.

Sources A and **B** are two Irish opinions on the Union with Britain.

Source A

> The Irish people have benefited greatly from the Union. We are better housed, fed and receive better wages for our work. Our freedom and rights have been protected and this has led to great success. In the past Ireland was a poor country with little or no future. Today Ireland works in partnership with Britain. It would be a disaster to listen to those who want to destroy all that Ireland has achieved.

Source B

> Until Ireland has the right to make its own laws we will have no freedom. For years we have been the losers in the Union with Britain. Although the Union is against the wishes of the people, the British are unwilling to listen. Unemployment and poor wages have made many Irish men and women desperate yet the British government does nothing to help. Conditions are so bad, Irish families are being forced to emigrate abroad in an attempt to try and improve their lives.

1.   How far do **Sources A** and **B** disagree about the Union?   4

2.   Describe the actions taken by the Unionists against the Home Rule Bill.   5

Source C explains why De Valera opposed the 1921 Treaty.

Source C

> After months of negotiations the Irish delegation in London reluctantly signed the 1921 Treaty. De Valera had remained in Dublin and was furious that terms had been agreed without consulting him. He refused to accept that six counties in the north of Ireland would be separated from the rest of the country. He also refused to swear an oath of allegiance to the British King. Although most people in Ireland wanted an end to the war, De Valera argued that only full independence would lead to peace.

3.   Why did De Valera oppose the 1921 Treaty? (Use **Source C** and recall.)   5

[END OF CONTEXT 9]

[END OF PART 2: SCOTTISH AND BRITISH CONTEXTS]

Marks

PART 3:

HISTORICAL STUDY: EUROPEAN AND WORLD

> ### CONTEXT 1: THE NORMAN CONQUEST, 1060–1153

Answer the following questions using recalled knowledge and information from the sources where appropriate.

Source A is about the events leading up to the Battle of Hastings.

Source A

> William arrived at Pevensey with a huge army. He had countless horsemen and archers. When it was reported that William had landed, Harold at once forced his exhausted army to march south. Although he knew that some of the bravest of the Saxons had fallen in the two previous battles he advanced with full speed into the south of England. On 14 October Harold fought with the Normans nine miles from Hastings. However some of his soldiers refused to remain loyal to him and deserted from his army.

1. Why did Harold lose the battle of Hastings? (Use **Source A** and recall.)   **5**

Source B describes how William gained control of England after the Battle of Hastings. It was written by his priest in 1077.

Source B

> William went to various parts of his kingdom. He tried to organise everything to suit his people as well as himself. Wherever he went the people surrendered to him. There was no resistance, but everywhere men submitted to him and asked for his peace. He gave rich fiefs to the men he had brought over from France but no Frenchman was given anything that had been unjustly taken from an Englishman.

2. How useful is **Source B** as evidence about William's attempts to control England after 1066?   **4**

3. In what ways did Scotland change during the reign of David I?   **5**

[END OF CONTEXT 1]

Marks

HISTORICAL STUDY: EUROPEAN AND WORLD

> ### CONTEXT 2: THE CROSS AND THE CRESCENT: THE FIRST CRUSADE, 1096–1125

Answer the following questions using recalled knowledge and information from the sources where appropriate.

Source A explains why Pope Urban II called the First Crusade.

Source A

> In 1095 Emperor Alexius sent messages to the Pope begging him for help against the Turks. Although Urban II had not been Pope for very long, he could see that the Turks were a threat to Christianity. Eight months later the Pope delivered a successful speech at Clermont. Almost immediately peasants and knights left their homes and took the cross. The Pope hoped the Crusade would stop western knights fighting amongst themselves and encourage them to recapture Jerusalem from the Turks.

1. Why did Pope Urban II call the First Crusade? (Use **Source A** and recall.)   **5**

2. Describe the siege and capture of Antioch by the First Crusade.   **5**

Source B describes the behaviour of the Crusaders at Marrat au Numan. It was written by a priest who went on the First Crusade.

Source B

> Although many knights stayed in Antioch or returned home, the main Crusading army continued the journey to Jerusalem. On the way we stayed at Marrat au Numan. Our men were starving and desperate for food. Some Crusaders began to rip up the bodies of their dead enemies. They cut their flesh into slices, cooked and ate them. Many of us were shocked by what we saw and could not wait to leave.

3. How useful is **Source B** as evidence of the Crusaders' behaviour in the Holy Land?   **4**

[END OF CONTEXT 2]

Marks

HISTORICAL STUDY: EUROPEAN AND WORLD

> CONTEXT 3: WAR, DEATH AND
> REVOLT IN MEDIEVAL EUROPE,
> 1328–1436

Answer the following questions using recalled knowledge and information from the sources where appropriate.

1. Describe the problem of succession to the French throne after 1328.   **5**

Source A is about the effects of the Battle of Poitiers on France. It was written by Froissart the chronicler in 1388.

Source A

> The battle was fought on the 19th day of September 1356. The finest knights of France died on that day. This severely weakened the realm of France. The country fell into great misery. In all, 17 lords were taken prisoner. Between 500 and 700 men-at-arms were killed. In all, 6,000 Frenchmen died.

2. How useful is **Source A** as evidence of the effects of the Battle of Poitiers on France?   **4**

Source B is about the end of the Peasants' Revolt.

Source B

> The King was determined that the revolt would not succeed. He sent out his messengers to capture those who had led the revolt. Many were hanged. Gallows were set up all around the city of London and in other cities and boroughs to put people off joining in the revolt. At last the King, seeing that too many of his subjects would die, took pity. He granted pardons to some of the troublemakers on condition that they should never rebel again on pain of losing their lives. So this wicked revolt ended.

3. Why was the King able to crush the Peasants' Revolt? (Use **Source B** and recall.)   **5**

[END OF CONTEXT 3]

Marks

HISTORICAL STUDY: EUROPEAN AND WORLD

> ### CONTEXT 4: NEW WORLDS:
> ### EUROPE IN THE AGE OF
> ### EXPANSION, 1480s–1530s

Answer the following questions using recalled knowledge and information from the sources where appropriate.

Source A is from a letter by Columbus to a friend of Queen Isabella, written in 1500.

Source A

> I was sent as a captain from Spain to the Indies to conquer a large and warlike people, who had customs and beliefs very different from ours. These people live in mountains and forest without any settled townships. Here by God's will I have brought this new world under the dominion of Spain. By doing this, Spain, which was thought of by some people as poor, has now become rich.

1. How useful is **Source A** as evidence of reasons for European exploration between 1480 and 1530?   **4**

2. In what ways did Vasco da Gama's voyage benefit Europe?   **5**

Source B explains some of the problems faced by Magellan on his voyage round the world.

Source B

> Magellan left Seville with five ships full of goods to trade in the east. As a Portuguese captain commanding a Spanish fleet he was unpopular. He kept the destination secret so that the crew would not be afraid but this made him seem untrustworthy. In Patagonia the other captains plotted a mutiny against him. He crushed this and brutally executed the ringleaders. Further south, his ships had to pass through a stormy narrow straight which now bears his name. Two of his ships were lost there.

3. Why did Magellan face difficulties during his voyage round the world? (Use **Source B** and recall.)   **5**

[END OF CONTEXT 4]

Marks

HISTORICAL STUDY: EUROPEAN AND WORLD

CONTEXT 5: "TEA AND FREEDOM":
THE AMERICAN REVOLUTION,
1763–1783

Answer the following questions using recalled knowledge and information from the sources where appropriate.

1. Describe the Boston Tea Party and the British government's response to it.   **5**

Source A is from a letter written by the leaders of the 13 colonies when they met in May 1775.

Source A

> On the 19th day of April, General Gage sent out a large detachment of his army who made an unprovoked attack on the inhabitants of the town of Lexington. They murdered eight of the inhabitants and wounded many others. The troops then proceeded to the town of Concord, where they cruelly slaughtered several people and wounded many more, until they were forced to retreat by a group of brave colonists suddenly assembled to repel this cruel aggression.

2. How useful is **Source A** as evidence about what happened at Lexington and Concord in April 1775?   **4**

Source B explains the effects of the involvement of foreign countries in the American War of Independence.

Source B

> Representatives of America and France signed an alliance on 6 February 1778. The entry of France into the war added enormously to Britain's difficulties. The French attacked Britain's colonies in the Caribbean and elsewhere undermining Britain's control. They harassed British shipping in the Atlantic interfering with Britain's trade. Spain and the Netherlands had joined the anti-British alliance by 1780. As a result, Britain lost control of the seas for the first time that century. It became ever more difficult for Britain to reinforce and supply its forces in America.

3. Why did the involvement of foreign countries cause difficulties for Britain in the War of Independence? (Use **Source B** and recall.)   **5**

[END OF CONTEXT 5]

Mark

HISTORICAL STUDY: EUROPEAN AND WORLD

> **CONTEXT 6: "THIS ACCURSED TRADE": THE BRITISH SLAVE TRADE AND ITS ABOLITION, 1770–1807**

Answer the following questions using recalled knowledge and information from the sources where appropriate.

1. Describe the different stages of the triangular trade.　　　　5

In **Source A**, a modern historian describes slave revolts in the West Indies.

Source A

> The British needed all the military help they could get in the 1790s when they faced slave unrest in Dominica, St Lucia, St Vincent and Grenada. Their greatest concern was for Jamaica, which was the biggest, the richest and most troublesome of their slave colonies. By the early nineteenth century, the island was undergoing what seemed like an endless series of revolts. In one of the worst rebellions, 226 properties were damaged at a cost estimated to be £1 million.

2. How useful is **Source A** as evidence of slave resistance in the West Indies?　　　　4

Source B explains why the slave trade was abolished in Britain.

Source B

> During the late nineteenth century, attitudes towards the slave trade were changing. More people began to think of Africans as fellow human beings and felt that they should be treated as such. Britain's trading interests were also changing. Trade with India and East Asia was growing while trade with the West Indies had become less important to Britain. Many merchants supported free trade. They argued that slavery was an inefficient way to produce sugar. In 1807, a new law made it illegal for British people to buy slaves in Africa.

3. Why was the slave trade abolished by Britain in 1807? (Use **Source B** and recall.)　　　　5

[END OF CONTEXT 6]

Marks

HISTORICAL STUDY: EUROPEAN AND WORLD

CONTEXT 7: CITIZENS! THE FRENCH REVOLUTION, 1789–1794

Answer the following questions using recalled knowledge and information from the sources where appropriate.

Source A is from the Tennis Court Oath agreed by the Third Estate in June 1789.

Source A

> Wherever the members of the Third Estate choose to meet, that is legally the National Assembly. No one has the right to prevent the members of the Assembly from gathering together when they want to. The National Assembly has the task of writing the constitution of France and to restore public order.

1. How useful is **Source A** as evidence of the relationship between the Third Estate and the King in June 1789?   **4**

Source B explains why France was at war with other European countries after 1791.

Source B

> Austria and Prussia went to war because they objected to the way that Marie Antoinette, an Austrian Princess, was being treated. Louis XVI also wanted war but only because he secretly hoped that a French defeat would mean an end to the Revolution. On the other hand the revolutionaries wanted to spread their ideas throughout Europe. Only some of the radical Jacobins opposed war, preferring to consolidate and expand the Revolution at home. Britain joined the war against France to prevent the French interfering in other countries.

2. Why did war break out between France and her neighbours after 1791? (Use **Source B** and recall.)   **5**

3. Describe the Reign of Terror.   **5**

[END OF CONTEXT 7]

Mark.

HISTORICAL STUDY: EUROPEAN AND WORLD

> ### CONTEXT 8: CAVOUR, GARIBALDI AND THE MAKING OF ITALY, 1815–1870

Answer the following questions using recalled knowledge and information from the sources where appropriate.

Source A is about the failure of the Italian nationalist movement up to 1850.

Source A

> Before 1848 there was little sign of Italian nationalism, except as a wild idea. Mazzini's dream of a democratic republic lost support. The nationalists failed to work together. The revolutionaries of Sicily wanted nothing to do with those of Naples. The revolutionary leaders did not encourage mass participation. The middle classes feared that democratic government would give power to the lower classes. The revolutions were not supported by autocratic leaders, such as King Ferdinand of Sicily.

1. Why did the revolutions of 1848–1849 fail to unite Italy? (Use **Source A** and recall.)   **5**

2. Describe the steps taken by Piedmont to bring about Italian unification up to 1860.   **5**

Source B was written by a politician in Piedmont in 1861.

Source B

> Count Cavour has the talent to assess a situation and the possibilities of exploiting it. It is this wonderful ability that has helped to bring about a united Italy. Cavour had to seek out opportunities wherever he could. He manipulated events to suit his purpose. He was Prime Minister of an unimportant country so he did not have the resources of a great power like Britain or France.

3. How useful is **Source B** as evidence of the skills of Cavour as a leader?   **4**

[END OF CONTEXT 8]

Marks

HISTORICAL STUDY: EUROPEAN AND WORLD

> ### CONTEXT 9: IRON AND BLOOD?
> ### BISMARCK AND THE CREATION OF
> ### THE GERMAN EMPIRE, 1815–1871

Answer the following questions using recalled knowledge and information from the sources where appropriate.

Source A is about the growth of Prussia before 1862.

Source A

> Prussia came to be regarded as the natural leader of a united Germany and therefore emerged as the champion of German nationalism. Prussia controlled the rivers Rhine and Elbe, which were vital communication and trade routes. Other states hoped to benefit from Prussia's industrial development. Prussia took the lead in improving roads and railways. After the revolutions of 1848 Frederick William IV of Prussia promised to work for a united Germany.

1. Why was Prussia able to take the lead in German unification by 1862? (Use **Source A** and recall.)   5

Source B is from the memoirs of Otto von Bismarck in 1898.

Source B

> I assumed that a united Germany was only a question of time, that the North German Confederation was only the first step in its solution. I did not doubt that a Franco-Prussian War must take place before the construction of a united Germany could be realised. At that time my mind was taken up with the idea of delaying the outbreak of war until our military strength had increased.

2. How useful is **Source B** as evidence of the methods used by Bismarck to bring about the unification of the German states in 1871?   4

3. Describe the events that led to war between France and Prussia in 1870.   5

[END OF CONTEXT 9]

HISTORICAL STUDY: EUROPEAN AND WORLD

Mark.

CONTEXT 10: THE RED FLAG: LENIN AND THE RUSSIAN REVOLUTION, 1894–1921

Answer the following questions using recalled knowledge and information from the sources where appropriate.

Source A explains the treatment of national minorities in the Russian Empire.

Source A

> The diversity of the Empire made it difficult to govern. Many minorities resented the policy of Russification. It made non-Russians use the Russian language instead of their own. Russian style clothes were to be worn and Russian customs were to be adopted. Russian officials were put in to run regional government in non-Russian parts of the Empire like Poland, Latvia and Finland. When Poles complained they were treated as second class citizens, they were told to change and become Russian citizens.

1. Why did national minorities dislike the policy of Russification? (Use **Source A** and recall.)   **5**

Source B is from a letter by the leader of the Provisional Government to his parents on 3 July 1917.

Source B

> Without doubt the country is heading for chaos. We are facing famine, defeat at the front and the collapse of law and order in the cities. There will be wars in the countryside as desperate refugees from the cities fight each other for food and land.

2. How useful is **Source B** as evidence of the problems facing the Provisional Government?   **4**

3. In what ways did the Civil War affect the Russian people?   **5**

[END OF CONTEXT 10]

Marks

HISTORICAL STUDY: EUROPEAN AND WORLD

> ### CONTEXT 11: FREE AT LAST? RACE RELATIONS IN THE USA, 1918–1968

Answer the following questions using recalled knowledge and information from the sources where appropriate.

1. Describe the problems facing European immigrants to the USA in the 1920s. **5**

Source A is from a speech made in 1954 by the Grand Dragon of the Federated Klans of Alabama.

Source A

> The Klan don't hate nobody! In fact, the Klan is the black man's best friend. He should behave himself and not allow himself to be fooled by the lies of Northerners. Then he will reap the rewards of hard work, instead of the disappointments of chasing unrealistic dreams!

2. How useful is **Source A** as evidence of attitudes towards Black Americans in the southern states at the time of the Civil Rights movement? **4**

Source B is about the Civil Rights march in Selma, Alabama in 1965.

Source B

> Late in 1964 President Johnson told King that there was little immediate hope that Congress would pass any more Civil Rights legislation. King decided that Johnson, like Kennedy before him, needed a "push". King decided to mount a new protest in Selma, Alabama. The local police chief, Sheriff Clark, was a crude, violent racist. Like Bull Connor he would make a wonderfully obvious enemy. King decided to lead a march from Selma to the state capital Montgomery to protest to Governor George Wallace about police brutality and racism.

3. Why did Martin Luther King plan a Civil Rights protest in Selma, Alabama in 1965? (Use **Source B** and recall.) **5**

[END OF CONTEXT 11]

Mark

HISTORICAL STUDY: EUROPEAN AND WORLD

CONTEXT 12: THE ROAD TO WAR,
1933–1939

Answer the following questions using recalled knowledge and information from the sources where appropriate.

1. In what ways did Britain appease Germany between 1933 and 1936? **5**

Source A explains why Germany wanted Anschluss with Austria.

Source A

> The Treaty of Versailles had forbidden unification with Austria. It was obvious that Austria was the key to south eastern Europe, where Germany wanted to spread her influence. Also, Austria had a close relationship with Hungary whom Germany wanted as an ally. Strategically, joining up with Austria would surround western Czechoslovakia and prevent it from being a base for Germany's enemies. Ever since 1918, German governments wanted to unite with Austria. Germany and Austria were joined economically in 1936 so political union was the next logical step.

2. Why did Germany want Anschluss in 1938? (Use **Source A** and recall.) **5**

Source B is from a report by the British ambassador to Germany, August 1938.

Source B

> No matter how badly the Germans behave, we must also condemn Czechoslovakia. No one has much faith in the Czech government's honesty or even their ability to do the right thing over the Sudetenland. We must not blame the Germans for preparing their army because they are convinced that the Czechs want to start a war as soon as possible so they can drag Britain and France into it.

3. How useful is **Source B** as evidence of Britain's attitude to Czechoslovakia in 1938? **4**

[END OF CONTEXT 12]

Marks

HISTORICAL STUDY: EUROPEAN AND WORLD

> **CONTEXT 13: IN THE SHADOW OF THE BOMB: THE COLD WAR, 1945–1985**

Answer the following questions using recalled knowledge and information from the sources where appropriate.

Source A explains why the Cold War broke out after 1945.

Source A

> The Allies met at Potsdam in July, 1945. The new American leader, Truman, distrusted the Russians and Stalin did not trust him. Stalin had good reason for being uneasy. While the Allies met at Potsdam a message had reached Truman informing him that America had successfully tested its first atomic bomb. On the 6th of August, the USA dropped an atomic bomb on Hiroshima; three days later, it dropped a second on Nagasaki. Truman had not told Stalin that this was about to happen. Wartime friends, who had fought together to defeat a common enemy, were about to become peacetime enemies.

1. Why did the Cold War break out after 1945? (Use **Source A** and recall.)   5

2. Describe the part played by the USSR in the Cuban Missile Crisis.   5

Source B is from a speech to the American people by President Reagan in March 1983.

Source B

> Our efforts to rebuild America's forces began two years ago. For twenty years the Soviet Union has been accumulating enormous military might. They didn't stop building their forces, even when they had more than enough to defend themselves. They haven't stopped now. I know that all of you want peace, and so do I. However, the freeze on building nuclear weapons would make us less, not more, secure and would increase the risk of war.

3. How useful is **Source B** as evidence of why the process of détente had come to a halt by the early 1980s?   4

[END OF CONTEXT 13]

[END OF PART 3: EUROPEAN AND WORLD CONTEXTS]

[END OF QUESTION PAPER]

[BLANK PAGE]

[BLANK PAGE]

X044/201

NATIONAL QUALIFICATIONS 2011	FRIDAY, 20 MAY 9.00 AM – 10.45 AM	HISTORY INTERMEDIATE 2

The instructions for this paper are on *Page two*. Read them carefully before you begin your answers.

Your Invigilator will tell you which contexts to answer in Parts 2 and 3 of the examination.

SQA

INSTRUCTIONS

Answer **one** question from Part 1, The Short Essay

Answer **one** context* from Part 2, Scottish and British

Answer **one** context* from Part 3, European and World

Answer **one** other context* from

>   **either**   Part 2, Scottish and British

>   **or**   Part 3, European and World

*Answer all the questions in each of your chosen contexts.

Contents

[Turn over

PART 1: THE SHORT ESSAY

Mark

Answer **one** question. For this question you should write a short essay using your own knowledge. The essay should include an introduction, development and conclusion. Each question is worth 8 marks.

SCOTTISH AND BRITISH CONTEXTS:

CONTEXT 1: MURDER IN THE CATHEDRAL: CROWN, CHURCH AND PEOPLE, 1154–1173

Question 1: Explain why Henry II and Archbishop Becket quarrelled so violently.

8

CONTEXT 2: WALLACE, BRUCE AND THE WARS OF INDEPENDENCE, 1286–1328

Question 2: Explain why some Scots were reluctant to accept the Maid of Norway as their ruler.

8

CONTEXT 3: MARY, QUEEN OF SCOTS AND THE SCOTTISH REFORMATION, 1540s–1587

Question 3: Explain why Mary, Queen of Scots, was forced to abdicate in 1567.

8

CONTEXT 4: THE COMING OF THE CIVIL WAR, 1603–1642

Question 4: Explain why the reign of Charles I was opposed in Scotland.

8

CONTEXT 5: "ANE END OF ANE AULD SANG": SCOTLAND AND THE TREATY OF UNION, 1690s–1715

Question 5: Explain why some people thought that Scotland would benefit from a Union with England in 1707.

8

CONTEXT 6: IMMIGRANTS AND EXILES: SCOTLAND, 1830s–1930s

Question 6: Explain why life was difficult for many Irish immigrants to Scotland between 1830 and 1930.

8

CONTEXT 7: FROM THE CRADLE TO THE GRAVE? SOCIAL WELFARE IN BRITAIN, 1890s–1951

Question 7: Explain why the Liberal Government reforms of 1906–1914 were important in improving the lives of children and the elderly.

8

Marks

CONTEXT 8: CAMPAIGNING FOR CHANGE: SOCIAL CHANGE IN SCOTLAND, 1900s–1979

Question 8:   Explain why Scottish education in the 1930s was in need of reform.   **8**

CONTEXT 9: A TIME OF TROUBLES: IRELAND, 1900–1923

Question 9:   Explain why the Unionists were against the Home Rule Bill.   **8**

EUROPEAN AND WORLD CONTEXTS:

CONTEXT 1: THE NORMAN CONQUEST, 1060–1153

Question 10:   Explain why there was so little opposition to William I after 1066.   **8**

CONTEXT 2: THE CROSS AND THE CRESCENT: THE FIRST CRUSADE, 1096–1125

Question 11:   Explain why people joined the First Crusade.   **8**

CONTEXT 3: WAR, DEATH AND REVOLT IN MEDIEVAL EUROPE, 1328–1436

Question 12:   Explain why the Black Death had serious consequences for England.   **8**

CONTEXT 4: NEW WORLDS: EUROPE IN THE AGE OF EXPANSION, 1480s–1530s

Question 13:   Explain why Christopher Columbus was an important figure in European exploration.   **8**

CONTEXT 5: "TEA AND FREEDOM": THE AMERICAN REVOLUTION, 1763–1783

Question 14:   Explain why the colonists were able to achieve victory in their war against the British by 1783.   **8**

CONTEXT 6: "THIS ACCURSED TRADE": THE BRITISH SLAVE TRADE AND ITS ABOLITION, 1770–1807

Question 15:   Explain why the Middle Passage was such a dreadful experience for slaves.   **8**

Mark

CONTEXT 7: CITIZENS!
THE FRENCH REVOLUTION, 1789–1794

Question 16: Explain why so many people were frightened of the Committee of Public Safety in 1793.

8

CONTEXT 8: CAVOUR, GARIBALDI
AND THE MAKING OF ITALY, 1815–1870

Question 17: Explain why the 1848–49 revolutions failed to bring about Italian unification.

8

CONTEXT 9: IRON AND BLOOD? BISMARCK AND THE
CREATION OF THE GERMAN EMPIRE, 1815–1871

Question 18: Explain why the 1848–49 revolutions failed to bring about German unification.

8

CONTEXT 10: THE RED FLAG:
LENIN AND THE RUSSIAN REVOLUTION, 1894–1921

Question 19: Explain why the Provisional Government had lost popular support by October 1917.

8

CONTEXT 11: FREE AT LAST?
RACE RELATIONS IN THE USA, 1918–1968

Question 20: Explain why the attitudes of Americans towards immigration changed after 1918.

8

CONTEXT 12: THE ROAD TO WAR, 1933–1939

Question 21: Explain why Britain did not want to go to war with Germany in the 1930s.

8

CONTEXT 13: IN THE SHADOW OF THE BOMB:
THE COLD WAR, 1945–1985

Question 22: Explain why the USA and USSR had begun the process of détente by the 1970s.

8

[END OF PART 1: THE SHORT ESSAY]

[Turn over for PART 2: SCOTTISH AND BRITISH CONTEXTS on *Page eight*

Mark

PART 2:

HISTORICAL STUDY: SCOTTISH AND BRITISH

> ### CONTEXT 1: MURDER IN THE CATHEDRAL: CROWN, CHURCH AND PEOPLE, 1154–1173

Answer the following questions using recalled knowledge and information from the sources where appropriate.

1. Describe the actions taken by Henry II to increase his power when he became king in 1154.   **5**

Source A was written in the twelfth century, by a French poet, about chivalry.

Source A

> Many knights are failing to live by the Code of Chivalry. They steal money from churches and rob pilgrims of their possessions. They attack whoever they please and show disrespect to children and the elderly. They speak of honour and bravery when they practise neither. Even though knights have spent years training to be the perfect soldier and role model they often forget their vows.

2. How useful is **Source A** as evidence of the behaviour of knights in the twelfth century?   **4**

Source B explains why priests were important in the twelfth century.

Source B

> Famine and disease meant that life in medieval times was uncertain and extremely difficult. The village priest offered support and hope that life after death would be better. At mass, the priest taught people how to behave and fulfil their Christian duties. In return the priest received some of the village's harvest to feed and keep him. Key ceremonies such as baptism, marriage and funerals were all carried out by the priest. They also taught boys to read and write and prepared them for a career in the Church.

3. Why were priests important in the twelfth century? (Use **Source B** and recall.)   **5**

[END OF CONTEXT 1]

Marks

HISTORICAL STUDY: SCOTTISH AND BRITISH

> **CONTEXT 2: WALLACE, BRUCE AND THE WARS OF INDEPENDENCE, 1286–1328**

Answer the following questions using recalled knowledge and information from the sources where appropriate.

Source A was written by the English chronicler, Walter of Guisborough in 1298.

Source A

> On one side of a little hill close to Falkirk, the Scots placed their soldiers in four round circles with their pikes held outwards at an angle. Between these circles, which are called schiltrons, were the archers and behind them was the cavalry. When our men attacked, the Scots horsemen fled without striking a sword's blow.

1. How useful is **Source A** as evidence about what happened at Falkirk?   **4**

2. Describe the events that led to the death of John Comyn at Dumfries in 1306.   **5**

Source B explains why Bruce was not fully accepted as King of Scots until 1328.

Source B

> It took almost twenty-two years of fighting before Bruce was accepted as King of Scots. He had to force many Scots to abandon King John Balliol, and others to reject the claims of Edward II as overlord. Bruce emphasised his own royal blood to justify his claim and his victory at Bannockburn as a sign of God's approval. However, he was unable to change the mind of Edward II. Bruce was also unsuccessful in his attempts to increase pressure on Edward II by spreading the war to other parts of Britain.

3. Why did it take so long for Robert Bruce to be accepted as King of Scots? (Use **Source B** and recall.)   **5**

[END OF CONTEXT 2]

Mark

HISTORICAL STUDY: SCOTTISH AND BRITISH

CONTEXT 3: MARY, QUEEN OF
SCOTS AND THE SCOTTISH
REFORMATION, 1540s–1587

Answer the following questions using recalled knowledge and information from the sources where appropriate.

Source A is John Knox's description of the way in which the Earl of Arran broke the Treaty of Greenwich in 1543.

Source A

> That dishonest man, Arran, sneaked away from the Palace of Holyrood and went to Stirling. There, he apologised to Cardinal Beaton and the people who were with him for making a treaty with England. He then made a deal with the Devil by giving up his Protestant faith and also by breaking the oath that he had made to keep the Treaty of Greenwich with England.

1. How useful is **Source A** as evidence about the way in which the Earl of Arran broke the Treaty of Greenwich?   4

Source B explains why the Scots rebelled against Mary of Guise in 1559.

Source B

> The marriage of Mary, Queen of Scots and the Dauphin of France took place in 1558. Her mother, Mary of Guise, continued to rule Scotland on behalf of her daughter who stayed in France. Guise took strong action against Protestants in Scotland, especially after Elizabeth became Queen of England in November of the same year. She made more use of French officials and used more French soldiers to control key strongholds in Scotland. She demanded a new tax, but the Scottish nobles were determined not to allow that.

2. Why did the Scots rebel against Mary of Guise in 1559? (Use **Source B** and recall.)   5

3. Describe the events that led to the execution of Mary, Queen of Scots, in 1587.   5

[END OF CONTEXT 3]

Marks

HISTORICAL STUDY: SCOTTISH AND BRITISH

CONTEXT 4: THE COMING OF
THE CIVIL WAR, 1603–1642

Answer the following questions using recalled knowledge and information from the sources where appropriate.

1. Describe the changes in the way Scotland was governed after 1603.   **5**

Source A explains how Charles I raised money during his reign.

Source A

> From 1629 until 1640 Charles I raised money without calling Parliament even though monarchs were supposed to ask Parliament for permission to raise taxes. In return MPs could express their concerns about issues. In the years 1626 and 1627 a forced loan was introduced and five knights who refused to pay it were put in prison without a fair trial. Ship money was also collected. This tax was normally paid by counties with coastlines to pay for the navy to protect them but Charles forced all counties to pay ship money. He increased his income from £600,000 a year to £900,000 a year.

2. Why was there opposition to the methods used by Charles I to raise money? (Use **Source A** and recall.)   **5**

Source B is from a letter written by Thomas Wiseman of London, on 6 January 1642.

Source B

> Twelve bishops were wrongly accused of high treason by the Parliament. This week five of the leading members of the House of Commons and the Lord Mandeville in the House of Lords were accused by the King. This has bred so much anger, and rightly so, both in the city and Houses of Parliament, that we are afraid of rebellion.

3. How useful is **Source B** as evidence of the causes of the Civil War?   **4**

[END OF CONTEXT 4]

Mark

HISTORICAL STUDY: SCOTTISH AND BRITISH

> ### CONTEXT 5: "ANE END OF ANE AULD SANG": SCOTLAND AND THE TREATY OF UNION, 1690s–1715

Answer the following questions using recalled knowledge and information from the sources where appropriate.

1. Describe Scotland's economic problems in the years before the Union. **5**

Source A explains why opponents of the Union were unable to stop it being passed in Scotland.

Source A

> There was very clear opposition to the Union in Scotland and some towns sent petitions against it to Edinburgh. Opponents of the Union in the Scottish Parliament were not well enough organised to take advantage of this popular opinion. Some were actually frightened by the riots and violence in the city. Their figurehead, Hamilton, was found to be unreliable. On the other hand, the government had sent secret agents to promote the advantages of a Union to Scotland and, if that did not work, the government had money to offer.

2. Why were opponents of the Union unable to stop it being passed in Scotland? (Use **Source A** and recall.) **5**

Source B was written by Daniel Defoe in 1727.

Source B

> Now that their Parliament is gone, the Scottish nobles and gentlemen spend their time and consequently their money in England. The Union has opened the door to English manufacturers and ruined Scottish ones. Their cattle are sent to England, but money is spent there too. The troops raised in Scotland are in English service and Scotland receives no money from them either.

3. How useful is **Source B** as evidence about the effects of the Union on Scotland? **4**

[END OF CONTEXT 5]

Marks

HISTORICAL STUDY: SCOTTISH AND BRITISH

CONTEXT 6: IMMIGRANTS AND
EXILES: SCOTLAND, 1830s–1930s

Answer the following questions using recalled knowledge and information from the sources where appropriate.

Source A is a picture showing an Irish family produced for a British magazine in the 1840s.

Source A

1. How useful is **Source A** as evidence of why so many people left Ireland for Scotland in the 1840s?　　　　　4

Source B explains why Scots moved away from the Highlands.

Source B

> The lairds had discovered that their land would yield far greater profits from sheep and therefore encouraged their tenant farmers to leave. Poor soil and harsh weather made farming difficult and life in the Highlands became even worse with the repeated failure of the potato crop after 1846. In fact the Highland Scot was affected by conditions over which he had no control. However, many Highlanders preferred the countries of the Empire to Scotland's dismal industrial cities. Many Lowland craftsmen were also leaving at this time.

2. Why did so many Highland Scots emigrate? (Use **Source B** and recall.)　　　5

3. Describe the ways emigrants created Scottish communities in their new homelands.　　　5

[END OF CONTEXT 6]

Mark

HISTORICAL STUDY: SCOTTISH AND BRITISH

> **CONTEXT 7: FROM THE CRADLE TO THE GRAVE? SOCIAL WELFARE IN BRITAIN, 1890s–1951**

Answer the following questions using recalled knowledge and information from the sources where appropriate.

Source A is by the Aberdeen Association for Improving the Conditions of the Poor, in the late 19th century.

Source A

> Our aims are to encourage, in every available way, the efforts of the poor to live sober lives and to discourage idleness. In general, we want to help those who are sober and hardworking but who through illness or accident are in danger of being plunged into poverty. These are the only people who deserve our help.

1. How useful is **Source A** as evidence of attitudes to the poor at the end of the 19th century?   **4**

Source B explains the effects of the Second World War on welfare reform.

Source B

> During the war the government had to take more responsibility for the welfare of its citizens. The Ministry of Food was established and raised standards of health among the poorer classes. Rationing helped establish the idea of a universal and equal share of the country's food supply. Damage to homes affected rich and poor, with the government assisting all who were affected. Classes were mixing in society who previously had little in common. War brought many problems for civilians that could only be overcome by government action.

2. Why did the Second World War change people's attitudes towards welfare reform? (Use **Source B** and recall.)   **5**

3. Describe the limitations of the Labour Government reforms of 1945–1951.   **5**

[END OF CONTEXT 7]

Marks

HISTORICAL STUDY: SCOTTISH AND BRITISH

> ### CONTEXT 8: CAMPAIGNING FOR CHANGE: SOCIAL CHANGE IN SCOTLAND, 1900s–1979

Answer the following questions using recalled knowledge and information from the sources where appropriate.

Source A is an extract from rules introduced by the British Museum in 1914 after a painting was slashed by a Suffragette.

Source A

> The British Museum is open to men and also to women if accompanied by men who are willing to guarantee their good behaviour and take full responsibility. Unaccompanied women are only allowed in if they present a letter of introduction from a responsible person guaranteeing the woman's good behaviour and accepting responsibility for her actions.

1. How useful is **Source A** as evidence of attitudes to Suffragettes by 1914?   **4**

2. Describe the effects of the economic slump in Scotland in the 1920s and 1930s.   **5**

Source B is about increasing use of the countryside for recreation in Scotland.

Source B

> The 1920s and 1930s was the time when the "Outdoor Movement" had popular appeal. New organisations such as youth hostels, cycling clubs and rambling associations were set up. Cheap motor bikes helped get people to the countryside. While mountaineering remained an upper class sport in most of Britain, by the 1930s the unemployed in the West of Scotland were joining climbing clubs. Many people were pleased to be away from the overcrowded cities. The Scottish Rights of Way and Recreation Society campaigned for walkers' rights to roam in private estates.

3. Why did more Scots use the countryside for recreation between the wars? (Use **Source B** and recall.)   **5**

[END OF CONTEXT 8]

Mark

HISTORICAL STUDY: SCOTTISH AND BRITISH

> **CONTEXT 9: A TIME OF TROUBLES: IRELAND, 1900–1923**

Answer the following questions using recalled knowledge and information from the sources where appropriate.

Source A is part of a letter written by an Irish MP to the British Government in 1916.

Source A

> I admit the rebels were wrong to start an uprising but they fought a clean fight and no cruel acts against the British army were committed. The rebels should have been tried in court, sentenced and sent to jail. Executing the leaders has only increased support and sympathy for them. Already people in Dublin, who ten days ago refused to help the rebels, have changed their minds. Their anger against the British is spreading dangerously across the country.

1. How useful is **Source A** as evidence of Irish attitudes to the executions following the Easter Rising?   **4**

2. Describe the terms of the Anglo-Irish Treaty of 1922.   **5**

Source B explains why the Free State Army won the Irish Civil War.

Source B

> In June 1922, the Free State Army were supplied with artillery by the British government which they used to attack the Republicans. Within days they had won back the Four Courts and other important buildings which gave them control of Dublin. Despite this success, the Free State Army suffered a blow when their leader, Michael Collins, was killed. In response, Republican leaders were captured and executed. These executions shocked Ireland but the Catholic Church and most of the public supported the Free State Army and their attempts to end the war. Although the fighting continued for another year, the Free State Army eventually won.

3. Why did the Free State Army win the Irish Civil War in 1923? (Use **Source B** and recall.)   **5**

[END OF CONTEXT 9]

[END OF PART 2: SCOTTISH AND BRITISH CONTEXTS]

Marks

PART 3:

HISTORICAL STUDY: EUROPEAN AND WORLD

> ### CONTEXT 1: THE NORMAN CONQUEST, 1060–1153

Answer the following questions using recalled knowledge and information from the sources where appropriate.

Source A explains William's success as Duke of Normandy.

Source A

> At the age of nineteen William was already capable of leading the Normans into battle. He soon showed he was willing to use ruthless methods. When the town of Alençon refused to surrender he ordered that 34 prisoners should have their eyes gouged out as a warning. However, he also realised that he needed allies. He married Matilda, the daughter of the powerful Count Baldwin of Flanders in order to gain his support. The couple looked strange together as William was over 6 feet tall while his wife was 4 feet 2 inches.

1. Why did William become a successful leader of Normandy? (Use **Source A** and recall.) **5**

Sources B and **C** describe the way in which David I ruled Scotland.

Source B

> David I supported the development of monasticism in Scotland by founding many abbeys including Holyrood and Dryburgh. The monks significantly improved the economy of Scotland through their expertise in sheep farming, coal working and salt production. David also established a series of royal burghs, such as Stirling, Perth and Dunfermline. He brought many Anglo-Normans into the southern half of the country to help strengthen his rule. He also took direct control of Moray after a revolt against him there.

Source C

> David established many of Scotland's most important towns. These became the King's burghs where traders were given special rights and privileges. They also benefited from the minting of Scotland's first coins. He extended the amount of land under direct royal control and used his Norman knights to put down rebellions against his rule. He helped to end the quarrel between Roman and Celtic churches and encouraged the work of Cistercian monks at Melrose and Kinloss.

2. How far do **Sources B** and **C** agree about the way in which David I ruled Scotland? **4**

3. Describe the features of Norman government which were introduced to Scotland after 1124. **5**

[END OF CONTEXT 1]

Mark

HISTORICAL STUDY: EUROPEAN AND WORLD

> ### CONTEXT 2: THE CROSS AND THE CRESCENT: THE FIRST CRUSADE, 1096–1125

Answer the following questions using recalled knowledge and information from the sources where appropriate.

Sources A and **B** describe what happened to Jewish communities during the First Crusade.

Source A

> After only a few weeks of travelling, Peter the Hermit and his followers came upon a Jewish community in Germany. Many of the Crusaders were poor and hungry so they began stealing food and possessions from the Jews. As the Crusaders thought the Jews were the enemy of Christ, most believed they could treat them as they wished. Some forced the Jews to change religion and become Christian. Others, against the orders of Peter the Hermit, slaughtered the Jews.

Source B

> A rumour spread amongst the Crusaders that whoever killed a Jew would have all their sins forgiven. Immediately Peter the Hermit's army began attacking and killing Jewish men, women and children. Although some Jews tried to fight back they had few weapons and were easily defeated. In the riot that followed, houses were robbed and valuables stolen. Those Jews who survived the massacre were forced to give up their faith and become Christians.

1. How far do **Sources A** and **B** agree about what happened to Jews during the First Crusade?　**4**

Source C explains why Emperor Alexius and the Crusaders had a poor relationship.

Source C

> When Emperor Alexius freed the Muslims inside Nicaea the Crusaders were outraged. They had taken a vow to kill all Muslims and did not expect them to be shown mercy. Worse still, Alexius insulted the Crusaders by denying them the chance to plunder the city to take their share of the treasure. Although the Crusaders needed the Emperor's help, many openly said they would no longer keep their oath of loyalty to him. Instead of returning any land they captured, the Crusaders agreed to keep it for themselves.

2. Why did Emperor Alexius and the Crusaders have a poor relationship? (Use **Source C** and recall.)　**5**

3. Describe the capture of Jerusalem in 1099.　**5**

[END OF CONTEXT 2]

Marks

HISTORICAL STUDY: EUROPEAN AND WORLD

CONTEXT 3: WAR, DEATH AND REVOLT IN MEDIEVAL EUROPE, 1328–1436

Answer the following questions using recalled knowledge and information from the sources where appropriate.

Source A explains the French defeat at Crecy.

Source A

> The English took up position on a hillside outside the village of Crecy. The French were forced to fight uphill. The French archers used crossbows which fired deadly iron-tipped bolts. However these weapons took time to reload. The first French cavalry charge was met by a hail of arrows. The knights were forced back and many French foot-soldiers were trampled by their own horsemen. The French charged 16 times but by midnight it was all over.

1. Why were the French defeated at Crecy? (Use **Source A** and recall.)   5

2. Describe the Jacquerie risings in France in 1358.   5

Sources B and **C** describe the effects of the Hundred Years War on France.

Source B

> By the end of the war there was not a chateau or a church in northern and western France which had not been destroyed by the English. No proper peace treaty was ever signed. The English regarded their expulsion from France as only temporary. In 1457 Charles VII wrote to the King of Scots that Frenchmen had to watch the coast daily for a new English invasion. The English still had the advantage of controlling Calais from where they could march out to re-conquer lost lands.

Source C

> Although Charles VII was at first worried that the English would return, he ensured that his coasts were well defended and encouraged attacks on English shipping in the Channel. The English were faced with the problem of having to pour resources into the defence of Calais. All in all the French emerged stronger from the war and the English weaker. The recovery by the French of much of their land in the north and west had been easy and had caused little destruction.

3. How far do **Sources B** and **C** disagree about the effects of the Hundred Years War on France?   4

[END OF CONTEXT 3]

Mark

HISTORICAL STUDY: EUROPEAN AND WORLD

> **CONTEXT 4: NEW WORLDS:**
> **EUROPE IN THE AGE OF**
> **EXPANSION, 1480s–1530s**

Answer the following questions using recalled knowledge and information from the sources where appropriate.

1. Describe the improvements in technology which made the voyages of discovery possible.   **5**

Source A explains the importance of Vasco da Gama's voyage.

Source A

> In 1497–8, Vasco da Gama made the longest voyage that any European vessel had achieved in the open sea. He sailed far out into the South Atlantic before heading east and crossing the Indian Ocean to Calicut. He returned the following year with three quarters of his crew and the first cargo of spices. When the cargo was sold it made a profit sixty times the cost of the voyage. The king of Portugal was delighted that he had found trade routes to Ethiopia, Arabia, Persia and India.

2. Why was Vasco da Gama's voyage important for European trade? (Use **Source A** and recall.)   **5**

Sources B and **C** describe the impact of Europeans on the native peoples of the New World.

Source B

> Great cities, their culture, their religion and their civilisations were destroyed by the Conquistadors. Kings who had gold and wealth were held captive and their people forced to pay ransoms in gold for them. The native people were used as slaves to make money for their new rulers in many ways such as in silver mines and even on sugar plantations. In return, the Europeans brought them new diseases which wiped them out in hundreds of thousands.

Source C

> The European explorers opened the New World to European settlers. Smallpox and measles spread rapidly and whole populations, such as the people of Hispaniola, had no resistance and died. Both the Spanish and Portuguese were keen to convert the native people to Christianity and their existing religions were harshly discouraged. However, this did not prevent the Europeans from taking gold and riches from the New World by any means, fair or unfair.

3. How far do **Sources B** and **C** agree about the impact of Europeans on the native peoples of the New World?   **4**

[END OF CONTEXT 4]

HISTORICAL STUDY: EUROPEAN AND WORLD

Marks

> ### CONTEXT 5: "TEA AND FREEDOM": THE AMERICAN REVOLUTION, 1763–1783

Answer the following questions using recalled knowledge and information from the sources where appropriate.

1. Describe what happened during the *Gaspée* incident in 1772.   **5**

Source A explains why many colonists were unhappy with British rule by 1776.

Source A

> The writer Thomas Paine was firmly opposed to British rule. In January 1776, he published a cleverly written pamphlet called "Common Sense". In it, he argued that the British government was abusing the rights of the American people and many colonists were persuaded by his arguments. The answer, Paine believed, was independence. Paine's ideas were very popular and 150,000 pamphlets were sold. The King's rejection of the Olive Branch Petition also moved many colonists towards independence, as did news that the British were hiring mercenary soldiers from Germany to help them control the colonies.

2. Why had many colonists turned against British rule by 1776? (Use **Source A** and recall.)   **5**

Sources B and **C** are about the defeat of British forces, led by General Cornwallis, at Yorktown.

Source B

> In 1781, Cornwallis moved into Virginia and began to build a base at Yorktown. By late summer, Cornwallis's position at Yorktown was deteriorating fast. While American forces prevented him from moving inland, a large French fleet carrying 3,000 troops had sailed up from the West Indies to join the siege. The fate of Cornwallis was sealed when the French defeated the British fleet in Chesapeake Bay. On October 19 Cornwallis surrendered his entire army of 7,000 men.

Source C

> To launch his campaign in Virginia, Cornwallis's army carried out raids, harassing the Americans wherever he could. In August 1781, Cornwallis set up camp at Yorktown but this turned out to be a poor position. American troops moved quickly to surround him and keep him there. The British could not help Cornwallis's army to escape or bring in reinforcements. In September, the French defeated the British fleet in a naval battle near Yorktown, giving the allies control over the sea in the area.

3. How far do **Sources B** and **C** agree about the reasons for the defeat of the forces led by Cornwallis at Yorktown?   **4**

[END OF CONTEXT 5]

Mark

HISTORICAL STUDY: EUROPEAN AND WORLD

> ### CONTEXT 6: "THIS ACCURSED TRADE": THE BRITISH SLAVE TRADE AND ITS ABOLITION, 1770–1807

Answer the following questions using recalled knowledge and information from the sources where appropriate.

Source A explains why resistance was difficult on slave plantations in the West Indies.

Source A

> Most slaves in the West Indies were involved in the production of sugar which was hard, heavy work. The life of the slave on the plantation was controlled by strict slave laws, or codes. Some slaves, however, refused to accept their circumstances and attempted to escape or plotted revolt. Those who escaped would be hunted down. Slave owners lived in constant fear of a revolt by their slaves. Slave risings took place throughout the colonies but very few had effective leadership and they were soon crushed by the better armed and organised whites.

1. Why was resistance difficult for slaves on the plantations? (Use **Source A** and recall.)   5

Sources B and **C** are about the importance of the slave trade for Britain.

Source B

> There were many reasons why it took so long to abolish the slave trade. One reason was that the slave trade had many powerful supporters. Plantation owners and merchants in British ports which relied on the slave trade were well organised and had political influence. They had enough wealth to bribe MPs to support them. They also had the support of King George III. Many people believed that the trade had helped them to make Britain wealthy and prosperous.

Source C

> The Abolitionists faced powerful opposition. The plantation owners allied themselves with important groups to promote the case for slavery and the slave trade. Their case seemed overwhelming. Dozens of British ports and surrounding areas relied on the slave trade. British consumers had become addicted to the products of the slave trade, most notably sugar. The Atlantic slave trade represented a large amount of British trade and seemed vital to the continuing prosperity of Britain and the Caribbean Islands.

2. How far do **Sources B** and **C** agree about the reasons the slave trade continued in Britain throughout the eighteenth century?   4

3. In what ways did the Abolitionists try to win support for their cause?   5

[END OF CONTEXT 6]

Marks

HISTORICAL STUDY: EUROPEAN AND WORLD

```
CONTEXT 7: CITIZENS! THE
FRENCH REVOLUTION, 1789–1794
```

Answer the following questions using recalled knowledge and information from the sources where appropriate.

1. Describe the complaints of the French peasants in 1789.   **5**

Sources A and **B** describe the supporters of the revolution who were known as the sans-culottes.

Source A

> The sans-culotte is an honest man who wants an honest reward for his work. The sans-culotte is a quiet, humble fellow who wishes only to live in peace with his fellow man. He feels at home in the poorest areas of Paris and lives only for the wife and children he loves so much. He is happy so long as he has a loaf of bread and a glass of wine, for his needs are simple.

Source B

> The main aim of these so-called sans-culottes is to get as much as they can for as little effort as possible. They have adopted a system of politics which puts them at the top of society and they care about little else. Violence is the only method they have to get what they want and the arrogance of these people from the gutter is astonishing.

2. How far do **Sources A** and **B** disagree about attitudes towards the sans-culottes?   **4**

Source C explains the unhappiness of the French people with the treatment of the Catholic Church.

Source C

> The National Assembly decided it was time to bring the Catholic Church under much tighter state control. The *assignat*, the new currency, was not being accepted and the government needed more money. Church lands were to be sold and the proceeds taken by the Assembly. Priests were to become government agents rather than servants of the Church. Bishops were to be elected which many French Catholics resented because even Protestants would be allowed to vote. However, the Assembly continued to support the teachings of the Church.

3. Why were many French people unhappy with the treatment of the Catholic Church during the French Revolution? (Use **Source C** and recall.)   **5**

[END OF CONTEXT 7]

Mark

HISTORICAL STUDY: EUROPEAN AND WORLD

> CONTEXT 8: CAVOUR, GARIBALDI
> AND THE MAKING OF ITALY,
> 1815–1870

Answer the following questions using recalled knowledge and information from the sources where appropriate.

Source A explains the influence of Napoleon Bonaparte on Italy.

Source A

> Napoleon proclaimed himself Emperor of France in 1804. He incorporated one third of Italy into the French Empire and created a Kingdom of Italy in the north. In this kingdom he encouraged the Italian language and literature. He took on the title of "King of Italy". Positive changes were introduced by Napoleon such as the abolition of internal customs barriers and the building of roads across the Alps, bringing Italians closer together.

1. Why did Napoleon Bonaparte have an important influence on Italian unification? (Use **Source A** and recall.)   5

2. Describe the events between 1850 and 1871 which led to the unification of Italy.   5

Sources B and **C** are about Cavour's contribution to unification.

Source B

> Cavour was not always a supporter of a united Italy. He took advantage of opportunities that came along rather than carrying out a clear plan of his own. He only united Italy to stop the activities of Garibaldi and not because he really believed in Italian unification. Cavour's actions in uniting Italy were a last desperate attempt to protect the power and influence of Piedmont.

Source C

> Cavour was a great diplomat and a brilliant planner. His ambition was always to unite Italy. To do this he raised the prestige of Italy and won the respect of foreign powers. Cavour allowed Garibaldi to win the south for Italy and for King Victor Emmanuel. Cavour himself gained the support of Napoleon III to break the power of Austria and keep Italy free from foreign intervention.

3. How far do **Sources B** and **C** disagree about the contribution of Cavour to the unification of Italy?   4

[END OF CONTEXT 8]

Marks

HISTORICAL STUDY: EUROPEAN AND WORLD

> **CONTEXT 9: IRON AND BLOOD?**
> **BISMARCK AND THE CREATION OF**
> **THE GERMAN EMPIRE, 1815–1871**

Answer the following questions using recalled knowledge and information from the sources where appropriate.

1. In what ways did German national feeling grow before 1848?   **5**

Source A explains the changing power of Austria and Prussia between 1850 and 1860.

Source A

> The balance of power between Austria and Prussia changed in the 1850s. During this time Austria had never been able to find anyone as skillful as Metternich in controlling the German states. Austria also lost an important alliance with Russia when it failed to help Russia in the Crimean War. In 1859 the French defeat of Austria destroyed her strong military reputation. Although Prussia had been humiliated at Olmutz, Prussian industrialisation led to economic growth and better trade links. This strengthened her position in the German Confederation.

2. Why had Austria lost her leading position in Germany by 1860? (Use **Source A** and recall.)   **5**

Sources B and **C** are about Bismarck's aims for unification.

Source B

> The British Prime Minister, Disraeli, had a conversation with Bismarck in 1862. Disraeli reported Bismarck's first vital task to strengthen Prussia's position in Germany was going to be the re-organisation of the army, with or without the help of the Prussian Parliament. Disraeli then said that Bismarck wanted to seize the first excuse to create war against Austria, control the smaller states and thus unite Germany under Prussian leadership.

Source C

> Bismarck's aims were to remove Austria and extend Prussia's power over the other German states in order to unite them under Prussian leadership. It was Bismarck's decision to reform the army which made Prussia dominant in Germany. After this he planned to force Austria to go to war with Prussia. The triumph of Bismarck's policy was to be seen on the battlefield at Koniggratz in 1866.

3. How far do **Sources B** and **C** agree about Bismarck's aims to unite Germany?   **4**

[END OF CONTEXT 9]

HISTORICAL STUDY: EUROPEAN AND WORLD

Mark

CONTEXT 10: THE RED FLAG:
LENIN AND THE RUSSIAN
REVOLUTION, 1894–1921

Answer the following questions using recalled knowledge and information from the sources where appropriate.

1.   Describe the hardships faced by industrial workers in Russia before 1914.   **5**

Source A explains why the Russian Royal Family had become increasingly unpopular by 1917.

Source A

> The Romanov dynasty had lasted for 300 years and Nicholas and Alexandra were unwilling to give up autocratic rule. Although the Tsar had been persuaded to set up the Duma he did not let it run the country and largely ignored it. When the Tsar left Alexandra in charge of the government this was a disastrous decision. Alexandra was influenced by Rasputin who advised her to sack many of the competent ministers if he simply disliked them. This made the situation even worse.

2.   Why had the Russian Royal Family become increasingly unpopular by 1917? (Use **Source A** and recall.)   **5**

Sources B and **C** describe Trotsky's leadership in the Civil War.

Source B

> For three years Trotsky lived on his armoured train travelling to all areas of the front. He covered 65,000 miles during the course of the war ensuring that the Red Army was well fed and properly armed. He was an inspirational leader and was dedicated to the cause. He made rousing speeches to the troops and raised morale even when other Bolshevik leaders were not convinced that they would defeat the Whites. Over 5 million men had joined the Red Army by 1920 of their own free will.

Source C

> Trotsky was appointed Commissar for War in early 1919 and quickly established a reputation as a ruthless leader who used strict discipline. He forced people to join the Red Army to raise the numbers of troops and introduced 50,000 former Tsarist officers to train the raw recruits. The death penalty was not only used for deserters. When 200 soldiers deserted at Svyazhsk, Trotsky arrived and ordered the execution of one in every ten men in the regiment, as a warning to the rest.

3.   How far do **Sources B** and **C** disagree about Trotsky's leadership in the Civil War?   **4**

[END OF CONTEXT 10]

Marks

HISTORICAL STUDY: EUROPEAN AND WORLD

CONTEXT 11: FREE AT LAST? RACE RELATIONS IN THE USA, 1918–1968

Answer the following questions using recalled knowledge and information from the sources where appropriate.

1. Describe the activities of the Ku Klux Klan in the 1920s and 1930s.   **5**

Sources A and **B** describe the results of the Montgomery Bus Boycott.

Source A

> Throughout the boycott a young black preacher inspired the black population of Montgomery. His name was Martin Luther King and this was to be his first step towards becoming the leading figure in the Civil Rights Movement. The boycott lasted over a year until eventually the courts decided that segregation on Montgomery's buses was illegal. On its own the bus boycott only had limited success. Montgomery remained a segregated town. There were still white-only theatres, pool rooms and restaurants.

Source B

> The bus company's services were boycotted by 99% of Montgomery's African Americans for over a year. As a result of the protest, the US Supreme Court announced that Alabama's bus segregation laws were illegal. However, most other facilities and services in Montgomery remained segregated for many years to come. As a result of the boycott, Martin Luther King became involved in the Civil Rights Movement. He went on to become an African American leader who was famous throughout the world.

2. How far do **Sources A** and **B** agree about the results of the Montgomery Bus Boycott?   **4**

Source C explains why Malcolm X opposed non-violent protest.

Source C

> Malcolm X was mistreated in his youth and this gave him a different set of attitudes to Martin Luther King. Later, while in jail, he was influenced by the ideas of Elijah Muhammad who preached hatred of the white race. In his speeches he criticised non-violence. He believed that the support of non-violence was a sign that Black people were still living in mental slavery. However, Malcolm X never undertook violent action himself and sometimes prevented it. Instead he often used violent language and threats to frighten the government into action.

3. Why did Malcolm X oppose non-violent protest? (Use **Source C** and recall.)   **5**

[END OF CONTEXT 11]

Mark

HISTORICAL STUDY: EUROPEAN AND WORLD

> ### CONTEXT 12: THE ROAD TO WAR, 1933–1939

Answer the following questions using recalled knowledge and information from the sources where appropriate.

Source A explains why Hitler wanted to rearm Germany in the 1930s.

Source A

> Hitler claimed that Germany alone was forced to leave herself defenceless as part of the punishment dictated by her enemies in 1919. He never missed an opportunity to attack the Treaty of Versailles. Hitler further stated that Germany was surrounded by hostile countries whose main purpose was to keep her in a weakened position and this could no longer be tolerated. A strong Germany would not only restore the balance of power in Europe but was also necessary to safeguard European civilisation against the threat from the east.

1. Why did Hitler want to rearm Germany in the 1930s? (Use **Source A** and recall.)   5

Sources B and **C** are about the Germans in the Sudetenland, Czechoslovakia.

Source B

> Germany's justification for interfering in Czechoslovakia was that the Sudetenland wanted to return to the German Fatherland. Ever since 1919 the Sudeten Germans had resented being part of the new state of Czechoslovakia which was based on the medieval kingdom of Bohemia. The German government claimed that the Germans in Czechoslovakia had suffered constant persecution because they were an ethnic minority.

Source C

> Sudeten German unrest grew only after the economic depression began in the early 1930s. Germany seemed to be the only country whose economy was improving. Although they shared the same language and culture, the Sudetenland had never been part of Germany. Since 1919, the Sudeten Germans had been treated with respect in Czechoslovakia because they had contributed greatly to the nation's wealth.

2. How far do **Sources B** and **C** disagree about the Germans living in Czechoslovakia?   4

3. Describe events in 1939 that led to the outbreak of war between Britain and Germany.   5

[END OF CONTEXT 12]

Marks

HISTORICAL STUDY: EUROPEAN AND WORLD

> ### CONTEXT 13: IN THE SHADOW OF THE BOMB: THE COLD WAR, 1945–1985

Answer the following questions using recalled knowledge and information from the sources where appropriate.

1. Describe the events which led to the formation of the Warsaw Pact in 1955.   **5**

Sources A and **B** are about the Cuban Missile Crisis.

Source A

> Under Fidel Castro, Cuba was a proud example of a Communist country and was a role model to other countries. Khrushchev had the idea of installing a small number of nuclear missiles on Cuba without letting the USA know until it was too late to stop them. Khrushchev said they only wanted to keep the Americans from invading Cuba. He stated they had no desire to start a war.

Source B

> To the American government, placing missiles on Cuba was a warlike act by the Soviets. They believed that the Soviet Union intended to supply a large number of powerful nuclear weapons. Spy photographs proved the offensive purpose of the missiles which were pointed directly at major American cities. It was estimated that within a few minutes of them being fired, 80 million Americans would be dead.

2. How far do **Sources A** and **B** disagree about the Soviet Union's actions during the Cuban Missile Crisis?   **4**

Source C explains why the United States became involved in a war in Vietnam.

Source C

> In its early stages, the war in Vietnam had nothing to do with the USA. American involvement began when it was asked by its ally, France, for assistance. France was fighting to regain control over its former colony. The Americans agreed. They disapproved of French colonialism, but feared Communism more. They believed that they could establish a friendly government in South Vietnam, under the leadership of President Diem. By the early 1960s an increase in Vietcong attacks in South Vietnam led to a fear that a civil war was developing.

3. Why did America become involved in a full scale war in Vietnam by 1964? (Use **Source C** and recall.)   **5**

[*END OF CONTEXT 13*]

[*END OF PART 3: EUROPEAN AND WORLD CONTEXTS*]

[*END OF QUESTION PAPER*]

[BLANK PAGE]

SQA

[BLANK PAGE]

X044/11/01

| NATIONAL QUALIFICATIONS 2012 | FRIDAY, 25 MAY 9.00 AM – 10.45 AM | HISTORY INTERMEDIATE 2 |

The instructions for this paper are on *Page two*. Read them carefully before you begin your answers.

Your Invigilator will tell you which contexts to answer in Parts 2 and 3 of the examination.

SQA
©

INSTRUCTIONS

Answer **one** question from Part 1, The Short Essay

Answer **one** context* from Part 2, Scottish and British

Answer **one** context* from Part 3, European and World

Answer **one** other context* from

> **either** Part 2, Scottish and British

> **or**   Part 3, European and World

*Answer all the questions in each of your chosen contexts.

Contents

[Turn over

PART 1: THE SHORT ESSAY

Mark

Answer **one** question. For this question you should write a short essay using your own knowledge. The essay should include an introduction, development and conclusion. Each question is worth 8 marks.

SCOTTISH AND BRITISH CONTEXTS:

CONTEXT 1: MURDER IN THE CATHEDRAL: CROWN, CHURCH AND PEOPLE, 1154–1173

Question 1: Explain the importance of monasteries in the twelfth century.   **8**

CONTEXT 2: WALLACE, BRUCE AND THE WARS OF INDEPENDENCE, 1286–1328

Question 2: Explain why the Scots won the Battle of Stirling Bridge.   **8**

CONTEXT 3: MARY, QUEEN OF SCOTS AND THE SCOTTISH REFORMATION, 1540s–1587

Question 3: Explain why Queen Elizabeth kept Mary, Queen of Scots, in prison for so long.   **8**

CONTEXT 4: THE COMING OF THE CIVIL WAR, 1603–1642

Question 4: Explain why James VI and I faced serious problems over religion.   **8**

CONTEXT 5: "ANE END OF ANE AULD SANG": SCOTLAND AND THE TREATY OF UNION, 1690s–1715

Question 5: Explain why support for the Jacobites grew between 1707 and 1715.   **8**

CONTEXT 6: IMMIGRANTS AND EXILES: SCOTLAND, 1830s–1930s

Question 6: Explain why so many Scots emigrated between 1830 and 1900.   **8**

CONTEXT 7: FROM THE CRADLE TO THE GRAVE? SOCIAL WELFARE IN BRITAIN, 1890s–1951

Question 7: Explain why the Labour Government reforms of 1945–1951 were important in creating a welfare state.   **8**

Marks

**CONTEXT 8: CAMPAIGNING FOR CHANGE:
SOCIAL CHANGE IN SCOTLAND, 1900s–1979**

Question 8: Explain why Scots had improved access to leisure opportunities by 1939.   8

**CONTEXT 9: A TIME OF TROUBLES:
IRELAND, 1900–1923**

Question 9: Explain why a civil war broke out in Ireland in 1922.   8

EUROPEAN AND WORLD CONTEXTS:

CONTEXT 1: THE NORMAN CONQUEST, 1060–1153

Question 10: Explain why Duke William won the Battle of Hastings in 1066.   8

**CONTEXT 2: THE CROSS AND THE CRESCENT:
THE FIRST CRUSADE, 1096–1125**

Question 11: Explain why the People's Crusade failed to capture Jerusalem.   8

**CONTEXT 3: WAR, DEATH AND REVOLT
IN MEDIEVAL EUROPE, 1328–1436**

Question 12: Explain why Joan of Arc was burnt at the stake in 1431.   8

**CONTEXT 4: NEW WORLDS:
EUROPE IN THE AGE OF EXPANSION, 1480s–1530s**

Question 13: Explain why European monarchs encouraged voyages of exploration.   8

**CONTEXT 5: "TEA AND FREEDOM":
THE AMERICAN REVOLUTION, 1763–1783**

Question 14: Explain why many colonists were unhappy with British rule by 1775.   8

**CONTEXT 6: "THIS ACCURSED TRADE":
THE BRITISH SLAVE TRADE AND ITS ABOLITION, 1770–1807**

Question 15: Explain why so many people in Britain continued to defend the slave trade.   8

Mark.

CONTEXT 7: CITIZENS!
THE FRENCH REVOLUTION, 1789–1794

Question 16:   Explain why Louis XVI was sentenced to death in 1792.   **8**

CONTEXT 8: CAVOUR, GARIBALDI
AND THE MAKING OF ITALY, 1815–1870

Question 17:   Explain why Italian nationalism grew between 1815 and 1848.   **8**

CONTEXT 9: IRON AND BLOOD? BISMARCK AND THE
CREATION OF THE GERMAN EMPIRE, 1815–1871

Question 18:   Explain why Prussia was successful in the wars of unification.   **8**

CONTEXT 10: THE RED FLAG:
LENIN AND THE RUSSIAN REVOLUTION, 1894–1921

Question 19:   Explain why the Russian people were so discontented by February 1917.   **8**

CONTEXT 11: FREE AT LAST?
RACE RELATIONS IN THE USA, 1918–1968

Question 20:   Explain why the Ku Klux Klan was so powerful in the South in the 1920s.   **8**

CONTEXT 12: THE ROAD TO WAR, 1933–1939

Question 21:   Explain why Hitler wanted to break the Treaty of Versailles in the 1930s.   **8**

CONTEXT 13: IN THE SHADOW OF THE BOMB:
THE COLD WAR, 1945–1985

Question 22:   Explain why the Cold War had broken out between 1945 and 1950.   **8**

[Turn over for PART 2: SCOTTISH AND BRITISH CONTEXTS on *Page eight*

Mark

PART 2:

HISTORICAL STUDY: SCOTTISH AND BRITISH

**CONTEXT 1: MURDER IN THE
CATHEDRAL: CROWN, CHURCH
AND PEOPLE, 1154–1173**

Answer the following questions using recalled knowledge and information from the sources where appropriate.

Source A explains why Henry II had problems when he became king in 1154.

Source A

> The civil war between Stephen and Matilda had given the barons a chance to increase their wealth and power. Many barons had private armies and used them to steal land and valuables from weaker neighbours. As soon as he became king, Henry ordered these armies to leave the country and introduced new laws to stop the theft of land. Next, Henry dealt with the barons who had refused to pay taxes and he attacked those who had started to rebel against him.

1. Why did Henry II have problems when he became king in 1154? (Use **Source A** and recall.)   5

2. Describe the duties of a medieval baron.   5

Sources B and **C** describe the murder of Archbishop Becket.

Source B

> The knights entered the cathedral and began shouting at Becket. They dragged him away and told him he was under arrest. Becket, who had just returned from exile in France, refused to leave. He knelt down and stated he was ready to die for God. The knights drew their swords, and in the scuffle that followed, injured Edward Grim. Becket was knocked to the ground and hit four times on the head.

Source C

> The knights told Becket he was the king's prisoner and forced him from the altar. Despite the threat of violence, Becket said he was willing to be a martyr for the Church and began to pray. Edward Grim tried to protect Becket but he was attacked by the knights and his arm was badly cut. Becket knew the king had sent the knights to murder him and so bowed his head and waited for the attack to begin.

3. How far do **Sources B** and **C** agree about the murder of Archbishop Becket?   4

[END OF CONTEXT 1]

Marks

HISTORICAL STUDY: SCOTTISH AND BRITISH

> ### CONTEXT 2: WALLACE, BRUCE AND THE WARS OF INDEPENDENCE, 1286–1328

Answer the following questions using recalled knowledge and information from the sources where appropriate.

Sources A and **B** are about who should be the next King of Scots.

Source A

> John Balliol said he had the strongest right to be King of Scots. He argued this was because he was descended from the eldest daughter in the family of David, Earl of Huntingdon, the brother of King William the Lion. Balliol said it did not matter that he was a generation younger than Bruce because the feudal law of primogeniture always supported the eldest line of a family.

Source B

> Robert Bruce was determined that he was to be the next King of Scots. He said that Imperial Law supported him because he was one generation closer to the Earl of Huntingdon's family than Balliol. Bruce argued that the feudal law of primogeniture did not apply to kingdoms. He argued that it did not matter that Balliol was descended from the eldest of Earl David's daughters.

1. How far do **Sources A** and **B** disagree about who should be the next King of Scots?   **4**

Source C explains the failure of John Balliol as King of Scots.

Source C

> John Balliol's final humiliation happened when King Edward publicly stripped him of his title. Consequently, John Balliol is often described as "toom tabard". In fact, he did not get this nickname until after his final defeat. The Bruces, who never supported him, encouraged the idea that Balliol had never been fit to be a king. Even before his final defeat, the Scottish nobles had appointed twelve men to force Balliol to stand up to King Edward. They realised that by himself Balliol was unable to stop Edward interfering in the government of Scotland.

2. Why was Balliol a failure as King of Scots? (Use **Source C** and recall.)   **5**

3. Describe how Robert Bruce made all the Scots accept him as king.   **5**

[END OF CONTEXT 2]

Mark

HISTORICAL STUDY: SCOTTISH AND BRITISH

> **CONTEXT 3: MARY, QUEEN OF SCOTS AND THE SCOTTISH REFORMATION, 1540s–1587**

Answer the following questions using recalled knowledge and information from the sources where appropriate.

Source A explains why King Henry VIII interfered in Scotland after 1542.

Source A

> King James V of Scots died in 1542, only eight days after the birth of his daughter Mary. King Henry VIII of England immediately realised the benefits of marrying the young Queen Mary to his son. It would also end French influence in Scotland and bring about an end to centuries of warfare between Scotland and England. The most recent war had contributed to the early death of James V. Henry VIII also saw an opportunity to spread Protestantism north of the border.

1. Why did King Henry VIII interfere in Scotland after 1542? (Use **Source A** and recall.)   5

2. Describe the problems Mary, Queen of Scots faced when she arrived in Scotland in 1561.   5

Sources B and **C** describe what happened in Scotland after Mary, Queen of Scots, fled to England.

Source B

> Queen Mary's supporters fought for several years after she fled to England. They hoped that the tribunal Elizabeth held in England would lead to their Queen's return. When this failed, one of Mary's supporters assassinated the Regent Moray. A year later, his replacement, the Earl of Lennox, was killed in a skirmish. The capture of Edinburgh Castle in 1573 removed Mary's last power base in Scotland.

Source C

> Mary's support in Scotland was undermined in 1569 when her Governor, Châtelherault and his deputy, the Earl of Argyll, changed sides. Nevertheless, her supporters killed both the Regent Moray and his successor. In 1573, after a few years of fighting, the Regent Morton finally persuaded most of Mary's supporters to recognise his authority. A few months later, Edinburgh Castle was forced to surrender.

3. How far do **Sources B** and **C** agree about what happened in Scotland after Mary, Queen of Scots, fled to England?   4

[END OF CONTEXT 3]

Marks

HISTORICAL STUDY: SCOTTISH AND BRITISH

> ### CONTEXT 4: THE COMING OF
> ### THE CIVIL WAR, 1603–1642

Answer the following questions using recalled knowledge and information from the sources where appropriate.

Source A explains why there were difficulties between James VI and I and the English Parliament.

Source A

> James found his Parliament to be argumentative and unco-operative. On the other hand the English Parliament thought James to be far too stubborn and that he spent too much money. In 1610, Parliamentary negotiations attempted to ease the tensions over James' requests for money. Negotiations failed and James annoyed MPs by dismissing his Parliament in anger. Negotiations in the 1614 Parliament again failed and James angered the nobility by deciding to govern without a Parliament and brought in his own favourites to find ways of raising money.

1. Why were there difficulties between James VI and I and the English Parliament between 1603 and 1625? (Use **Source A** and recall.)   5

2. Describe the reaction in Scotland to the introduction of the new Prayer Book in 1637.   5

Sources B and **C** are about the activities of the Long Parliament between 1640 and 1641.

Source B

> The Long Parliament opened on 3 November 1640 and attempted to create political reform. The King's Ministers were accused of High Treason and Strafford and Laud were impeached and imprisoned. Strafford was later executed. In 1641, the Triennial Act meant that a new Parliament would be held every three years whether the King liked it or not. Parliament was also successful in ending taxes on Tonnage and Poundage and in declaring Ship Money illegal.

Source C

> In February 1641 Charles gave in to Parliament by signing an Act which ensured Parliament could meet even without the King's consent. Charles signed Strafford's death warrant. Strafford had been accused by Parliament of High Treason and Charles felt pressured into making an example of him. By the summer of 1641, Charles felt isolated and was compelled to agree to new laws such as the Ship Money Act and the abolition of the Courts of Star Chamber.

3. How far do **Sources B** and **C** agree about the activities of the Long Parliament between 1640 and 1641?   4

[END OF CONTEXT 4]

Mark

HISTORICAL STUDY: SCOTTISH AND BRITISH

> **CONTEXT 5: "ANE END OF ANE AULD SANG": SCOTLAND AND THE TREATY OF UNION, 1690s–1715**

Answer the following questions using recalled knowledge and information from the sources where appropriate.

Source A explains why many Scots decided to invest in the Darien Scheme.

Source A

> After the Union of the Crowns, the Scots became aware that the prosperity of their country depended on farming which suffered from bad weather and poor soil. In fact, very little was done to improve Scottish farming for another fifty years. Scottish overseas trade was limited and it did not make huge amounts of money for the country. The Scots thought that England's prosperity came from its overseas trade with its colonies. William Paterson promised them a colony where "trade will increase and money will make money".

1. Why did the Scots invest in the Darien Scheme? (Use **Source A** and recall.)   5

Sources B and **C** are about why some Scots suggested a Union.

Source B

> Queen Anne had always wanted a union between her two kingdoms. A number of Scots supported the idea believing that trading with England's colonies would make Scotland a wealthier country. Many English people worried that a union would make England poorer. England's frequent wars with France annoyed the Scots because Scotland's trade with France was badly affected. The Scottish "Act of Security" offered England a shared monarch in return for access to its colonies.

Source C

> Bad feelings between Scotland and England erupted into a crisis when Anne became Queen in 1702. The Scots were angry because the ban from trading with England's colonies stopped them from increasing their wealth, especially since they blamed England for the failure of Darien. In 1703, they demanded access to England's colonies in return for sharing a monarch. Then they passed the Wine Act to reduce the bad effects of England's wars against France on Scotland's trade.

2. How far do **Sources B** and **C** agree about why some Scots suggested a Union?   4

3. Describe how Queen Anne's government won support for the Act of Union.   5

[END OF CONTEXT 5]

Marks

HISTORICAL STUDY: SCOTTISH AND BRITISH

CONTEXT 6: IMMIGRANTS AND EXILES: SCOTLAND, 1830s–1930s

Answer the following questions using recalled knowledge and information from the sources where appropriate.

1. Describe the "pull" factors which attracted Irish immigrants to Scotland.   5

Source A explains why the Catholic Church was important for many Irish immigrants in the nineteenth century.

Source A

> The Irish immigrants were not very well-off and the native Scots often did not welcome them. The church gave them a place to worship and a sense of security. Immigrants knew that they could be baptised, married and buried according to their religion. The priests usually spoke Irish so there was someone to whom they could explain their problems. Over time a number of Catholic churches were established in the west of Scotland. The church became a centre of social life and gave the immigrants an opportunity to meet their fellow countrymen.

2. Why was the Catholic Church important to many Irish immigrants in the nineteenth century? (Use **Source A** and recall.)   5

Sources B and **C** are about the experiences of Scottish emigrants.

Source B

> I feel that everything the agent told me about this country has turned out to be false and I dearly wish to return home. I am very much dissatisfied with the poor quality of the land which will never be of much use. The nearest town is two days' journey away and my daughter and I suffer a great deal from loneliness.

Source C

> I have already prepared 14 acres of good land and, if I am spared, I shall have 40 ready next year. I got a splendid horse and a good cow and a calf, plenty milk and butter, plenty to eat of everything. Our wee community is doing well and our fellow immigrants have already built a church and a school-house. There is not a better place in the whole world.

3. How far do **Sources B** and **C** disagree about the experiences of Scottish emigrants?   4

[END OF CONTEXT 6]

Mark

HISTORICAL STUDY: SCOTTISH AND BRITISH

> **CONTEXT 7: FROM THE CRADLE TO THE GRAVE? SOCIAL WELFARE IN BRITAIN, 1890s–1951**

Answer the following questions using recalled knowledge and information from the sources where appropriate.

1. Describe the problems facing the poor between 1890–1905.   **5**

Sources A and **B** are about the limitations of the Liberal welfare reforms of 1906–1914.

Source A

> The Liberal reforms were just a beginning. They were a long way short of solving all the problems. Medical care was only provided for the worker, it did not cover wives and children. Other benefits were only to last for a short period of time and the amounts paid were very small. The old age pensions covered people of over 70. This meant a lot of old people still got nothing at all.

Source B

> The Liberal reforms sought to provide help in a way that would not bring shame to the poor, yet the reforms had many limitations. Unemployment, sickness benefits and pension amounts were not enough to live on. Pensions were paid for the first time in 1909 but were only available to those over 70. Health insurance saw the government take on more responsibility for looking after people but the benefits did not extend to the worker's family.

2. How far do **Sources A** and **B** agree about the limitations of the Liberal welfare reforms of 1906–1914?   **4**

Source C is about the Beveridge Report.

Source C

> Beveridge proposed setting up a welfare system which was open to everyone, regardless of their wealth. There would be no return to the hated Means Test. The system was to establish a set of minimum standards. No matter how poor people were, the system would ensure that everyone had a reasonable standard of living. It would also include a free National Health Service for everyone. Poor people would now be able to receive good medical attention. Within a year the report had sold over half a million copies.

3. Why was the Beveridge Report popular with so many people? (Use **Source C** and recall.)   **5**

[END OF CONTEXT 7]

Marks

HISTORICAL STUDY: SCOTTISH AND BRITISH

CONTEXT 8: CAMPAIGNING FOR CHANGE: SOCIAL CHANGE IN SCOTLAND, 1900s–1979

Answer the following questions using recalled knowledge and information from the sources where appropriate.

1. Describe the peaceful activities of women campaigning for the vote.   **5**

Sources A and **B** are about the reasons for the failure of traditional industries after the First World War.

Source A

> The Scottish economy was very dependent on the traditional industries. However, the decline of shipbuilding had a knock-on effect on the iron and steel industries. Many of the companies had depended on shipbuilding for their orders. Scotland's share of Britain's steel production fell to 15% by 1937. Despite increased competition from abroad, Scotland's manufacturers failed to invest in new technology. Not surprisingly, overseas buyers lost to Scotland during the war often preferred to stay with their new suppliers.

Source B

> Scotland had always depended more than England on the export market but during the war her industry had to concentrate on the war effort, so customers overseas were lost. The fall in world trade in the 20s and 30s, with its disastrous effect on shipbuilding, hurt Scotland's coal, iron and steel production. Scottish industry continued to suffer because new technology made foreign goods cheaper, making them more attractive to customers.

2. How far do **Sources A** and **B** agree about reasons for the failure of traditional industries after the First World War?   **4**

Source C is about employment opportunities for women after the Second World War.

Source C

> Between 1946 and 1951 Scotland attracted 70% of all American investment into Britain. Many firms set up factories in Scotland's new towns. Women seemed suited to work in the developing light industries, such as making cash registers and typewriters. Women workers were popular as they did not have a tradition of joining trade unions so were not expected to cause trouble over wages or hours. The Government created jobs in the new NHS and welfare agencies which were attractive to women. Expanding service industries also created further jobs open to women.

3. Why were there more employment opportunities for women after the Second World War? (Use **Source C** and recall.)   **5**

[END OF CONTEXT 8]

Mark

HISTORICAL STUDY: SCOTTISH AND BRITISH

> CONTEXT 9: A TIME OF
> TROUBLES: IRELAND, 1900–1923

Answer the following questions using recalled knowledge and information from the sources where appropriate.

Sources **A** and **B** are about the Curragh Mutiny in 1914.

Source A

> Fearing Unionist opposition to Home Rule, the British government asked the army for help in Ulster. Almost immediately fifty eight officers threatened to resign if sent to fight. Most of the soldiers based in Ireland were from Protestant families and were against the new law. The government wanted to punish the rebel soldiers but they had the support and sympathy of the whole army. Powerless to take any action the government was forced to accept defeat.

Source B

> The Curragh Mutiny began when officers based in Dublin said they would rather leave the army than serve in Ulster. Unable to make the officers change their minds, the government had no choice but to give in to their demands. The Mutiny was extremely popular amongst the armed forces and as a result the officers could not be disciplined. In Ulster the Mutiny was used by Unionists to strengthen their protests against Home Rule.

1. How far do **Sources A** and **B** agree about the Curragh Mutiny?   **4**

2. Describe the events of the 1916 Easter Rising.   **5**

Source **C** explains why the Anglo-Irish War began in 1919.

Source C

> In 1919, Sinn Fein MPs declared their independence and established the Dail. They refused to acknowledge British laws and officials and instead set up their own administrative system. The British government had no desire to start a war in Ireland but the actions of Sinn Fein were too dangerous to ignore. In many parts of the country, the Dail was recognised as the official government and its influence grew. Although the British army had just returned from the First World War, they were told to prepare for action.

3. Why did the Anglo-Irish War begin in 1919? (Use **Source C** and recall.)   **5**

[END OF CONTEXT 9]

[END OF PART 2: SCOTTISH AND BRITISH CONTEXTS]

Marks

PART 3:

HISTORICAL STUDY: EUROPEAN AND WORLD

CONTEXT 1: THE NORMAN CONQUEST, 1060–1153

Answer the following questions using recalled knowledge and information from the sources where appropriate.

Source A was written by a Norman priest in 1073.

Source A

> King Edward loved Duke William like a son and promised he would be the next King of England. He sent Earl Harold to Duke William to repeat the promise and make it stronger by swearing an oath. Edward thought that Harold would use his power to stop any unrest when William became king. The English are treacherous and usually try to go against what has been decided.

1. How useful is **Source A** as evidence of Duke William's claim to the English throne? **4**

Source B is about King David's early life in England.

Source B

> King David was brought up in the royal court of William Rufus where he fell under the influence of Norman ways. King William prepared David to become a knight. He learned how to fight like a Norman and how to serve his lord, the king. During this training he befriended other young men of the court who would inherit wealth and land. When William Rufus died his brother Henry became king. Shortly afterwards, David married a wealthy widow. This made him one of the largest landowners in England.

2. Why was King David deeply influenced by Norman England? (Use **Source B** and recall.) **5**

3. In what ways did King David support the Church in Scotland? **5**

[END OF CONTEXT 1]

Mark.

HISTORICAL STUDY: EUROPEAN AND WORLD

CONTEXT 2: THE CROSS AND THE CRESCENT: THE FIRST CRUSADE, 1096–1125

Answer the following questions using recalled knowledge and information from the sources where appropriate.

Source A explains why Antioch was difficult to capture.

Source A

> When the Crusaders arrived at Antioch they were amazed by what they saw. One of the great cities of the east, Antioch, had twenty five miles of wall and nearly four hundred towers. Almost immediately, the Crusaders realised their siege machines would be of no use. The wall around the city had been reinforced and each tower was well defended by Muslim guards. Although the Crusaders had successfully captured other cities, they soon believed Antioch would be an impossible task.

1. Why did the First Crusade find Antioch difficult to capture? (Use **Source A** and recall.)　　**5**

Source B was written by Raymond of Aguilers who was on the First Crusade.

Source B

> After several hours of digging, many began to despair that the story of the Holy Lance was false. Then, just as our fate seemed doomed, Peter Bartholomew took off his shoes and jumped into the pit. Within minutes he returned with the sacred Holy Lance. Throughout the city there was joy and celebration as God had given us a sign we would defeat the Muslims.

2. How useful is **Source B** as evidence of Peter Bartholomew's discovery of the Holy Lance?　　**4**

3. Describe the problems faced by the Crusaders after they captured Jerusalem in 1099.　　**5**

[END OF CONTEXT 2]

Marks

HISTORICAL STUDY: EUROPEAN AND WORLD

> ### CONTEXT 3: WAR, DEATH AND REVOLT IN MEDIEVAL EUROPE, 1328–1436

Answer the following questions using recalled knowledge and information from the sources where appropriate.

Source A explains why England and France went to war in 1337.

Source A

> A situation that had long been smouldering burst into flame in 1337. Philip VI declared that Edward III was a disobedient vassal and that Aquitaine was therefore confiscated. Edward's response was to challenge the legitimacy not of the king's decision but of Philip's right to be king. His decision to make his claim to the French throne by force led to a conflict that would last for five generations and cause untold death and destruction.

1. Why did war break out between England and France in 1337? (Use **Source A** and recall.)   5

2. Describe the events leading up to the Peasants' Revolt in 1381.   5

Source B is from an account of the Battle of Agincourt written by a French chronicler around 1342.

Source B

> On the morning after the battle King Henry V returned to the field with his army. He ordered that any surviving French soldiers be put to death. Then he marched away despite the fact that three quarters of his army were exhausted from the battle and suffering from lack of food. Despite this the King of England returned to Calais, rejoicing at his great victory, and leaving the French in the utmost distress.

3. How useful is **Source B** as evidence about the actions of Henry V following the Battle of Agincourt?   4

[END OF CONTEXT 3]

Mark

HISTORICAL STUDY: EUROPEAN AND WORLD

> **CONTEXT 4: NEW WORLDS:**
> **EUROPE IN THE AGE OF**
> **EXPANSION, 1480s–1530s**

Answer the following questions using recalled knowledge and information from the sources where appropriate.

Source A is from "The Age of Discovery 1400–1550" written by Dan O'Sullivan in 1984.

Source A

> Vasco da Gama was a ruthless and cruel leader. In the Indian Ocean he set fire to a ship full of pilgrims returning from Mecca because they refused to give him suitable respect. Another time he ordered the hands and feet to be cut off innocent fishermen and sent them floating home in a small boat in order to frighten the local king into obeying him.

1. How useful is **Source A** as evidence of Vasco da Gama's attitude to native people?   **4**

2. In what ways were the native people of the Americas unable to resist the Conquistadors?   **5**

Source B is about the success of the explorer Jacques Cartier.

Source B

> Jacques Cartier was one of the most successful explorers of the age. He made three voyages to unknown waters without losing a ship. On his first voyage he left France with three ships to look for a passage to China. Although he did not find the route, the land he found became the basis for France's colonisation of Canada. He formed friendships with the natives. He was trusted to take the sons of King Donnacona to meet the French king in Paris and brought them home the following year.

3. Why was Jacques Cartier a successful explorer? (Use **Source B** and recall.)   **5**

[END OF CONTEXT 4]

Marks

HISTORICAL STUDY: EUROPEAN AND WORLD

> **CONTEXT 5: "TEA AND FREEDOM": THE AMERICAN REVOLUTION, 1763–1783**

Answer the following questions using recalled knowledge and information from the sources where appropriate.

Source A is from the trial of a British officer which followed the Boston Massacre in 1770.

Source A

> One of my soldiers received a severe blow with a stick, which caused him to fire his weapon accidentally. There followed a general attack on my men by a great number of heavy clubs. At this point our lives were in imminent danger and three or four of my soldiers fired, claiming that they heard an order to shoot. I can assure you that I gave no such order.

1. How useful is **Source A** as evidence of why the Boston Massacre took place?   **4**

Source B explains why some colonists remained loyal to the British during the War of Independence.

Source B

> Most colonists were of British descent. There were people from other lands, such as former Dutch settlers in New York and German newcomers in Pennsylvania. By the 1760s, all sorts of farms and businesses were well established throughout the colonies and many colonists had become quite wealthy through trade with Britain. There was much debate in cities such as Philadelphia and New York about the war. Some Americans felt that the conflict was the fault of troublemakers. Many others felt a great sense of loyalty to the King.

2. Why did some colonists remain loyal to Britain during the War of Independence? (Use **Source B** and recall.)   **5**

3. Describe the ways in which foreign countries helped the colonists in the war against the British.   **5**

[END OF CONTEXT 5]

Mark

HISTORICAL STUDY: EUROPEAN AND WORLD

> ### CONTEXT 6: "THIS ACCURSED TRADE": THE BRITISH SLAVE TRADE AND ITS ABOLITION, 1770–1807

Answer the following questions using recalled knowledge and information from the sources where appropriate.

1. Describe the way slave factories operated on the West African coast.   **5**

In **Source A** a modern historian describes the treatment of slaves on the middle passage.

Source A

> Troublesome slaves were kept in chains and only let on the deck a few at a time for exercise. To keep the slaves as healthy as possible the crew would whip them to make them dance during exercise time. In desperation some slaves tried to jump overboard. Many slaves died during the middle passage from harsh treatment, poor food and disease. So did many of the crew.

2. How useful is **Source A** as evidence of how slaves were treated on the middle passage?   **4**

Source B is about the role of William Wilberforce in the campaign to abolish the slave trade.

Source B

> John Newton persuaded William Wilberforce to join the Society for the Abolition of the Slave Trade and Wilberforce soon became its leader. Newton was a former slave trader who became an anti-slavery campaigner. Wilberforce used evidence gathered by abolitionists to try to persuade parliament to end the slave trade. For 18 years he introduced anti-slavery motions in parliament. However, the slave traders put their case to parliament and Wilberforce's arguments failed to win enough support. As a consequence, Wilberforce published even more horrific accounts of the slave trade.

3. Why was William Wilberforce an important figure in the campaign for the abolition of the slave trade? (Use **Source B** and recall.)   **5**

[END OF CONTEXT 6]

Marks

HISTORICAL STUDY: EUROPEAN AND WORLD

> ### CONTEXT 7: CITIZENS! THE FRENCH REVOLUTION, 1789–1794

Answer the following questions using recalled knowledge and information from the sources where appropriate.

1. Describe the problems faced by Louis XVI in 1789.   5

Source A explains why the Declaration of the Rights of Man was important to the French people.

Source A

> The Declaration stated "that all men are born free and equal and no one has the right to deprive them of their liberty". Delegates to the National Assembly believed that a lack of knowledge of these rights led to bad government. All French people were also to have the right to own property and avoid oppression. Nobody should be forced to do something unless it was demanded by the law and all persons must obey the same laws no matter what their status in society. A large majority of the delegates voted in favour of the Declaration.

2. Why was the Declaration of the Rights of Man important to the French people? (Use **Source A** and recall.)   5

Source B is about the execution of Danton during the Reign of Terror. It was written by a British historian in 1837.

Source B

> Danton held his head high in the death-cart and told the others to be calm and courageous. At the foot of the guillotine he was heard to say, "O my well beloved wife, I will never see you again", but then he was heard to say to himself, "Danton, show no weakness". His greatness will live for a long time in the memory of men.

3. How useful is **Source B** as evidence about the execution of Danton?   4

[END OF CONTEXT 7]

Marks

HISTORICAL STUDY: EUROPEAN AND WORLD

CONTEXT 8: CAVOUR, GARIBALDI AND THE MAKING OF ITALY, 1815–1870

Answer the following questions using recalled knowledge and information from the sources where appropriate.

1. Describe the events of the 1848–1849 revolutions in Italy. 5

Source A explains why Piedmont became the dominant state in Italy.

Source A

> Cavour was the leading politician in Piedmont between 1850 and 1861. He modernised the Piedmont economy and trebled its trade within ten years. Roads and railways were built under his guidance, meaning raw materials and machinery could be brought in to develop industry. The main port of Genoa was also modernised to help improve trade. Significantly, Piedmont was able to keep its liberal constitution after 1850 which meant that it became the centre of Italian nationalist thought. By the mid 1850s Piedmont had become the dominant state in Italy.

2. Why did Piedmont become the dominant state in Italy after 1850? (Use **Source A** and recall.) 5

Source B was written shortly after Garibaldi's death, by his personal secretary.

Source B

> This is the century of the ordinary people and no one could see this better than Garibaldi. He gave strong leadership to the people of Naples and Sicily whilst understanding the sufferings of the working man. Although Garibaldi only ruled Naples and Sicily for a short while, it was his leadership that made the unification of Italy possible. He knew what the people of Italy wanted and dedicated his life to achieving their common aim.

3. How useful is **Source B** as evidence of Garibaldi's contribution to Italian unification? 4

[END OF CONTEXT 8]

Marks

HISTORICAL STUDY: EUROPEAN AND WORLD

> **CONTEXT 9: IRON AND BLOOD?**
> **BISMARCK AND THE CREATION OF**
> **THE GERMAN EMPIRE, 1815–1871**

Answer the following questions using recalled knowledge and information from the sources where appropriate.

Source A is a popular German song written in 1840 by someone living in the Rhineland.

Source A

> Wherever speaks the German tongue
> And God is praised in German song,
> There shall it be!
> There, German, make your Germany!
> There shall the German's country lie,
> Where France reaps hatred from the land,
> And German clasps a German hand!
> There shall it be!
> There is the whole of Germany!
> There is the whole of Germany!

1. How useful is **Source A** as evidence of the growth of nationalist feeling in Germany between 1815 and 1850?   **4**

Source B explains why the Frankfurt Parliament failed.

Source B

> The 596 men elected to the assembly were intellectually well qualified. However, the parliament suffered from a lack of clear, agreed objectives which made decision making difficult. They had to decide on a constitution, which took nearly a year. It also took nine months finally to decide on the fundamental rights of the German citizens. So much valuable time and effort was used on debating these matters and coming to a conclusion. The assembly gradually disintegrated after King Frederick refused to accept the Frankfurt Parliament's offer of the crown.

2. Why did the Frankfurt Parliament fail? (Use **Source B** and recall.)   **5**

3. Describe the events of the Franco-Prussian War of 1870–1871.   **5**

[END OF CONTEXT 9]

Mark

HISTORICAL STUDY: EUROPEAN AND WORLD

> ### CONTEXT 10: THE RED FLAG: LENIN AND THE RUSSIAN REVOLUTION, 1894–1921

Answer the following questions using recalled knowledge and information from the sources where appropriate.

Source A is from "History of the Russian Revolution" by Leon Trotsky, written in 1932.

Source A

> Nicholas II was unreliable and not to be trusted. He kept his gentlest smiles and kindest words for officials whom he planned to dismiss. He drew back with distaste from anyone gifted or capable. He only felt relaxed among very average and unimaginative people such as so-called holy men—people who could not show up his stupidity.

1. How useful is **Source A** as evidence about Nicholas II?   **4**

2. Describe the events of Bloody Sunday in January 1905.   **5**

Source B explains why the Bolsheviks were able to stay in power in Russia in 1917–1918.

Source B

> The successful seizure of power in Petrograd was only a beginning. Almost immediately the Congress of Soviets pleased the peasants by declaring that landlords' rights to property were abolished so that the land could be redistributed. A new Bolshevik Cabinet, Sovnarkom, was set up and given authority to pass new laws. In November, the Bolsheviks allowed the long-awaited elections to the Constitutional Assembly to be held; over 47 million Russians, including many peasants, voted. In December, Sovnarkom created a new secret police, the Cheka, to wipe out any counter-revolutionary activity.

3. Why were the Bolsheviks able to stay in power in Russia in 1917–1918? (Use **Source B** and recall.)   **5**

[END OF CONTEXT 10]

Marks

HISTORICAL STUDY: EUROPEAN AND WORLD

CONTEXT 11: FREE AT LAST? RACE RELATIONS IN THE USA, 1918–1968

Answer the following questions using recalled knowledge and information from the sources where appropriate.

1. In what ways did the Civil Rights Movement improve the lives of black Americans?   **5**

Source A is from a statement made by President Kennedy in May 1963.

Source A

> I think that the situation in Birmingham will be peacefully settled in the next 24 hours. Quite obviously the situation was damaging the reputation of Birmingham and the United States. It seems to me that the best way to prevent that kind of serious damage is to take steps to provide equal treatment for all of our citizens. That is the best remedy in this case and other cases.

2. How useful is **Source A** as evidence of the effects of the Civil Rights protest in Birmingham?   **4**

In **Source B** Stokely Carmichael explains his opposition to non-violent protest.

Source B

> It is clear that the non-violent movement has failed young black people living in the urban ghettos. Each time these people saw little black girls bombed to death in a church and civil rights workers ambushed and murdered, they became angry and when nothing happened, they were steaming mad. Non-violent protest had nothing to offer except to go out and be beaten again. It said that the black minority would get power by bowing its head and getting whipped. To all of us now the very idea of non-violent protest seems absurd.

3. Why did Stokely Carmichael oppose non-violent protest? (Use **Source B** and recall.)   **5**

[END OF CONTEXT 11]

Mark

HISTORICAL STUDY: EUROPEAN AND WORLD

> ### CONTEXT 12: THE ROAD TO WAR, 1933–1939

Answer the following questions using recalled knowledge and information from the sources where appropriate.

Source A is from one of the school textbooks introduced by the Nazis in 1934.

Source A

> For many centuries the Germans have protected Europe from the dangers of the east. It was German blood that defended Europe from Slav invaders and proved the superiority of our race. It is important that the Aryan race remains pure to fulfil its historic sacred mission to dominate inferior peoples and spread German culture and civilisation wherever possible.

1. How useful is **Source A** as evidence of Nazi ideas on race?   **4**

Source B explains why Britain and France were worried about Germany's actions.

Source B

> From 1933 onwards it looked as if Germany's policies were beginning to change. As soon as he could, Hitler removed the German representatives from the Disarmament Conference in Geneva. Hitler was working hard to create an image of strong leadership among his own people and most of them supported him when Germany gave up her membership of the League of Nations. Germany's non-aggression treaty with Poland meant that France lost a valuable ally in Eastern Europe. In 1935 Germany announced the creation of an air force and navy.

2. Why were Britain and France worried about Germany's actions by 1936?   (Use **Source B** and recall.)   **5**

3. Describe the events that led to the takeover of Czechoslovakia.   **5**

[END OF CONTEXT 12]

Marks

HISTORICAL STUDY: EUROPEAN AND WORLD

> **CONTEXT 13: IN THE SHADOW OF THE BOMB: THE COLD WAR, 1945–1985**

Answer the following questions using recalled knowledge and information from the sources where appropriate.

Source A explains why there was a crisis in Berlin in 1961.

Source A

> By 1960 the situation in East Berlin was very dangerous. A new East German labour law, which stopped workers from going on strike, had led to growing unrest in the factories. The East German government's reforms of agriculture had led to shortages of food and higher prices. All of this led to a massive increase in the numbers of refugees fleeing to the West. At a meeting of the Warsaw Pact states, Khrushchev had been informed about the situation. In the six months up to June 1961, 103,000 East Germans had fled through Berlin. The decision to act was taken.

1. Why was there a crisis in Berlin in 1961? (Use **Source A** and recall.)   5

2. In what ways did people show their opposition to the war in Vietnam?   5

Source B is from a speech by President Leonid Brezhnev, in 1976.

Source B

> We are attempting to follow the path of peaceful co-existence. We are trying to bring about lasting peace to reduce, and in the longer term to eliminate, the danger of another world war. This is the main element of our policy towards the capitalist states. It may be noticed that considerable progress in this area has been achieved in the last five years.

3. How useful is **Source B** as evidence of the Soviet attitude towards détente?   4

[END OF CONTEXT 13]

[END OF PART 3: EUROPEAN AND WORLD CONTEXTS]

[END OF QUESTION PAPER]

[BLANK PAGE]

[BLANK PAGE]

X044/11/01

NATIONAL QUALIFICATIONS 2013	TUESDAY, 14 MAY 9.00 AM – 10.45 AM	HISTORY INTERMEDIATE 2

The instructions for this paper are on *Page two*. Read them carefully before you begin your answers.

Your Invigilator will tell you which contexts to answer in Parts 2 and 3 of the examination.

✗SQA

©

INSTRUCTIONS

Answer **one** question from Part 1, The Short Essay

Answer **one** context* from Part 2, Scottish and British

Answer **one** context* from Part 3, European and World

Answer **one** other context* from

> **either**   Part 2, Scottish and British
>
> **or**   Part 3, European and World

*Answer all the questions in each of your chosen contexts.

Contents

[Turn over

PART 1: THE SHORT ESSAY

Mark

Answer **one** question. For this question you should write a short essay using your own knowledge. The essay should include an introduction, development and conclusion. Each question is worth 8 marks.

SCOTTISH AND BRITISH CONTEXTS:

CONTEXT 1: MURDER IN THE CATHEDRAL: CROWN, CHURCH AND PEOPLE, 1154–1173

Question 1:   Explain why the church was important in the twelfth century.   8

CONTEXT 2: WALLACE, BRUCE AND THE WARS OF INDEPENDENCE, 1286–1328

Question 2:   Explain why Scots had accepted Bruce as their king by 1328.   8

CONTEXT 3: MARY, QUEEN OF SCOTS AND THE SCOTTISH REFORMATION, 1540s–1587

Question 3:   Explain why Mary's marriage to Darnley led to her downfall in 1567.   8

CONTEXT 4: THE COMING OF THE CIVIL WAR, 1603–1642

Question 4:   Explain why the reign of King James VI and I caused problems with the English Parliament between 1603 and 1625.   8

CONTEXT 5: "ANE END OF ANE AULD SANG": SCOTLAND AND THE TREATY OF UNION, 1690s–1715

Question 5:   Explain why support for the Jacobites had risen by 1715.   8

CONTEXT 6: IMMIGRANTS AND EXILES: SCOTLAND, 1830s–1930s

Question 6:   Explain why many Scots who emigrated became successful in their new homelands.   8

CONTEXT 7: FROM THE CRADLE TO THE GRAVE? SOCIAL WELFARE IN BRITAIN, 1890s–1951

Question 7:   Explain why the Second World War changed attitudes towards government involvement in the welfare of its people.   8

Marks

CONTEXT 8: CAMPAIGNING FOR CHANGE: SOCIAL CHANGE IN SCOTLAND, 1900s–1979

Question 8:　　Explain why standards of living fell for many Scots in the 1930s.　　**8**

CONTEXT 9: A TIME OF TROUBLES: IRELAND, 1900–1923

Question 9:　　Explain why the Easter Rising of 1916 failed.　　**8**

EUROPEAN AND WORLD CONTEXTS:

CONTEXT 1: THE NORMAN CONQUEST, 1060–1153

Question 10:　　Explain why David I's reign has been described as the "Normanisation" of Scotland.　　**8**

CONTEXT 2: THE CROSS AND THE CRESCENT: THE FIRST CRUSADE, 1096–1125

Question 11:　　Explain why the relationship between Emperor Alexius and the Crusaders was difficult.　　**8**

CONTEXT 3: WAR, DEATH AND REVOLT IN MEDIEVAL EUROPE, 1328–1436

Question 12:　　Explain why war broke out between England and France in 1337.　　**8**

CONTEXT 4: NEW WORLDS: EUROPE IN THE AGE OF EXPANSION, 1480s–1530s

Question 13:　　Explain why the lives of Native Peoples in the New World were changed by the voyages of discovery.　　**8**

CONTEXT 5: "TEA AND FREEDOM": THE AMERICAN REVOLUTION, 1763–1783

Question 14:　　Explain why the British had lost the war against the Americans by 1783.　　**8**

Marks

CONTEXT 6: "THIS ACCURSED TRADE": THE BRITISH SLAVE TRADE AND ITS ABOLITION, 1770–1807

Question 15:   Explain why the British Parliament voted to end the slave trade in 1807.

8

CONTEXT 7: CITIZENS! THE FRENCH REVOLUTION, 1789–1794

Question 16:   Explain why French peasants were angry before the revolution in 1789.

8

CONTEXT 8: CAVOUR, GARIBALDI AND THE MAKING OF ITALY, 1815–1870

Question 17:   Explain why Italy had failed to become a united country before 1848.

8

CONTEXT 9: IRON AND BLOOD? BISMARCK AND THE CREATION OF THE GERMAN EMPIRE, 1815–1871

Question 18:   Explain why the German states were united by 1871.

8

CONTEXT 10: THE RED FLAG: LENIN AND THE RUSSIAN REVOLUTION, 1894–1921

Question 19:   Explain why the First World War was important in causing the downfall of the Tsar.

8

CONTEXT 11: FREE AT LAST? RACE RELATIONS IN THE USA, 1918–1968

Question 20:   Explain why there was a growing demand for civil rights between 1945 and 1965.

8

CONTEXT 12: THE ROAD TO WAR, 1933–1939

Question 21:   Explain why the events of 1939 caused the Second World War to break out.

8

CONTEXT 13: IN THE SHADOW OF THE BOMB: THE COLD WAR, 1945–1985

Question 22:   Explain why a crisis had broken out over Cuba by 1962.

8

[Turn over for PART 2: SCOTTISH AND BRITISH CONTEXTS on *Page eight*

Mark

PART 2:

HISTORICAL STUDY: SCOTTISH AND BRITISH

> ### CONTEXT 1: MURDER IN THE CATHEDRAL: CROWN, CHURCH AND PEOPLE, 1154–1173

Answer the following questions using recalled knowledge and information from the sources where appropriate.

Source A is from the Assize of Northampton written in 1176.

Source A

> Anyone accused of forgery or arson must face the ordeal of water. If they fail and are found guilty of breaking the law then their right hand and foot are to be cut off. This punishment is to be enforced throughout the entire kingdom and should serve as a warning to those who wish to challenge the authority of the King.

1. How useful is **Source A** as evidence of the laws introduced by Henry II?   **4**

2. Describe the use of castles in the twelfth century.   **5**

Source B explains why Henry II and Archbishop Becket quarrelled.

Source B

> When Becket failed to appear at the Northampton trial, the quarrel between the two men became worse. Henry humiliated Becket by confiscating Becket's lands, accusing him of fraud and charging him with contempt of court. Fearing for his life, Becket fled to France without Henry's permission. Under the protection of Louis VII, Becket appealed to the Pope and continued to defend the rights of the Church. Finally, after six years of exile, Becket agreed to return to England. In exchange for his lands Becket promised to crown Henry's son.

3. Why did Henry II and Archbishop Becket quarrel? (Use **Source B** and recall.)   **5**

[END OF CONTEXT 1]

Marks

HISTORICAL STUDY: SCOTTISH AND BRITISH

> ### CONTEXT 2: WALLACE, BRUCE AND THE WARS OF INDEPENDENCE, 1286–1328

Answer the following questions using recalled knowledge and information from the sources where appropriate.

1. Describe the events which allowed Edward I to interfere in Scotland between 1286 and 1292.   **5**

Source A is from "The Bruce", written by the Scots poet John Barbour in 1375.

Source A

> Unlike Robert Bruce, John Balliol agreed to obey King Edward. So Edward made Balliol King of Scots. This was a disaster for Scotland. Balliol, however, was king for only a little while before the Scots realised he was incompetent. He was arrested and both his crown and kingdom were taken away. Then, King Edward quickly occupied the whole land.

2. How useful is **Source A** as evidence about King John Balliol?   **4**

Source B explains why William Wallace resigned after the Battle of Falkirk.

Source B

> Stirling Bridge is important in understanding the career of William Wallace. Wallace's victory at Stirling Bridge was the only reason he was made Guardian. He was the successful leader of a successful army. Many nobles, however, had always resented Wallace for stealing their traditional position of leadership. Although he may have chosen a bad position to fight at Falkirk many claim that, as much as anything, it was jealous snobbishness that made the Scottish nobles withdraw from the battlefield at Falkirk.

3. Why did William Wallace resign after the Battle of Falkirk? (Use **Source B** and recall.)   **5**

[END OF CONTEXT 2]

Mark

HISTORICAL STUDY: SCOTTISH AND BRITISH

CONTEXT 3: MARY, QUEEN OF SCOTS AND THE SCOTTISH REFORMATION, 1540s–1587

Answer the following questions using recalled knowledge and information from the sources where appropriate.

Source A explains why Cardinal Beaton was unpopular with Scottish Protestants by 1545.

Source A

> After taking power, Governor Arran agreed to the Treaty of Greenwich with Henry VIII whose son would marry Mary, Queen of Scots. This treaty would break the Auld Alliance with France and strengthen Protestants in Scotland. To prevent this, Cardinal Beaton acted quickly. He persuaded Arran to return to the Catholic Church and to surrender his son into Beaton's care. To restore French influence, Arran was then made to share power with Beaton and Mary of Guise. Finally, Beaton persuaded the Scots to reject the Treaty of Greenwich and, to Henry's fury, they confirmed the Auld Alliance.

1. Why was Cardinal Beaton unpopular with Scottish Protestants by 1545? (Use **Source A** and recall.)   **5**

2. Describe the events in Scotland which led it to become a Protestant country in 1560.   **5**

Source B was written by a historian in 2005.

Source B

> Knox was horrified to find out that Mary and her ladies danced at royal balls and banquets and warned that the country would be ruined if this devilish practice was allowed to continue. He said it was "offensive in the sight of God". Another Protestant, David Calderwood, wrote that "when she, her fiddlers and other dancing companions were alone, there might be unseemly skipping and dancing".

3. How useful is **Source B** as evidence about Protestants' attitude to Mary, Queen of Scots?   **4**

[END OF CONTEXT 3]

Marks

HISTORICAL STUDY: SCOTTISH AND BRITISH

> ### CONTEXT 4: THE COMING OF THE CIVIL WAR, 1603–1642

Answer the following questions using recalled knowledge and information from the sources where appropriate.

1. Describe the attempts made by Charles I to raise money between 1629 and 1640.   **5**

Source A explains why the religious policies of Charles I caused resentment in England and Scotland.

Source A

> Charles appointed Laud as Archbishop of Canterbury. Laud's preference for elaborate church services caused opposition amongst Puritans who believed in simple church services. However, Laud allowed priests to wear decorated robes and permitted stained-glass windows in churches. The Puritans thought Laud's changes were making the Church of England look too much like the Catholic Church, which they opposed. In 1637 a Puritan criticised Laud in a pamphlet. Laud had him arrested, his ears cut off and his face branded with red-hot irons. This harsh treatment created more opposition for Charles.

2. Why did the religious policies of Charles I cause resentment in England and Scotland? (Use **Source A** and recall.)   **5**

Source B is part of a list of demands made by Parliament in November 1640.

Source B

> Parliament shall be willing to agree to the King's request for money should he agree to the following:
>
> • Laud and Strafford to be removed as advisors and put on trial
>
> • Parliament can never be dismissed without Parliament agreeing to this. If, for whatever reason, Parliament is dismissed, a new one must be called within three years.

3. How useful is **Source B** as evidence of the relations between Charles I and Members of Parliament?   **4**

[END OF CONTEXT 4]

Mark

HISTORICAL STUDY: SCOTTISH AND BRITISH

> ### CONTEXT 5: "ANE END OF ANE AULD SANG": SCOTLAND AND THE TREATY OF UNION, 1690s–1715

Answer the following questions using recalled knowledge and information from the sources where appropriate.

Source A was written by a historian in 1998.

Source A

> Scotland was in a desperate situation in 1700. Everything had gone wrong for its economy. The foolish venture to set up a colony at Darien had wiped out most of the country's money. The Scots blamed King William for this disaster. The weather had not helped any recovery; a series of bad harvests, known as the "Seven Ill Years", had left many Scots destitute.

1. How useful is **Source A** as evidence about the Scottish economy in 1700?   **4**

2. Describe the Succession Problem which Queen Anne wanted to solve before her death.   **5**

Source B explains why there was so much opposition to the Union in Scottish burghs.

Source B

> There were protests and demonstrations against the Union in many Scottish burghs. People opposed surrendering Scotland's honour to the "Auld Enemy", England. Wine merchants were concerned that Scotland's well-established wine trade with its "Auld Ally", France, would end after the Union. Shopkeepers worried that they would lose business if Scottish MPs and lords moved to London and spent their money there. Mobs burned copies of the Union in the streets while respectable people criticised it at home. Ministers, fearing for the future of the Church of Scotland, preached against it.

3. Why was there so much opposition to the Union in Scottish burghs? (Use **Source B** and recall.)   **5**

[END OF CONTEXT 5]

Marks

HISTORICAL STUDY: SCOTTISH AND BRITISH

CONTEXT 6: IMMIGRANTS AND
EXILES: SCOTLAND, 1830s–1930s

Answer the following questions using recalled knowledge and information from the sources where appropriate.

1. Describe the work done by Irish immigrants in Scotland. **5**

Source A explains why many Scots resented Irish immigrants.

Source A

> Many Scots had developed a resentment of Irish immigrants in the nineteenth century. Newspapers were eager to describe the violent activities of groups of Irish men. One of the most notorious stories was about drunken Irishmen rampaging around the town of Hamilton and terrifying the inhabitants until soldiers arrived to restore order. Many Irishmen often worked for weeks with little opportunity for a rest. In Ayr the Irish were blamed for using up most of the money available to support the poor. In Glasgow they were blamed for crimes of theft and burglary.

2. Why did many Scots resent Irish immigrants? (Use **Source A** and recall.) **5**

Source B was written by a visitor to Skye in 1865.

Source B

> When the landlord appeared the tenants all greeted him respectfully. One by one the people approached him to let him know what they needed in order to emigrate. One man had not yet saved up his passage-money and required a loan; a woman desired a pair of blankets; an old man wished the landlord to buy his cow for a fair price. For each the way to Canada was eased.

3. How useful is **Source B** as evidence of emigration from the Highlands? **4**

[END OF CONTEXT 6]

Mark

HISTORICAL STUDY: SCOTTISH AND BRITISH

> ### CONTEXT 7: FROM THE CRADLE TO THE GRAVE? SOCIAL WELFARE IN BRITAIN, 1890s–1951

Answer the following questions using recalled knowledge and information from the sources where appropriate.

Source A is about the poorest district of York, described by Seebohm Rowntree in 1901.

Source A

> About one-fourth of the whole population of the district are living in overcrowded conditions–ie more than two persons to each room. Of these 1613 persons, 200 are living under conditions of extreme overcrowding, ie more than four persons to each room. This fact alone would be enough to seriously affect the standard of health, but the problem of overcrowding does not fully represent the extent of the evil.

1. How useful is **Source A** as evidence of the problem of poverty at the beginning of the twentieth century? **4**

2. In what ways did the Liberal government's reforms of 1906–1914 fail to meet the needs of the people? **5**

Source B explains why the Labour reforms of 1945–1951 were considered a success.

Source B

> The Labour Government started to tackle poverty by introducing social reforms. Most social problems would be solved by a single insurance payment, for which the government provided the people with a much improved National Insurance system. Labour were committed from the start to improve the lives of everyone in society. Acts passed to help the workers included unemployment and sickness benefits. Families were also helped with schemes such as maternity and widows' benefits. For those who were not covered by insurance schemes, the National Assistance Act was created.

3. Why were the Labour reforms of 1945–1951 considered by many to be a success? (Use **Source B** and recall.) **5**

[END OF CONTEXT 7]

Marks

HISTORICAL STUDY: SCOTTISH AND BRITISH

CONTEXT 8: CAMPAIGNING FOR
CHANGE: SOCIAL CHANGE IN
SCOTLAND, 1900s–1979

Answer the following questions using recalled knowledge and information from the sources where appropriate.

Source A explains why Suffragette actions were important in getting women the vote.

Source A

> Until the outbreak of war, the Suffragettes kept the campaign for votes for women in the news every other day. They often put their own lives in danger so women could win the right to vote. Some people said the Suffragettes' militant actions alienated the government. It was also argued they had sacrificed valuable public support. However, the dramatic death of Emily Davison had given the movement its first martyr and left no doubt about the Suffragettes' dedication. Their courage in prison continued to win sympathy and admiration.

1. Why were Suffragette actions important in getting women the vote? (Use **Source A** and recall.)   5

2. In what ways did job opportunities change in Scotland after the Second World War?   5

Source B is a postcard produced in 1935 showing Portobello beach near Edinburgh.

Source B

THE CALL OF THE SEASIDE. PORTOBELLO

3. How useful is **Source B** as evidence about popular leisure activities in Scotland in the 1930s?   4

[END OF CONTEXT 8]

Mar

HISTORICAL STUDY: SCOTTISH AND BRITISH

> ### CONTEXT 9: A TIME OF TROUBLES: IRELAND, 1900–1923

Answer the following questions using recalled knowledge and information from the sources where appropriate.

Source A explains why Unionists campaigned against Home Rule before 1914.

Source A

> Edward Carson, a powerful Irish MP, argued that Home Rule threatened the Protestant way of life. A gifted speaker and able leader, Carson stated that the Bill was part of a Catholic plot to take over Belfast and must be stopped. At rallies across Ulster, Carson warned that Home Rule would eventually lead to full independence for Ireland and separation from the United Kingdom. He encouraged thousands of Unionists to unite together and fight to keep Ireland a part of the British Empire.

1. Why did Unionists campaign against Home Rule before 1914? (Use **Source A** and recall.)   5

2. Describe the actions of both sides during the Anglo-Irish War of 1919–1921.   5

Source B is part of a speech given by Eamon De Valera in 1923.

Source B

> Fellow Republicans, it saddens me to tell you that we can no longer successfully defend our country. Our army has been overrun and many of our soldiers are in prison or have been executed. Any further loss of Republican life would be in vain. For now we must accept defeat until a time when we are strong enough to fight again.

3. How useful is **Source B** as evidence of why Republicans ended the Civil War in 1923?   4

[END OF CONTEXT 9]

[END OF PART 2: SCOTTISH AND BRITISH CONTEXTS]

PART 3:   *Marks*

HISTORICAL STUDY: EUROPEAN AND WORLD

CONTEXT 1: THE NORMAN CONQUEST, 1060–1153

Answer the following questions using recalled knowledge and information from the sources where appropriate.

1. Describe the methods William I used to crush opposition to his rule in England.   **5**

Sources A and **B** are about the effects of the feudal system on England.

Source A

> Each of William's subjects depended on someone else for their land and livelihood. They had to be loyal to survive. In this way, William was able to extend his influence throughout England. William cleverly used religion to support the feudal system by making people swear an oath of loyalty to him. Breaking this oath meant breaking a pledge to God. Only the peasants did not swear an oath because they were assumed to be too unimportant.

Source B

> When William granted land to his followers an important ceremony took place. The baron would kneel before him and swear to be his man. To break this oath was the worst crime in Norman England. The baron would then perform similar acts with his knights. Under this system William was able to tighten his control over England. The peasants, who were rated lowest in the feudal system, were not even required to take an oath. Despite this they benefited from the protection of their lord.

2. How far do **Sources A** and **B** agree about the effects of the feudal system on England?   **4**

Source C explains the development of burghs in Scotland under David I.

Source C

> Tolls were charged at the burgh gates and market dues had to be paid on all sorts of goods. The King took his share of this new wealth and filled his treasury. On market day the gates were thrown open to the people of the local farms and villages allowing them to bring goods to sell. This helped the local economy. Burghs also attracted foreign merchants to Scotland who also paid tolls and brought goods to sell. The King gave permission for burghs to hold an annual fair from which he gained more wealth.

3. Why did David I encourage the development of burghs in Scotland? (Use **Source C** and recall.)   **5**

[END OF CONTEXT 1]

HISTORICAL STUDY: EUROPEAN AND WORLD

Mark

> **CONTEXT 2: THE CROSS AND THE CRESCENT: THE FIRST CRUSADE, 1096–1125**

Answer the following questions using recalled knowledge and information from the sources where appropriate.

Sources A and **B** explain why Pope Urban II called the First Crusade.

Source A

> When Pope Urban II spoke at Clermont in 1095 he said Jerusalem must be recaptured. The city had been overrun by Turks and the Pope wanted to stop Christian churches from being destroyed. Urban II demanded that an army be raised to fight God's enemy. He called upon the knights of Europe to stop fighting amongst themselves and unite. He promised that in return for fighting, knights would have their sins forgiven.

Source B

> When Emperor Alexius sent a letter asking for help, the Pope decided to act. During a passionate speech, he told knights they must end their bad behaviour and use their skills to fight the infidel. Urban II said he would not rest until every Christian church in the East was protected. He encouraged the Christians who had gathered in Clermont to help reclaim Jerusalem in any way they could. Inspired by his words thousands took the cross.

1. How far do **Sources A** and **B** agree about why Pope Urban II called the First Crusade?   **4**

2. Describe the problems faced by the People's Crusade on their journey to Jerusalem.   **5**

Source C explains why the Crusaders were able to keep control of the Latin States after 1099.

Source C

> Within days of the capture of Jerusalem, Godfrey of Bouillon was elected ruler of the city. A strong and able Crusader, he re-organised the knights and prepared them for battle. Despite their small numbers and insufficient supplies, the Crusaders were able to defeat the advancing Muslim army. This success allowed the Crusaders to extend their territory in the East and push their enemies back. Additionally Godfrey ordered castles to be built to protect the land conquered. By doing so he ensured the Latin States remained in Christian hands.

3. Why were the Crusaders able to keep control of the Latin States after 1099? (Use **Source C** and recall.)   **5**

[END OF CONTEXT 2]

Marks

HISTORICAL STUDY: EUROPEAN AND WORLD

> ### CONTEXT 3: WAR, DEATH AND REVOLT IN MEDIEVAL EUROPE, 1328–1436

Answer the following questions using recalled knowledge and information from the sources where appropriate.

Source A explains why the English were successful at the Battle of Poitiers.

Source A

> The first line of French knights charged towards the English front line. English archers shot at them from the cover of the hedgerows causing panic. Many Frenchmen fled. The second line under the Dauphin's command was also resisted. The French king then advanced with a large force, threatening to move around the English. The Black Prince dealt with this threat by sending forward reinforcements whom he had wisely kept in reserve. He also sent horsemen through the woods reappearing at the King's rear and cutting him off from the rest of his army.

1. Why were the English successful at the Battle of Poitiers? (Use **Source A** and recall.)   5

2. Describe the effects of the Black Death on England.   5

Sources B and **C** explain the reasons for French success in the Hundred Years War.

Source B

> Joan of Arc led the French armies to victory over the English until she was captured and burned by the English as a witch. The end of their long and bitter civil war meant that the French now had greater unity. This allowed the French King to field massive armies. In addition, however, French leaders began to understand the new style of warfare, and began to make use of these methods of fighting.

Source C

> Joan of Arc played a vital role by inspiring the army to victory and persuading the Dauphin to accept the crown in 1429. However, the following year she was betrayed to the Burgundians and burned as a heretic. In 1435 the Burgundians made peace with the French King ending the feud which had divided France. From that point England was doomed. The French learned from earlier defeats and built a more efficient, tactical army.

3. How far do **Sources B** and **C** agree about the reasons for the success of France in the Hundred Years War?   4

[END OF CONTEXT 3]

Mark

HISTORICAL STUDY: EUROPEAN AND WORLD

> **CONTEXT 4: NEW WORLDS**
> **EUROPE IN THE AGE OF**
> **EXPANSION, 1480s–1530s**

Answer the following questions using recalled knowledge and information from the sources where appropriate.

Source A explains why explorers went on voyages of discovery.

Source A

> Voyages of exploration were not carried out simply to bring fame. At this time in Europe, there was a great desire to know more about the world. Prince Henry the Navigator had already established a port at Ceuta in Morocco and was well aware that most of the surrounding lands were controlled by the Moors. Many people believed it was their Christian duty to spread their faith to people who had no knowledge of it. Others realised successful explorers could become very rich.

1. Why did explorers go on voyages of discovery? (Use **Source A** and recall.)   5

Sources B and **C** are about some of the problems faced by commanders of voyages of discovery.

Source B

> After Columbus's fleet sailed out of sight of land, the crews threatened to mutiny. They protested about the length of the voyage so Columbus pretended they had travelled a shorter distance than they had to reassure them. He himself had no real idea of how far the journey was as his calculations were wrong. After they reached land, the Pinta set off on its own to look for gold and the Santa Maria ran aground.

Source C

> Magellan did not tell his sailors that their destination was the Spice Islands by the western route before they sailed because he knew this long journey would terrify them. As it was, even before he reached Cape Horn a mutiny broke out and he was forced to execute the ringleaders. When the fleet entered the stormy seas leading to the Straits, one ship sank and the captain of another disobeyed him and turned back to Spain.

2. How far do **Sources B** and **C** agree about the problems faced by commanders of voyages of discovery?   4

3. Describe the voyage of Vasco da Gama in 1497.   5

[END OF CONTEXT 4]

HISTORICAL STUDY: EUROPEAN AND WORLD

Marks

**CONTEXT 5: "TEA AND FREEDOM":
THE AMERICAN REVOLUTION,
1763–1783**

Answer the following questions using recalled knowledge and information from the sources where appropriate.

Sources A and **B** are about why the colonists were unhappy with British rule by 1775.

Source A

> The British government collected money from their American colonies through taxes. Many colonists regarded the taxes as unfair as they were not represented in the British parliament. Colonists were furious with the passing of the Stamp Act in 1765. This led to violent clashes between British soldiers and colonists. Tension was highest in Boston. In one incident, British soldiers opened fire, killing five colonists. This was reported as a brutal massacre across the colonies.

Source B

> During the war with France the British government had passed new laws to extend its control of the American colonies. Many colonists resented British interference in their lives and businesses. The Stamp Act produced a furious storm of protest. Under the banner "no taxation without representation", mobs took to the streets in Boston and other large towns. In 1770, the shooting of five protestors by British soldiers in Boston was portrayed as a terrible crime committed by the British.

1. How far do **Sources A** and **B** agree about the reasons why the colonists had become unhappy with British rule by 1775?   **4**

2. Describe what happened at Lexington and Concord in 1775.   **5**

Source C explains why some people sympathised with America in the Wars of Independence.

Source C

> The writer Thomas Paine opposed British rule. In 1776, he published a pamphlet called Common Sense. He argued that Britain was abusing the rights of the American people. Many people were persuaded by his arguments. The answer, Paine believed, was independence. Paine's ideas were popular and 150,000 pamphlets were sold. The King's rejection of the Olive Branch Petition moved many colonists towards independence and angered radicals in Britain. The news that Britain was hiring mercenary soldiers from Germany to help them control the colonies also led some people in Britain to question the point of the war.

3. Why did some British people sympathise with America in the Wars of Independence? (Use **Source C** and recall.)   **5**

[END OF CONTEXT 5]

Mar.

HISTORICAL STUDY: EUROPEAN AND WORLD

> ### CONTEXT 6: "THIS ACCURSED TRADE": THE BRITISH SLAVE TRADE AND ITS ABOLITION, 1770–1807

Answer the following questions using recalled knowledge and information from the sources where appropriate.

Source A explains why the slave trade was important to many British cities.

Source A

> Cities in the west of Britain benefited from the Atlantic slave trade. By 1800, Liverpool profited most directly from the transportation of human beings as slaves. Glasgow and Bristol developed their own specialist areas which were linked to the trade. Glasgow had the largest share of the British tobacco trade and this helped the city's economic development. Profits from the tobacco trade also contributed to the development of industry in Glasgow. In Bristol, merchants profited from the sugar trade. All of these activities were based on Britain's involvement in the Atlantic slave trade.

1. Why was the slave trade important to many British cities? (Use **Source A** and recall.)   5

Sources B and **C** are about the capture of slaves in Africa.

Source B

> The ships which had arrived on the African coast from Europe landed armed raiders who attacked African villages and seized as many men, women and children as possible. As soon as they saw a ship the Africans left their villages and took to the forests to hide. Another way Europeans obtained slaves was simply to buy them from their African masters. As the trade increased, Europeans built forts on the coast and established factories to hold captured slaves.

Source C

> The slave trade across the Atlantic Ocean changed the whole course of African history. The kings and chiefs of the African tribes became trading partners with European merchants. They swapped their people for European goods such as horses, guns and alcohol. As the demand for slaves grew, raiding and kidnapping spread terror deep into Africa. Frightened villagers, trying to escape the raiders, moved into remote areas which often had poor soil and produced few crops.

2. How far do **Sources B** and **C** agree about the effect of the slave trade on Africa?   4

3. Describe the ways in which slaves were prepared and sold in the West Indies.   5

[END OF CONTEXT 6]

HISTORICAL STUDY: EUROPEAN AND WORLD   *Marks*

CONTEXT 7: CITIZENS! THE FRENCH REVOLUTION, 1789–1794

Answer the following questions using recalled knowledge and information from the sources where appropriate.

1. Describe the events of July 1789 which led to the attack on the Bastille.   **5**

Source A explains the unhappiness of the French people with the results of the Revolution by 1792.

Source A

> The revolution had been supported by a large number of ordinary French people, both city dwellers and peasants. Many of them now questioned a system which was benefiting mainly the middle class. Only the middle class had the right to vote for the Assembly and if that were not bad enough, only the wealthy could elect Assembly members. The peasants were pleased that the old regime had been swept away. They were still unhappy that it was so easy for the nobility to buy the lands taken from the Catholic Church.

2. Why were many French people unhappy with the results of the Revolution by 1792? (Use **Source A** and recall.)   **5**

Sources B and **C** describe the activities of the Committee of Public Safety in 1793.

Source B

> The Committee of Public Safety was created in order to protect the gains of the Revolution and the rights of the citizens. Its members are committed to the cause of perfect justice at a time when the enemies of the Revolution are working to bring a great darkness back to France. The Committee ensures that trials and punishments are fair so that society runs according to the rules of freedom.

Source C

> The enemies of the Revolution are everywhere, both in France and abroad. Only the Committee for Public Safety can ensure that the great achievements of the Revolution are saved. Never before in the history of France have the courts of law ensured that innocent citizens are protected from false accusation. Dare anyone accuse the Committee of failing to create the fairest system of justice the people have ever known?

3. How far do **Sources B** and **C** agree about activities of the Committee of Public Safety?   **4**

[END OF CONTEXT 7]

Mark

HISTORICAL STUDY: EUROPEAN AND WORLD

> ### CONTEXT 8: CAVOUR, GARIBALDI AND THE MAKING OF ITALY, 1815–1870

Answer the following questions using recalled knowledge and information from the sources where appropriate.

Sources A and **B** are about the revolutions of 1848.

Source A

> The revolutions in the Italian states failed to unite Italy. Each revolution had different aims and the revolutionaries failed to work together. Furthermore, Austria was strengthened by quickly defeating its own revolution and this played a decisive role in halting those in Italy. All revolts were put down by Austria, apart from the Roman Republic. General Radetzky was important in the Austrian victories as his decisive military leadership was superior to that of Charles Albert.

Source B

> Austria had recovered quickly from its revolutions of 1848, and this allowed it to control the revolutions in Italy. If the Italian states were to have a chance at uniting then Austria must be defeated. However, the Italian revolutionaries failed to unite in a common aim and could not fully co-operate. Although the men involved in the Italian revolutions fought bravely, this was not enough against the better trained and better led Austrian forces.

1. How far do **Sources A** and **B** agree about the failures of the 1848 revolutions?   **4**

Source C explains the importance of Cavour to Italian unification.

Source C

> Cavour was very important to Italian unification. He was responsible for developing Piedmont into a modern industrial state capable of uniting Italy. Piedmont became the richest Italian state because of Cavour, resulting in it eventually dominating the rest of Italy. Cavour reduced Austrian domination over the Italian states by provoking Austria into starting the war of 1859. Prior to this his diplomatic skills secured an alliance with France to support a war with Austria, which led to the Austrians being quickly defeated.

2. Why was Cavour important to Italian unification? (Use **Source C** and recall.)   **5**

3. Describe Garibaldi's contribution to Italian unification.   **5**

[END OF CONTEXT 8]

HISTORICAL STUDY: EUROPEAN AND WORLD   *Marks*

> ### CONTEXT 9: IRON AND BLOOD?
> ### BISMARCK AND THE CREATION OF
> ### THE GERMAN EMPIRE, 1815–1871

Answer the following questions using recalled knowledge and information from the sources where appropriate.

Source A explains why the ideas of liberalism and nationalism failed to spread in Germany after 1815.

Source A

> The German Confederation of 1815 allowed the German Princes to hold on to their power. This upset liberals and nationalists who wanted a united Germany and the right to vote for their leaders. However, these ideas appealed mainly to a minority of educated people such as intellectuals and students. These nationalist students held a mass meeting in 1817 where they made speeches supporting liberal ideas and criticising Austria. Metternich feared a revolution so created the Carlsbad Decrees, which outlawed the student movement. They also regulated universities to stop liberal ideas spreading.

1. Why did the ideas of liberalism and nationalism fail to spread in Germany after 1815? (Use **Source A** and recall.)   **5**

2. Describe the revolutions which began in Germany in 1848.   **5**

Sources B and **C** are about Bismarck's appointment as Minister-President of Prussia.

Source B

> Bismarck soon gained a powerful hold over the King by force of his personality and powers of persuasion. He had annoyed Parliament with the tactics he used to maintain royal authority over it when he ended the argument about army reforms in the King's favour. Parliament's distaste with Bismarck was officially noted in 1863, when its members took a vote and declared to the King that they could no longer work with Bismarck.

Source C

> Tough and with a strong personality, Bismarck easily gained influence over the King. The dispute over army reforms did not help relations between Bismarck and Parliament. It objected to Bismarck's methods of ensuring royal authority was upheld. In 1863 Parliament informed the King that it was not willing to deal with Bismarck. He had only been Minister-President for eight months and had failed to achieve agreement with Parliament.

3. How far do **Sources B** and **C** agree about Bismarck's appointment as Minister-President of Prussia?   **4**

[END OF CONTEXT 9]

Mar.

HISTORICAL STUDY: EUROPEAN AND WORLD

CONTEXT 10: THE RED FLAG: LENIN AND THE RUSSIAN REVOLUTION, 1894–1921

Answer the following questions using recalled knowledge and information from the sources where appropriate.

Source A explains why the Orthodox Church was important in maintaining the Tsar's rule.

Source A

> As well as teaching Christian beliefs, the Russian Orthodox Church taught the people to be loyal to the Tsar. Followers of other religions were encouraged to convert and Jews were often persecuted. As the head of the Orthodox Church the Tsar himself appointed the chief bishops and its ruling organisation known as the Holy Synod which was essentially a government department. As a result, the Orthodox Church had influence, power and wealth. Its most important bishops wore fabulous jewelled robes and lived comfortable lives.

1. Why was the Orthodox Church important in maintaining the Tsar's rule? (Use **Source A** and recall.)   5

Sources B and **C** are about the first Duma.

Source B

> The Duma was set up in 1906. It was a parliament without real power. It was never intended to represent the majority of the ordinary Russian people, that is, the workers and the peasants. The Tsar made it clear he retained control. He personally appointed all government ministers and the Duma could not make laws without his consent. He could simply dismiss the Duma if it displeased him and rule alone.

Source C

> The first Duma lasted a mere 10 weeks before its demands upset the Tsar. He dissolved it and another election was called. The voting system meant that very few of the lower classes ever voted. The Tsar had chosen Stolypin as Prime Minister and he planned to introduce reforms to increase the Tsar's support in the countryside, hoping this would make it easier to govern.

2. How far do **Sources B** and **C** agree about the ineffectiveness of the first Duma?   4

3. Describe the weaknesses of the Whites in the Civil War.   5

[END OF CONTEXT 10]

HISTORICAL STUDY: EUROPEAN AND WORLD

Marks

CONTEXT 11: FREE AT LAST? RACE
RELATIONS IN THE USA, 1918–1968

Answer the following questions using recalled knowledge and information from the sources where appropriate.

Sources A and **B** are about the experience of immigrants in the USA in the 1920s.

Source A

> Italians did not want to buy land as few planned to stay in America for long. They headed for the great cities where other jobs were available. Italian Americans succeeded in jobs requiring little formal education such as small business ownership. However, like other immigrants, they found other ways to get rich. Politics, sports, and crime, were ladders for upward mobility. Italian Americans achieved notable success in classical and popular music.

Source B

> My family lived in the city of Chicago. My father came there from Montfalcone, in Italy and always hoped to return there. When I was 14 years old I started dodging school and turned to stealing. At first I stole from clothes lines, later I stole bicycles, as did others in the neighbourhood. We sold the bicycles and made about $75 a week. Then we joined an older gang because although they were only around 20 years old they were in the big money and drove around in fancy automobiles.

1. How far do **Sources A** and **B** agree about the experience of immigrants in the USA during the 1920s?   **4**

2. Describe the effects of the Jim Crow laws on black Americans in the 1920s and 1930s.   **5**

Source C is about the split in the Civil Rights Movement in the mid 1960s.

Source C

> By the mid 1960s some Civil Rights campaigners were wondering if the cost in injuries and human life was worth the gains achieved through non-violent protest. They had also become frustrated with the slow pace of change. A split emerged in the Civil Rights Movement. New leaders like Malcolm X offered hope of a better future in northern ghettos. This message reached great cities such as Chicago and Los Angeles. In places like these there was a growing resentment at the way white police officers bullied the young black citizens living in their precinct.

3. Why was there a split in the Civil Rights Movement in the mid 1960s? (Use **Source C** and recall.)   **5**

[END OF CONTEXT 11]

Mark

HISTORICAL STUDY: EUROPEAN AND WORLD

> ### CONTEXT 12: THE ROAD TO WAR, 1933–1939

Answer the following questions using recalled knowledge and information from the sources where appropriate.

Sources A and **B** are about the Nazi view on race.

Source A

> The Nazi theory of racial superiority was not original even though Hitler had stated, in Mein Kampf, that differences between the races was a matter of scientific fact. There could be no argument that the Aryan people of northern Europe were superior in every way. This was not just a matter of physical superiority but also of intellectual strength. It was logical that people like this should be in control of all other races.

Source B

> The stereotype of the blond and blue-eyed warrior took a powerful hold on many young Germans who were taught that the Aryans of Germany and Scandinavia were the Master Race. According to Nazi propaganda, which continually stressed the importance of "pure blood", biological research had shown that there was a distinction between races. This gave them the authority to rule over the peoples of the world.

1. How far do **Sources A** and **B** agree about the Nazi view on race?   4

2. Describe Hitler's foreign policy plans after 1933.   5

Source C explains why Britain followed a policy of appeasement in the 1930s.

Source C

> By the 1930s many British people felt that the Treaty of Versailles had been unfair to Germany. The Germans had expected the treaty to be based on the reasonable aims of the Americans. The Peace Ballot had shown that a large section of the population was against war in principle. Since technology had advanced rapidly in the previous twenty years there were also more practical reasons for avoiding war such as the fear of bombing from the air. The Prime Minister was convinced that Hitler could be persuaded to keep the peace.

3. Why did Britain follow a policy of appeasement in the 1930s?   (Use **Source C** and recall.)   5

[END OF CONTEXT 12]

HISTORICAL STUDY: EUROPEAN AND WORLD

Marks

**CONTEXT 13: IN THE SHADOW
OF THE BOMB: THE COLD WAR,
1945–1985**

Answer the following questions using recalled knowledge and information from the sources where appropriate.

Sources A and **B** are about why a Cold War broke out between the superpowers.

Source A

> The alliance against a common enemy during the Second World War broke down almost as soon as the war ended and was replaced by a climate of suspicion. Soviet and American leaders held opposing ideological views and attempted to spread their beliefs to other countries. Tensions continued to grow over the next few years. America's decision to develop and use the atomic bomb against the Japanese without consulting the Soviets placed further strain on relations.

Source B

> As soon as the war ended the Soviet Union and the Americans developed open hostility towards each other. The meetings at Yalta and Potsdam did little to improve relations. The new President Truman and Stalin seemed hostile to one another and this emphasised their ideological divisions. The tension at Potsdam was increased by America's use of the atomic bomb against Japan.

1. How far do **Sources A** and **B** agree about the reasons why a Cold War broke out between the Soviet Union and the USA?   **4**

2. Describe the tactics used by the USA in the Vietnam War.   **5**

Source C explains why relations between the superpowers improved in the 1970s.

Source C

> By the early 1970s President Nixon had begun to withdraw US troops from Vietnam. Although the fighting did not end immediately, it seemed like the beginning of peace. Gradually the Vietnamese peace had a positive influence over other areas of superpower relations. The personalities involved were also important. Presidents Nixon and Carter enjoyed the increased popularity they won as peace-makers. The Soviet leader Brezhnev welcomed the improved relations with America because he recognised the perils of all-out nuclear war. Brezhnev was also keen on peace because it left him free to concentrate on problems within the Soviet Union.

3. Why did relations between the superpowers improve in the 1970s? (Use **Source C** and recall.)   **5**

[END OF CONTEXT 13]

[END OF PART 3: EUROPEAN AND WORLD CONTEXTS]

[END OF QUESTION PAPER]

Acknowledgements

Permission has been sought from all relevant copyright holders and Hodder Gibson is grateful for the use of the following:

An extract from 'History of Britain' by Andrew Langley. Published by Heinemann Educational Publishers, 1996. (2009 page 11);

An extract from 'Scotland: A Concise History' by Fitzroy MacLean. Copyright © 1970, 1993 and 2000 Thames & Hudson Ltd., London. (2009 page 11);

An extract from 'Highland News, 8th April 1911, reproduced in 'Adventurers and Exiles: The Great Scottish Exodus' by Marjory Harper, published by Profile Books, 2003 (2009 page 13);

An extract from 'From the Cradle to the Grave: Social Welfare in Britain 1890s–1951' by Simon Wood and Claire Wood, published by Hodder & Stoughton, 2002 (2009 page 14);

A cartoon from the Daily Herald newspaper in 1942 © Daily Herald Archive/Science & Society Picture Library (2009 page 14);

A poster produced by the Irish National Party in 1915. Courtesy of the National Library of Ireland (2009 page 16);

An extract from 'Understanding Global Issues 10/92 Columbus and after: The beginnings of Colonisation' edited by Richard Buckley, published by European Schoolbooks, 1992 (2009 page 20);

An extract from http://www.en.wikipedia-org/wiki/AgeofDiscovery (2009 page 20);

An extract from 'The Unification of Italy', by Andrina Stiles, published by Hodder & Stoughton, 2006 (2009 page 24);

An extract from 'Cavour, Garibaldi and the Making of Italy 1815–70', published by Scottish Consultative Council on the Curriculum © Learning and Teaching Scotland, 2000 (2009 page 24);

Two extracts from 'Germany 1815–1939' by Jim McGonigle, published by Hodder Gibson 2006 (2009 page 25);

An extract from 'The Growth of Nationalism: Germany and Italy 1815–1939' by Ronald Cameron, Christine Henderson & Charles Robertson, published by Pulse Publications (2009 page 25);

An extract from 'The Civil Rights Movement' by Mark Newman, published by Edinburgh University Press (BAAS Paperbacks) 2004 (2009 page 27);

Two extracts from 'Free at Last? Race Relations in the USA 1918–1968' by John A Kerr, published by Hodder & Stoughton, 2000 (2009 page 27);

A picture taken from Illustrated London News, December 22, 1849. Public Domain (2011 page 13);

An extract from 'The Middle Ages' by Achland and Burt, published by Hodder & Stoughton 1978 (2012 page 17);

An extract from 'David I – A Medieval King' by Robert Scott and Alasdair Hogg, published by Chambers 1978 (2012 page 17);

An extract from 'The Age of Discovery 1400–1550' written by Dan O'Sullivan, published by Longman 1984 © Pearson Education (2012 page 20);

An extract from 'History of the Russian Revolution' by Leon Trotsky, published by Pathfinder Press, 1932 2012 page 26);

'The Call of the Seaside, Portobello'. Reproduced with acknowledgement to Peter Stubbs, www.edinphoto.org.uk (2013 page 15).

HISTORY INTERMEDIATE 2
2009

PART 1 THE SHORT ESSAY

Scottish and British

Context 1: Murder in the Cathedral: Crown, Church and People, 1154-1173

1. The candidate explains why knights were important in medieval times by referring to evidence such as:
   * they were an important part of a feudal army
   * they were part of the feudal system and gave part of their land to peasants
   * they were used in local government/member of a jury
   * they protected the weak, young and old in society
   * they fought for the Church against non-Christians eg crusade
   * their behaviour made them role models for the rest of society
   * they performed services such as castle-guard in return for their land.

Context 2: Wallace, Bruce and the Wars of Independence, 1286-1328

2. The candidate explains why John Balliol lost his position as King of Scots in 1296 by referring to evidence such as:
   * John Balliol had accepted Edward I as his overlord
   * John Balliol had been bullied by King Edward (eg orders, legal decisions overturned)
   * John Balliol refused King Edward's order to join him in a war against France
   * John Balliol withdrew his homage to King Edward
   * John Balliol had made an alliance with the King of France against Edward ie treason
   * King Edward defeated John Balliol at Dunbar
   * King Edward forced John Balliol to surrender to him
   * King Edward had stripped John Balliol of his crown and title
   * Robert Bruce had been plotting against John Balliol
   * not all the Scots supported Balliol in his campaign against King Edward.

Context 3: Mary, Queen of Scots and the Scottish Reformation, 1540s-1587

3. The candidate explains why Mary, Queen of Scots, faced difficulties ruling Scotland when she returned in 1561 by referring to evidence such as:
   * Mary was female – many people were suspicious of a female ruler (eg Knox)
   * Mary was young – possibly inexperienced in governing a country
   * nobles were in competition to win her support eg Huntly, Moray
   * there had recently been a revolt in Scotland against her mother, Mary of Guise
   * Mary had come from France but the French were unpopular in Scotland
   * Mary was Roman Catholic and Scotland had recently become Protestant
   * Elizabeth of England was hostile to Mary because she claimed to be Queen of England.

Context 4: The Coming of the Civil War, 1603-1642

4. The candidate explains why there were problems between Crown and Parliament during the reign of James VI and I by referring to evidence such as:
   * James VI and I's belief in the Divine Right of Kings
   * over-confident/naive character of James VI and I
   * extravagant spending/debts of James VI and I eg clothing, banquets, gifts, pensions
   * raised taxes without consulting Parliament eg feudal dues, customs duties
   * James VI and I's desire for a union between Scotland and England
   * gave money and power to favourites at court
   * impositions and the "Bates Case" 1606/resentment over extra customs duties
   * failure of the "Great Contract" 1610 resulted in James VI and I dismissing Parliament
   * failure of "Addled" Parliament 1614
   * monopolies caused anger/resentment within Parliament
   * war with Spain 1621 caused debates between James and Parliament.

Context 5: "Ane End of Ane Auld Sang": Scotland and the Treaty of Union, 1690s-1715

5. The candidate explains why there was so much opposition to a Union in Scotland before 1707 by referring to evidence such as:
   * the Scots felt key members of Parliament had been bribed
   * the Scots felt their friendship/trade with France would be affected
   * Scots were critical of the joint monarchy and feared the effects of a Parliamentary union
   * the Scots blamed England for the failure of their colony at Darien
   * the Scots feared that Union would bring economic ruin
   * the Scots feared for the position of their Presbyterian church
   * Scots feared that their legal system would be changed
   * Jacobites opposed the Union
   * the Scots were not being offered sufficient compensation
   * the Scots were afraid of increased taxes.

Context 6: Immigrants and Exiles: Scotland, 1830s-1930s

6. The candidate explains why Scots emigrants made a valuable contribution in Canada and the United States by referring to evidence such as:
   * Scots were comparatively well educated
   * had a pioneering spirit
   * many Scots had practical farming skills
   * others had financial and commercial ability
   * Scots often managed to arrive with some capital to invest
   * skilled craftsmen contributed their skills
   * played an important role in education and politics
   * reference to individual Scots whose contribution was valuable.

Context 7 (a): From the Cradle to the Grave? Social Welfare in Britain, 1890s-1951

7. (a) The candidate explains why the Liberal reforms, 1906-14, failed to solve the problems of the poor by referring to evidence such as:
   * Liberals had no overall plan – tackled problems one by one
   * legislation gave powers to local authorities – some did not introduce free school meals at first
   * medical inspections did not provide treatment
   * amount of old age pensions was inadequate
   * pension age was set too high at 70 for most people to benefit
   * health insurance only provided free treatment for worker not family

- unemployment insurance was only for certain industries
- benefit rates were not sufficient to overcome poverty
- Liberals did not tackle poor housing at all.

Context 7 (b): Campaigning for Change: Social Change in Scotland, 1900s-1979

(b) The candidate explains why many industries in Scotland experienced problems in the years between the two world wars by referring to evidence such as:
- the end of the Great War had led to a drop in demand for warships
- the slump of the 1920s had led to a drop in demand for merchant ships
- there was a decline in the old industries producing coal and steel
- British markets had been lost to foreign competition
- industrial unrest undermined the reputation of Scottish industries
- the Great Depression made matters even worse for the heavy industries – shipyards, coal mines closed
- there was little investment in new technology
- the Government did little to help industry in the 1930s
- new industries eg light engineering, cars were mainly located in England.

Context 8: A Time of Troubles: Ireland, 1900-1923

8. The candidate explains why support for Sinn Fein increased after 1916 by referring to evidence such as:
- execution of rebel leaders in the Easter Rising caused resentment against the British
- Sinn Fein opposed the First World War eg organised strikes against conscription
- Sinn Fein was supported by the Catholic Church
- leadership of De Valera and Collins encouraged support
- returning Easter Rising rebels were treated as heroes. Many stood as Sinn Fein candidates in local by-elections
- Sinn Fein were successful in the 1918 General Election encouraging others to support them
- Sinn Fein became the leading Irish Political Party
- Sinn Fein refused to go to London to work in Parliament as a protest
- Sinn Fein set up an illegal Irish Parliament in Dublin i.e. they stood for independence.

European and World

Context 1: The Norman Conquest, 1060-1153

9. The candidate explains why David I introduced feudalism to Scotland by referring to evidence such as:
- influence of David's experiences at the court of King Henry as a young man
- Scotland was difficult for David to control eg different tribes had their own leaders
- feudalism gave the king a means of control over his subjects
- it made administration of the country easier
- encouraged the development of castles across the kingdom
- church received large amounts of land which encouraged its support for the king
- charters were given to encourage the development of burghs
- David was provided with knights for his army.

Context 2: The Cross and the Crescent: The First Crusade, 1096-1125

10. The candidate explains why Pope Urban II called the First Crusade by referring to evidence such as:
- to recapture Jerusalem
- to help the Christians in the east who were being persecuted
- to protect Christian churches and relics which were being destroyed

- to help Emperor Alexius, who had sent ambassadors asking for help
- to reopen the trade/pilgrim routes to the east
- to heal the schism between the western and eastern churches
- to place himself as head of a united church
- to show European rulers eg The Holy Roman Emperor that he could call an army
- to prevent knights in the west from killing each other.

Context 3: War, Death and Revolt in Medieval Europe, 1328-1436

11. The candidate explains why the Hundred Years' War broke out between England and France in 1337 by referring to evidence such as:
- French kings claimed overlordship of English possessions in France
- English economic interests in France – wine, wool and grain
- English reaction to the continuing French alliance with Scotland
- English kings claimed the throne of France
- dispute over the succession following the death of Charles IV in 1328
- French attacks on English and Flemish merchants in the Channel
- King Philip IV declared Edward III's land in France forfeit
- King Philip IV's invasion of Gascony.

Context 4: New Worlds: Europe in the Age of Expansion, 1480s-1530s

12. The candidate explains why European countries wanted to search for new lands between the 1480s and the 1530s by referring to evidence such as:
- religious motives/they wanted to spread Christianity
- there was rivalry between countries eg Spain and Portugal
- countries/individuals wanted fame and fortune
- they wished to find valuable spices
- they wished to increase trading links with the East
- the Turks had disrupted the old spice routes
- there was a desire for increased knowledge about the world
- improvements in technology made voyages easier ie caravels, quadrants
- there was a search for new fishing grounds.

Context 5: "Tea and Freedom": The American Revolution, 1763-1783

13. The candidate explains why the colonists won the American War of Independence by referring to evidence such as:
- the skill of George Washington and his leadership of the Colonial army
- knowledge of the terrain gave the colonists an advantage
- poor leadership and tactics by British officers
- difficult to supply the British army across the Atlantic
- British surrender at Saratoga in October 1777 was a decisive event
- French involvement in 1778
- involvement of Spain and Holland in 1779
- Britain lost control of the Atlantic
- defeat at Yorktown persuaded British government to negotiate the end of the war.

Context 6: "This Accursed Trade": The British Slave Trade and its Abolition, 1770–1807

14. The candidate explains why there was increasing support for the campaign against the slave trade by referring to evidence such as:
- influence of Christian groups who believed slavery was against the ten commandments
- role of William Wilberforce in taking the campaign to parliament

- testimony of former slaves
- awareness of conditions on middle passage
- awareness of conditions in slave factories
- awareness of treatment of slaves on plantations
- public meetings, petitions being used to inform people about trade
- British economy no longer so reliant on slave trade.

Context 7: Citizens! The French Revolution, 1789-1794

15. The candidate explains why few French people supported Louis XVI in 1789 by referring to evidence such as:
    - the peasants blamed the king for the power of the landlords
    - the peasants blamed the king for having to pay most of the taxes
    - the workers in the cities were suffering from poor wages and conditions
    - Louis XVI was a weak and ineffective king
    - Marie Antoinette was blamed for spending too much money on luxuries
    - there were new political ideas saying that kings must share power
    - the middle class resented the political power of the nobility and the king
    - the peasants and middle class wanted more power for the Estates General
    - the king refused to listen to the demands of the Third Estate.

Context 8: Cavour, Garibaldi and the Making of Italy, 1815-1870

16. The candidate explains why Cavour was important to Italian unification by referring to evidence such as:
    - he adopted a realistic and opportunist approach to situations
    - as PM of Piedmont from 1852 his main aim was expansion of territory and expulsion of Austria from Italy
    - modernised Piedmont's economy eg built railways, roads, modernised port of Genoa
    - made treaties with Britain and France
    - built up military strength of Piedmont
    - following Crimean War, recognised that diplomacy alone would not work
    - met with Napoleon III at Plombieres 1858 to agree to drive Austria out of Italy
    - provoked Austria into war in April 1859
    - following reinstatement in 1860 he signed a deal with France: Piedmont would take 3 duchies of Tuscany, Modena and Parma; France would take Nice and Savoy.

Context 9: Iron and Blood? Bismarck and The Creation of the German Empire, 1815-1871

17. The candidate explains why Bismarck's leadership was important to the unification of the German states by referring to evidence such as:
    - he encouraged the nationalist ambitions of the Liberals in the Prussian Parliament
    - he backed army reforms which strengthened the Prussian army
    - he wanted to unify Germany under Prussian leadership
    - he followed policies of "realpolitik" eg "iron and blood" speech
    - he engineered war between Prussia and Denmark in 1864
    - he outmanoeuvred Austria at the Treaty of Vienna
    - he engineered war with Austria in 1866 to secure dominance of Prussia
    - his leniency in the Treaty of Prague left open possibility of Austria as an ally in future
    - he masterminded the formation of the North German Confederation

- he edited the Ems telegram to bring about Franco-Prussian War
- the defeat of France led to the creation of the German Empire in 1871.

Context 10: The Red Flag: Lenin and the Russian Revolution, 1894-1921

18. The candidate explains why the Reds won the Civil War by referring to evidence such as:
    - Red army had good supplies of food – mostly taken from the peasants
    - Reds controlled the industrial centres of Russia
    - Reds had good rail routes/communications
    - Whites were divided/did not always act together
    - peasants were afraid that they would lose land if the Whites won
    - Trotsky moulded his army into a good fighting unit
    - Reds controlled main cities
    - large proportion of the population supported the Reds.

Context 11: Free at Last? Race Relations in the USA, 1918-1968

19. The candidate explains why black people rioted in many American cities in the 1960s by referring to evidence such as:
    - poverty – 40% of black Americans still lived in poverty
    - nothing had been done about slum housing with overcrowding and high rents
    - blacks were in low paid jobs or had no jobs
    - they had poor quality schools and facilities
    - blacks had poor health and little access to health care
    - ghettos were places of crime, gangs and drugs
    - feeling that Civil Rights Act had not solved problems in northern cities
    - assassination of Martin Luther King
    - riots broke out during summer heatwaves
    - disillusionment with the draft/Vietnam War
    - influence of Radical leaders encouraged action
    - heavy-handed policing/brutality caused anger among blacks.

Context 12: The Road to War, 1933-1939

20. The candidate explains why events after Munich, September 1938, led to the outbreak of war in 1939 by referring to evidence such as:
    - the take-over of the Sudetenland gave Germany dominance in Central Europe
    - Hitler threatened Czechoslovakia despite his promise of no more territorial demands
    - Germany invaded Czechoslovakia in March 1939 and so broke the Munich settlement of 1938
    - Britain realised appeasement had failed
    - Great Britain no longer trusted Hitler and sped up her rearmaments programme/led to conscription
    - Hitler's aggression against Poland and the demand for the return of Danzig increased tension
    - Britain promised to defend Poland if she were attacked
    - August 1939, Germany and Russia signed the Nazi-Soviet Non-Aggression Pact which left Hitler free to attack Poland
    - September, Germany invaded Poland
    - Germany ignored the British ultimatum to stop the attack so Britain declared war on Germany.

Context 13: In the Shadow of the Bomb: The Cold War, 1945-1985

21. The candidate explains why the USA became involved in a crisis over Cuba in 1962 by referring to evidence such as:
    - Cuban leader Castro had formed a close alliance with the Soviet Union

- Castro had angered American businesses by nationalising key industries
- evidence of missile bases being constructed in Cuba
- Cuba lay close to the American mainland
- American public opinion would not accept the threat posed by Soviet missiles on the island
- fear in America that their country was falling behind in the Cold War
- Kennedy was looking for an opportunity to gain revenge after Bay of Pigs fiasco.

PART 2 HISTORICAL STUDY

Scottish and British

Context 1: Murder in the Cathedral: Crown, Church and People, 1154-1173

1. The candidate evaluates the usefulness of the source by referring to evidence such as:
   - primary source written at the time of Henry II's reign
   - author knew Henry/possible bias
   - to describe Henry's character/to flatter the king
   - states that Henry was honest, polite and generous.

   Maximum of 1 mark for commenting on content omission such as:
   - does not mention Henry's famous temper
   - does not mention that Henry was stubborn eg quarrel with Becket.

2. The candidate describes the life of a monk in medieval times by referring to evidence such as:
   - took vows of poverty, obedience and chastity
   - spent much of the day in prayer or attending religious services
   - lived strictly according to the rules of his order
   - had a simple diet eg fruit, bread and water
   - owned no personal possessions
   - prayed for the souls of the dead
   - wrote chronicles, recording events
   - worked in monastic fields eg rearing sheep
   - looked after the sick in the monastery's infirmary.

3. The candidate explains why Henry II and Archbishop Becket quarrelled by referring to evidence such as:

   from the source
   - Becket resigned as Chancellor
   - Becket refused to sign the Constitutions of Clarendon
   - Becket would not reduce the power of the Church
   - Becket fled to France without the king's permission

   from recall
   - Henry wanted all clergymen (criminous clerks) to be tried in the king's court
   - Henry charged Becket with contempt of court and confiscated his lands
   - Becket appealed to the Pope and gained his full support
   - Becket excommunicated the Archbishop of York and sacked the bishops who had crowned Henry's son.

Context 2: Wallace, Bruce and the Wars of Independence, 1286-1328

1. The candidate evaluates the usefulness of the source by referring to evidence such as:
   - primary source/secondary source written some time after the events it describes
   - a chronicle was to record what happened/the author would have to research the events
   - to describe the events of that night
   - it describes the bad weather which contributed to the accident/states that the King's horse stumbled and he was killed.

   Maximum of 1 mark for commenting on content omission such as:
   - King Alexander III fell over a cliff.

2. The candidate describes what happened at the Battle of Stirling Bridge by referring to evidence such as:
   - the Scots and English were on different sides of the bridge
   - the Scots were formed up on the high ground (Abbey Craig)
   - the English were slow in getting organised (slept in and/or a knighting ceremony)
   - the English debated whether to use Stirling Bridge or a slightly distant ford
   - the English crossed the bridge (which was narrow) slowly
   - Wallace ordered the Scots to attack the English when enough had crossed to defeat them
   - the Scots cut off the end of the bridge and isolated the English/many were drowned
   - the English were defeated and/or Cressingham was killed.

3. The candidate explains why the Scots sent the Declaration of Arbroath to the Pope in 1320 by referring to evidence such as:

   from the source
   - the Scots wanted Bruce recognised internationally as king
   - the raids on northern England had not been successful
   - the invasion of Ireland had failed to put pressure on Edward II
   - they wanted the Pope to recognise Bruce as King

   from recall
   - Edward II would not agree that Bruce was King of Scots
   - the Pope was a person of international authority
   - the Pope could put pressure on Edward II to change his policy
   - the Church had excommunicated Bruce and would not accept him as king.

Context 3: Mary, Queen of Scots and the Scottish Reformation, 1540s-1587

1. The candidate explains why Protestantism spread in Scotland in the 1540s and 1550s by referring to evidence such as:

   from the source
   - some Scots began to question the teachings of the Catholic Church
   - English translations of the Bible were distributed
   - religious pamphlets were smuggled from abroad
   - the Good and Godly Ballads spread Protestant ideas

   from recall
   - criticism of the wealth of the Church in Scotland and its concerns with money
   - criticism of the lack of spirituality among some members of that Church
   - criticism of how some Protestant preachers had been treated (eg Wishart)
   - resentment of French/Catholic influence over Scotland.

2. The candidate describes the events surrounding the murder of Darnley by referring to evidence such as:
   - Darnley was killed in Edinburgh in 1567
   - Mary had encouraged Darnley to return to Edinburgh because he was ill
   - Darnley had settled in lodgings in Kirk o' Fields
   - Mary was supposed to stay with Darnley on his last night in Kirk o' Fields, but she left
   - the house was blown up by gunpowder
   - Darnley's body was found in the garden behind the house
   - Darnley had not died in the explosion, he had been suffocated.

3. The candidate evaluates the usefulness of the source by referring to evidence such as:
   - primary source written by Mary while she was in an English prison
   - it was a personal letter from Mary to Elizabeth/possible bias against Elizabeth
   - to accuse Elizabeth of helping cause trouble in Scotland
   - English agents, spies etc encouraged rebellion in Scotland/these agents had been very well rewarded afterwards.

   Maximum of 1 mark for commenting on content omission such as:
   - Mary was Elizabeth's prisoner/Elizabeth would not let Mary return to Scotland.

Context 4: The Coming of the Civil War, 1603-1642

1. The candidate evaluates the usefulness of the source by referring to evidence such as:
   - secondary source written more than 300 years after the religious disagreements developed between the king and the Scots
   - the historian is well informed as he will have studied the Scottish records
   - written to show that the (ordinary) Scots were opposed to the Prayer Book/to show that women took the lead in the opposition
   - it says there was a riot in St Giles when the Prayer Book was first used/that Jenny Geddes egged the women on.

   Maximum of 1 mark for commenting on content omission such as:
   - Jenny Geddes threw her stool at the Dean
   - the Scots objected because they thought the new Prayer Book seemed to be going back to mass (Roman Catholicism).

2. The candidate explains why Charles I became unpopular in England by referring to evidence such as:

   from the source
   - the King imposed the "Ship Money" tax on inland areas
   - he imposed "Ship Money" tax without the consent of Parliament
   - anyone who refused to pay the taxes was tried in special courts
   - he imposed fines on people who built on common land or in royal forests

   from recall
   - appointment of Archbishop Laud/introduction of Laudianism unpopular with the Puritans
   - Standing Army was unpopular with the people
   - Charles raised taxes to pay for own extravagances eg art
   - Royal Monopolies were unpopular.

3. The candidate describes the events between 1640 and 1642 which led to the outbreak of the Civil War by referring to evidence such as:
   - Long Parliament led by Pym led to "anti-court" consensus
   - Strafford impeached by Parliament 1640/executed 1641
   - Triennial Act 1641 restricted power of king to call Parliament
   - emergence of Hyde/"Constitutional Royalists"
   - Ten Propositions 1641 put further restrictions on king's power
   - the Grand Remonstrance 1641 divided House of Commons
   - formation of "King's Party" in House of Commons
   - Five Members Coup January 1642 made Civil War likely
   - rebellion in Ireland
   - widespread social disorder eg weavers, fens
   - Militia Ordinance 1642 issued by Parliament/Commission of Array issued by king
   - the Nineteen Propositions June 1642 were rejected by Charles I
   - Committee of Public Safety appointed by Parliament
   - Charles declares war on Parliament 22 August 1642.

Context 5: "Ane End of Ane Auld Sang": Scotland and the Treaty of Union, 1690s-1715

1. The candidate evaluates the usefulness of the source by referring to evidence such as:
   - primary source, published at the time they were recruiting for the expedition
   - published by the Directors who were in charge of the expedition
   - to recruit people to go to Darien
   - it tells that the ships were loaded with everything needed for the expedition/it promises them fifty acres of good ground.

   Maximum of 1 mark for commenting on content omission such as:
   - the expedition was badly equipped/the ground at Darien was not good.

2. The candidate explains why many Scottish nobles agreed to the Act of Union by referring to evidence such as:

   from the source
   - they were convinced of the prosperity it would bring to Scotland
   - they saw the opportunities of investing in England's colonies
   - they saw it would guarantee the Protestant Succession (v. Jacobites)
   - they would gain royal approval and its benefits

   from recall
   - they received money through the Equivalent
   - they received bribes
   - they received new titles
   - they were offered government jobs for their families
   - they received back payment of their salaries.

3. The candidate describes how Scotland changed as a result of the Act of Union by referring to evidence such as:
   - the Pound Sterling replaced the Pound Scots and coins changed
   - English weights and measures replaced Scottish ones
   - a Union flag replaced the Scottish flag
   - new taxes applied in Scotland (Malt Tax)
   - Customs and Excise men appeared in Scotland
   - Scottish Parliament and Scottish nobles moved to London
   - Scots Law was affected by appeals to the House of Lords
   - The Patronage Act (1712) affected the Kirk.

Context 6: Immigrants and Exiles: Scotland, 1830s-1930s

1. The candidate evaluates the usefulness of the source by referring to evidence such as:
   - primary source from 1836 when Irish people were coming to Scotland
   - authorship: a Catholic priest in Aberdeen would know why the Irish came to the city
   - to show the kind of work done by the Irish in Aberdeen
   - they came to Scotland as jobs were easy to find and wages were fairly high.

   Maximum of 1 mark for commenting on content omission such as:
   - Scotland was close to Ireland so a short voyage
   - Scotland was cheap to get to.

2. The candidate describes the experience of Irish immigrants in the west of Scotland by referring to evidence such as:
   - found work in factories, mines and farms
   - lived in poorest housing – overcrowded, little furniture, poor sanitation
   - hit by disease such as cholera and typhus
   - kept to themselves in their own communities
   - welcomed by employers
   - disliked by Scots for taking their jobs and keeping wages low

- received support from Catholic Church/used church as centre for social activities
- those from the north of Ireland settled more easily.

3. The candidate explains why many Scots emigrated overseas in the twentieth century by referring to evidence such as:

from the source
- former pupils who had gone to Canada were succeeding
- money and letters sent home encouraged people to go
- Canada had great opportunities for farming
- agents persuaded people by enthusiasm and slides

from recall
- poverty in Scotland encouraged emigration
- unemployment eg in fishing after World War I or during depression
- some countries paid fares
- advertisements persuaded people of benefits.

Context 7 (a): From the Cradle to the Grave? Social Welfare in Britain, 1890s-1951

1. The candidate explains why attitudes towards poverty changed in the early twentieth century by referring to evidence such as:

from the source
- Trade Unions did not feel Liberals and Conservatives did enough for the poor
- Socialists felt a high level of poverty was wrong
- the new Labour Party stood for practical reforms to tackle poverty
- Liberals thought of ways to help the poor because they thought they would lose votes to Labour

from recall
- reports of Booth and Rowntree showed the scale of poverty
- worries about effect of poverty on health and the defence of the country
- concern that industrial output was being held back because of poverty
- countries such as Germany showed poverty could be tackled eg with pensions.

2. The candidate evaluates the usefulness of the source by referring to evidence such as:
- primary source from 1942 when the Beveridge Report issued
- authorship: newspaper reporting events/cartoonist may exaggerate
- to show clearly the problems Beveridge identified
- problems were want, squalor, disease, ignorance and idleness/shows "Giants".

Maximum of 1 mark for commenting on content omission such as:
- Beveridge wanted to introduce a comprehensive national insurance scheme
- Beveridge assumed the existence of eg a National Health Service.

3. The candidate describes the reforms introduced by Labour after 1945 to improve the lives of the British people by referring to evidence such as:
- National Insurance Act 1946 – comprehensive, universal scheme
- National Assistance Act 1948 – to help those not covered by Insurance
- National Health Service set up in 1948
- huge house building programme started
- New Towns were set up throughout the country
- investment in education eg built new schools

- had a policy of full employment/kept unemployment at a very low level
- nationalised industries eg coal.

Context 7 (b): Campaigning for Change: Social Change in Scotland, 1900s-1979

1. The candidate describes the ways sport became more popular in Scotland between 1900 and 1939 by referring to evidence such as:
- introduction of half day on Saturday gave people more time to participate/watch sport
- football and rugby became better organised in leagues
- sports such as football became professionalised
- large stadiums were built for the growing number of fans
- better transport meant nationwide competitions could be organised
- better transport meant people had more access to the countryside for activities such as hill-walking
- local councils built golf courses so golf was available to more people
- local councils built swimming pools that were cheap to use.

2. The candidate explains why women had not gained the right to vote by 1914 by referring to evidence such as:

from the source
- votes for women was not an important issue for the government
- the Prime Minister was opposed to the female franchise
- most men believed that women had no place in politics
- militant actions led to women being accused of irresponsibility

from recall
- suffragette militancy hindered progress towards getting the vote
- actions such as setting fire to buildings were seen as very serious crimes
- the press were mostly opposed to votes for women
- the government refused to be blackmailed/intimidated into granting the vote.

3. The candidate evaluates the usefulness of the source by referring to evidence such as:
- primary source from a Scottish school in the 1930s, photograph is likely to be accurate/could be posed
- to show that pupils are being trained in practical skills
- it shows girls washing clothes/girls are wearing aprons

Maximum of 1 mark for commenting on content omission such as:
- girls were also taught to cook
- boys were taught technical subjects.

Context 8: A Time of Troubles: Ireland, 1900-1923

1. The candidate explains why the Ulster Unionists were against Home Rule by referring to evidence such as:

from the source
- believed it would destroy their way of life
- believed they would be forced into poverty
- feared isolation from the empire
- feared the Protestant Church could be weakened

from recall
- Catholic Church could dominate
- businesses and trade could be harmed
- industries such as ship building could be harmed
- agriculture could become main business
- Ireland was too weak to exist on its own, needed to be in the union
- living conditions in Ireland had improved, these improvements could be compromised.

2. The candidate evaluates the usefulness of the source by referring to evidence such as:
   - primary source produced at the time of the First World War
   - poster produced by the Irish National Party who supported the First World War
   - to encourage Irishmen to join the army/postpone the campaign for Home Rule
   - it says their first duty was to take part in ending the war/join an Irish regiment.

   Maximum of 1 mark for commenting on content omission such as:
   - not all Irish Nationalists supported the First World War
   - the Nationalist movement split, Sinn Fein gained more support as a result of this.

3. The candidate describes the Civil War by referring to evidence such as:
   - Republicans occupied a number of buildings in Dublin including the Four Courts
   - Republicans occupied ex-British and RIC barracks
   - Free Staters attacked the Four Courts
   - the Republicans were defeated within nine days in Dublin
   - the Republicans continued the fight in the countryside
   - guerrilla warfare was used by both sides
   - Free State General, Henry Wilson MP for North Down was kidnapped and murdered by Republicans
   - Michael Collins was assassinated in a Republican ambush
   - Republican leader Liam Lynch was murdered
   - fighting lasted for a year
   - as many as 4000 people are believed to have been killed
   - Free State Government had imprisoned 1100 Republicans without trial
   - Special Powers Act was issued by the Dail offering amnesty for Republicans until October 1922
   - 77 Republicans were executed by the Irish Free State government after October 1922
   - De Valera conceded defeat/men were ordered to lay down their arms.

PART 3 HISTORICAL STUDY

European and World

Context 1: The Norman Conquest, 1060-1153

1. The candidate makes an accurate comparison of the sources by referring to evidence such as:

   The sources disagree completely

Source A	Source B
• Edward had nominated Harold as his rightful successor.	• Harold broke his oath to support William's rightful claim.
• Harold was chosen as King by all the powerful lords of England.	• Harold did not wait for public support/with the help of a few of his supporters.
• Harold was crowned legitimately by Aldred.	• He was illegally crowned by Stigund who had been excommunicated.

2. The candidate describes the methods used by William to increase his royal authority by referring to evidence such as:
   - built castles throughout England eg Tower of London
   - Norman barons were given land
   - established feudal ties based on homage

- ruthless destruction of challengers eg Harrying of the North
- used knights as basis for the royal army
- heavy taxation was ruthlessly enforced
- the church was controlled by Norman bishops
- produced Domesday Book to show who held land from him.

3. The candidate explains why there was an increase in the number of abbeys and monasteries during the reign of David I by referring to evidence such as:

   from the source
   - David was very religious
   - David poured wealth from his burghs into building abbeys and monasteries
   - David encouraged his nobles to leave land to the church
   - master craftsmen were brought from England and France

   from recall
   - David gave charters providing land for the church
   - David's link with Europe encouraged monks to come to Scotland from abroad
   - churchmen had important position in David's government
   - the support of the church helped strengthen royal control.

Context 2: The Cross and the Crescent: The First Crusade, 1096-1125

1. The candidate explains why the People's Crusade failed by referring to evidence such as:

   from the source
   - many of the people's army had been killed
   - the Crusaders ignored the Emperor Alexius' advice not to attack without the knights
   - the Crusaders argued amongst themselves
   - Peter the Hermit left the Crusade

   from recall
   - the Crusaders were not trained soldiers/they were disorganised
   - Peter the Hermit was not a good military leader
   - the Crusaders had split up and were easy to attack
   - the Crusaders had lost their money and supplies
   - their poor reputation meant people were unwilling to help the Crusaders.

2. The candidate describes the capture of Nicaea by the First Crusade by referring to evidence such as:
   - the Crusaders failed to starve the Muslims inside Nicaea into surrendering
   - the governor of Nicaea, Kilij Arslan was away fighting his Muslim neighbours, he did not return to protect the city
   - the Crusaders asked Emperor Alexius for boats to blockade the city
   - the city was surrounded and the Muslims inside had their supplies cut off
   - Emperor Alexius agreed to let the Muslims go free in return for the city
   - without the knowledge of the Crusaders the city was returned to Emperor Alexius in the middle of the night
   - the Crusaders were denied their plunder of the city
   - the relationship between Emperor Alexius and the Crusaders was damaged.

3. The candidate makes an accurate comparison of the sources by referring to evidence such as:

The sources disagree

Source B	Source C
• Attacked the minute they left the city.	• Did not attack when they left the city.
• Bohemond organised the knights.	• Bohemond could not organise the knights.
• Muslims were forced to flee the battlefield.	• Muslims refused to fight, fled the battlefield.
• Muslims were brave.	• Muslims were cowardly.

Context 3: War, Death and Revolt in Medieval Europe, 1328-1436

1. The candidate explains the spread of the Black Death in the fourteenth century by referring to evidence such as:

from the source
- fleas carried the disease to humans
- people lived in close proximity to rats
- plague infected rats from trading ships spread the disease to ports of call
- diseased rats got on to merchants' wagons and were carried across the country

from recall
- insanitary conditions in towns encouraged large populations of rats
- people escaped plague affected towns often carrying the fleas with them
- people did not understand what caused the Black Death
- other theories eg Black Death was an ebola viral infection.

2. The candidate makes an accurate comparison of the sources by referring to evidence such as:

The sources mainly disagree

Source B	Source C
• He believed strongly in his right to the French throne.	• Henry had no right to the crown of France.
• Henry inspired victory.	• Henry's success in the war with France was due to gambler's luck.
But • he could be cruel towards defeated enemies.	But • Henry massacred prisoners after Agincourt in defiance of the conventions of war.

3. The candidate describes the part played by Joan of Arc in reawakening French national pride by referring to evidence such as:
- she inspired the Dauphin to restart the war against England
- led the Dauphin's army to lift the siege of Orleans
- showed defiance towards the English eg sent messages
- showed bold military leadership
- restored the pride of the French soldiers
- claimed that God had called her to drive the English out of France
- helped to bring about the coronation of the Dauphin at Reims
- defeated English forces at Patay.

Context 4: New Worlds: Europe in the Age of Expansion, 1480s-1530s

1. The candidate explains why developments in shipbuilding and navigation made voyages of exploration easier between the 1480s and 1530s by referring to evidence such as:

from the source
- lateen sails made ships more manoeuvrable and faster
- longer voyages were now possible
- astrolabes helped sailors identify location at sea
- loglines were used to calculate speed and longitude.

from recall
- caravels also used lateen sails
- bigger ships could carry more men
- better compasses/cross-staff improved navigation
- quadrants helped sailors calculate position/direction.

2. The candidate makes an accurate comparison of the sources by referring to evidence such as:

The sources agree fully

Source B	Source C
• The local people came to watch them.	• Watched by silent, naked natives.
• Took possession of the said island for the King and Queen.	• Took control of the island in the name of the King and Queen of Spain.
• He presented the natives with red caps and strings of beads.	• Gifts were exchanged with the natives.

3. The candidate describes the exploration of North America up to 1540 by referring to evidence such as:
- exploration of Canada by Cabot 1497
- Cabot mapped North American coast from Nova Scotia to Newfoundland
- Ponce de Leon explored south and west coasts of Florida in 1513
- De Vaca explored Gulf coast to Rockies 1528-36 eg Texas, New Mexico, Arizona
- Jacques Cartier explored the Gulf of the St Lawrence in 1534
- Cartier sailed past Newfoundland looking for a north west passage to China in 1535-36
- Cartier discovered the area which became known as Montreal
- Spanish exploration of Florida, North and South Carolinas by de Soto.

Context 5: "Tea and Freedom": The American Revolution, 1763-1783

1. The candidate explains why colonists were unhappy with British rule by referring to evidence such as:

from the source
- colonists blamed the British government for trade being poor
- Granville's tough trade policies made the economic situation more difficult
- British officials were seen as greedy
- the British government was seen as distant and unsympathetic

from recall
- anger at unfair taxation – Stamp Act, Sugar Act etc
- lack of representation in British Parliament
- George III was viewed as a tyrant
- acts of violence by British, eg Boston massacre
- anger at continuing presence of British soldiers in colonies.

2. The candidate makes an accurate comparison of the sources by referring to evidence such as:

The sources agree fully

Source B	Source C
• Poor leadership – American forces were often led by inefficient, incompetent commanders.	• Poor leadership – many American officers lacked training in the different types of warfare.
• They were badly armed and lacked supplies.	• Were short of artillery, cavalry and almost all sorts of supplies; many did not have a uniform.
• Most men were part-time soldiers.	• Many militia men met and trained in their spare time; part-time soldiers within each state.

3. The candidate describes the events leading up to the British surrender at Saratoga by referring to evidence such as:
  • capture of 1000 British on 26/12 1776 at Trenton
  • General Howe sends Cornwallis with 5000 men to take revenge
  • Cornwallis postpones attack and allows Washington's army to escape
  • poor leadership/tactics of British forces during 1777
  • lack of communication between the British armies
  • overconfidence of General Burgoyne
  • native Americans desert the British
  • defeat of Burgoyne's forces at Saratoga
  • surrender of 6000 men and 30 cannon.

Context 6: "This Accursed Trade": The British Slave Trade and its Abolition, 1770–1807

1. The candidate describes conditions for slaves during the Middle Passage by referring to evidence such as:
  • slaves were held in chains below deck
  • description of different methods of packing slaves – loose pack/tight pack
  • violence against slaves was common
  • illness and disease were common
  • dead slaves were thrown overboard
  • occasional exercise on deck was forced on the slaves
  • slaves were fed unfamiliar food which made them ill
  • there was a lack of sanitation
  • abuse of female slaves was common.

2. The candidate makes an accurate comparison of the sources by referring to evidence such as:

The sources mainly agree

Source A	Source B
• Slaves were treated like animals (cattle).	• Examined like they were animals (horses).
• Slaves sold to highest bidder.	• Sold to man who offered most money.
• Wives sold to different owners than their husbands/owner wouldn't buy the baby.	• Son sold on his own.

3. The candidate explains why some people were in favour of the slave trade by referring to evidence such as:

from the source
  • businessmen made large profits – 30% from a single voyage
  • Triangular Trade contributed to Britain's industrial development
  • helped growth of manufacturing in Manchester
  • provided jobs at the port of Liverpool

from recall
  • slave trade was supported by powerful people (many MPs, King George III)
  • slave trade created wealth for powerful individuals and for Britain
  • British cities such as Bristol, Glasgow benefited from the trade and the raw material produced
  • steady supply of slaves were needed to work on plantations
  • end of slave trade might threaten the position of the British Empire.

Context 7: Citizens! The French Revolution, 1789-1794

1. The candidate describes the changes introduced by the Legislative Assembly in 1791 by referring to evidence such as:
  • the king no longer "owned" France
  • the king could not suggest nor delay laws/king lost a great deal of authority
  • only Active Citizens were to be given the vote
  • Active Citizens elected "Electors" to represent them
  • only the Assembly had the right to pass laws
  • the Assembly recognised local government
  • France was divided into departments
  • Courts were reorganised and judges were elected.

2. The candidate explains why there was a growing dislike of the monarchy in France in 1792 by referring to evidence such as:

from the source:
  • king disliked sharing power with the assembly
  • wanted French army to be defeated to restore his power
  • Louis refused to implement the constitution
  • many suspected that he supported counter-revolution

from recall
  • the royal family had attempted to escape from Paris
  • Marie Antoinette was held responsible for France being attacked
  • the Brunswick Manifesto was seen as a threat against the people of Paris
  • the king's dealings with foreign counter-revolutionaries had been discovered.

3. The candidate makes an accurate comparison of the sources by referring to evidence such as:

The sources mainly agree

Source B	Source C
• Danton encouraged the Paris mobs to rise up.	• Working class people rioted to defend the revolution.
• One and a half thousand people were killed.	• At least fifteen hundred women, priests and soldiers were brutally murdered.
• Danton encouraged the mob to rise up.	• Danton must take the blame for having stirred up the sans-culottes.

Context 8: Cavour, Garibaldi and the Making of Italy, 1815-1870

1. The candidate describes the growth of nationalism in Italy between 1815 and 1847 by referring to evidence such as:
  • impact of French Revolution encouraged Italian intellectuals

- invasions of Napoleon brought Italian states closer in terms of transport links
- resentment of Austrian domination of Lombardy and Venetia
- emergence of secret societies eg Carbonari inspired Italians to join struggle for change
- Romantic Movement eg novelists, poets, composers, philosophers, spread nationalist ideas
- business classes wanted greater economic integration
- Mazzini formed Young Italy and inspired young Italians to dedicate energies to campaigning for a united Italy
- 1831 King Charles Albert of Piedmont wanted to drive Austrians from Italy/allowed publication of liberal newspapers
- Pope Pius IX 1846 gave amnesty to political opponents/encouraged nationalist feeling.

2. The candidate makes an accurate comparison of the sources by referring to evidence such as:

The sources mainly agree

Source A	Source B
• Small-scale fights broke out.	• There were clashes between the people and troops.
• Followed by larger riots and eventually a full scale revolution.	• Protests grew as peasants from outside the city arrived to join the rising.
• The revolutionaries set up a provisional government.	• Middle and upper class nationalists set up a provisional government.

3. The candidate explains why Garibaldi was important to the unification of Italy in 1861 by referring to evidence such as:

from the source
- brilliant commander/excellent at sizing up the situation
- inspired great enthusiasm and devotion in his men
- conquest of the south was a remarkable achievement
- he was totally devoted to the idea of national unity

from recall
- helped Mazzini defend the Roman Republic, 1849
- Garibaldi and the Thousand sailed to Sicily in 1860/defeated forces of King Ferdinand II
- he had a military success on River Volturno near Naples in October
- won over mass support from the peasants
- handed over South to King Victor Emmanuel at Teano in 1860.

Context 9: Iron and Blood? Bismarck and The Creation of the German Empire, 1815-1871

1. The candidate makes an accurate comparison of the sources by referring to evidence such as:

The sources agree fully

Source A	Source B
• The Austrian government was determined to prevent further incidents.	• Metternich and the Austrian government were determined to stop the nationalist feeling in the universities.
• At the Confederation at Carlsbad student organisations were outlawed.	• At the Confederation of Carlsbad in 1819 decrees were passed which suppressed the student societies.
• The effects of the decrees was the dismissal of a number of professors.	• Many university teachers were dismissed.

2. The candidate explains why there was a growth in nationalism in the German states between 1815 and 1850 by referring to evidence such as:

from the source
- Grimm folk tales celebrated Germany's past and looked to a day when it would be one nation
- many felt that their common language could lead to being united by the same government
- the Zollverein brought 25 German states together by 1836
- the development of railways pushed German states into greater cooperation

from recall
- growing middle class were won over to nationalism because of economic reasons
- the Zollverein set up an economic free trade area
- student movements promoted idea of national unity
- other cultural developments eg music, (Beethoven); German authors (Hegel, Goethe) encouraged unity
- 1848 revolutions/Frankfurt Parliament gave German states first taste of political unity.

3. The candidate describes the events leading to Prussia's war with Austria in 1866 by referring to evidence such as:
- the war lasted 7 weeks
- decisive battle at Konnigtratz/Sadowa 3 July 1866
- Prussians used railway network to mobilise armies and supplies
- superior Prussian tactics and weapons/Austrians had old-fashioned weapons
- Prussian generals used the telegraph system to communicate with Berlin
- Austria was forced to fight a war on two fronts with Italy
- Austrians lost 240,000; 13,000 taken prisoner.

Context 10: The Red Flag: Lenin and the Russian Revolution, 1894-1921

1. The candidate explains why there was a revolution in Russia in 1905 by referring to evidence such as:

from the source
- repression in Russia by the Tsar and his government
- there was a great deal of poverty in the cities and countryside
- defeat by Japan strengthened the revolutionary movement
- revolutionary groups became more organised eg formation of St Petersburg soviet

from recall
- impact of Bloody Sunday which angered people
- shortages of food and fuel made people desperate
- high unemployment caused distress
- discontent in the armed forces was increasing.

2. The candidate describes the effects of the First World War on the Russian people by referring to evidence such as:
   - outbreak of war led to patriotic demonstrations
   - increasing economic hardship was caused by shortages of fuel and food
   - there was increasing bereavement due to heavy losses in battles
   - the increase in conscription left fewer people to work the land
   - rising inflation meant prices rose ahead of wages
   - people lost faith in their leaders
   - anti-German feeling led to distrust of the Tsarina
   - there was a growing desire for peace by 1917.

3. The candidate makes an accurate comparison of the sources by referring to evidence such as:

   The sources disagree completely

Source B	Source C
• The party is ready and can seize power.	• An uprising now would put the party and revolution at risk.
• Our supporters in Petrograd and Moscow are strong.	• Our supporters among workers and soldiers are not ready to take to the streets now.
• By seizing power in Moscow and Petrograd we shall be successful.	• An uprising war will destroy what we have achieved/it will ruin us.

Context 11: Free at Last? Race Relations in the USA, 1918-1968

1. The candidate describes the problems that faced black Americans who moved north in the 1920s and 1930s by referring to evidence such as:
   - skin colour identified them as "different" and marked them out for discrimination
   - Whites felt they were superior to black migrants
   - seen as uneducated and unskilled so poorly paid jobs
   - White unskilled workers saw them as a threat to their jobs
   - there was competition for jobs with immigrants to USA
   - there were riots between Blacks and Whites in north
   - they were separated into ghetto communities in northern cities
   - housing conditions were very poor.

2. The candidate explains why black Americans felt that progress towards civil rights had been made between 1945 and 1959 by referring to evidence such as:

   from the source
   - NAACP were the moving force behind Supreme Court decisions
   - the Supreme Court declared segregated schools unconstitutional
   - black pressure forced Eisenhower to propose a Civil Rights Act
   - Civil Rights Movement was gaining heroes such as Rosa Parks

   from recall
   - mass action such as Montgomery Bus Boycott was successful
   - protest at Little Rock saw black students admitted to a white school
   - details of Brown v Topeka Board of Education decision
   - rise of new civil rights' leaders such as Martin Luther King and SCLC.

3. The candidate makes an accurate comparison of the sources by referring to evidence such as:

   The sources agree fully

Source B	Source C
• Sit-ins showed students/young people could take action themselves.	• Students believed they could make a difference. • Sit-ins gave students/young people a sense of their own worth.
• Could make a difference by winning support of both blacks and whites.	• Actions encouraged black community support and won the respect of whites.
• Only limited success in some towns and cities.	• Only enjoyed success in a few Southern states. Refusal to desegregate in Deep South.

Context 12: The Road to War, 1933-1939

1. The candidate explains why Britain followed a policy of Appeasement in the 1930s by referring to evidence such as:

   from the source
   - the Great Depression meant there was no money for rearmament
   - the British people were opposed to war
   - Chamberlain believed that he could negotiate directly with Hitler
   - communist Russia was the real threat to peace

   from recall
   - British opinion felt that the Treaty of Versailles had been too harsh
   - there was the fear of bombing from the air
   - Chiefs of Staff warned the government that British forces were unprepared
   - Britain had no reliable allies – Empire unwilling, France was not trusted and USA was neutral.

2. The candidate describes the aims of Hitler's foreign policy between 1933 and 1936 by referring to evidence such as:
   - he wanted to destroy the Treaty of Versailles
   - he wanted to regain the territory that Germany had lost
   - he wanted to remilitarise the Rhineland
   - he wanted to increase Germany's power in Europe
   - he wanted to create a Greater Germany for all Germans
   - he wanted to gain *Lebensraum* for the German people
   - he wanted to achieve Anschluss with Austria
   - he wanted to isolate France.

3. The candidate makes an accurate comparison of the sources by referring to evidence such as:

   The sources disagree completely

Source B	Source C
• Anschluss is popular among the Austrian people.	• The population has no love for Nazism.
• Versailles had been wrong to keep Germany and Austria apart.	• The decision of 1919 to forbid Anschluss had been sensible.
• Europe will benefit from a period of peace and prosperity.	• A powerful Germany is a threat to the peace and stability of Europe.

Context 13: In the Shadow of the Bomb: The Cold War, 1945-1985

1. The candidate explains why the Soviet Union built the Berlin Wall in 1961 by referring to evidence such as:

from the source

- record numbers of East Germans were escaping to the West
- those who left East Berlin were young and well educated
- enemy agents (spies) were stationed in East Berlin
- agents were using West Berlin as a centre of operations against East Germany and the Soviet Union

from recall

- West Berlin was in the middle of communist East Germany
- future of Berlin had been in dispute since the end of World War II
- West Berlin was a shining example of capitalism
- Khrushchev needed a foreign policy success to divert attention from domestic problems.

2. The candidate evaluates the sources by referring to evidence such as:

The sources mainly disagree

Source B	Source C
• The Vietcong generally avoided large scale attacks.	• Thousands of Vietcong launched wave after wave of attacks on our camp.
• The Vietcong travelled light carrying few supplies and basic weapons.	• They had all kinds of weapons such as Chinese flamethrowers, Russian rocket launchers.
• The Vietcong caused heavy American casualties.	• Americans only lost 7 guys/Vietcong body count was reported to have been 800.

3. The candidate describes steps taken to reduce tensions between the USA and USSR during the 1960s and 1970s by referring to evidence such as:

- they set up a "hot line" post Cuba
- non-proliferation treaty was signed in the 1960s
- SALT talks agreed to limit testing of nuclear weapons
- USA begins to sell the USSR wheat in 1970s
- the end of the Vietnam War eased tension
- USA and USSR signed Helsinki agreement in 1975
- changing personalities among the leadership of the USA and USSR
- joint space mission between USA and USSR in 1975.

PART 1 THE SHORT ESSAY

Scottish and British

Context 1: Murder in the Cathedral: Crown, Church and People, 1154-1173

1. The candidate explains why Henry II faced difficulties on becoming king in 1154 by referring to evidence such as:
   - Henry's empire was vast with no common language or traditions
   - barons had built illegal castles
   - barons hired mercenaries/had illegal private armies to protect their land
   - some barons openly challenged Henry eg Earl of York, Scarborough Castle
   - barons were stealing land from their weaker neighbours
   - sheriffs were corrupt and were keeping fines and possessions which should have gone to the king
   - there was no uniform law in the kingdom/sheriffs decided the law in their local area
   - the Church had increased its authority eg Criminous Clerks/Canon Law.

Context 2: Wallace, Bruce and the Wars of Independence, 1286-1328

2. The candidate explains why the Scots won the battle at Bannockburn by referring to evidence such as:
   - Robert Bruce's leadership was a key factor
   - Robert Bruce had trained his men to fight as mobile schiltrons
   - Robert Bruce fought the battle on ground which suited his men/tactics
   - the English did not expect Bruce to attack them (they expected to attack)
   - the English had moved onto ground which was too marshy for them to manoeuvre
   - the English were trapped in an area which was too small for their army to manoeuvre
   - the English were arguing with each other before the battle
   - the English did not have confidence in King Edward II
   - the English were disheartened after the death of de Bohun etc
   - English bowmen were defeated by the Scottish cavalry
   - the English panicked when the "small folk" charged towards the battle.

Context 3: Mary, Queen of Scots and the Scottish Reformation, 1540s-1587

3. The candidate explains why Riccio became unpopular with Darnley and the Scottish nobles by referring to evidence such as:
   - Darnley thought he had persuaded Mary not to give him the crown matrimonial
   - Scottish nobles persuaded Darnley that Riccio was too friendly with his Mary
   - Riccio was behaving like a noble although he was below them in status
   - Riccio was dressing like a nobleman
   - Riccio was humiliating the Scottish nobles by making them ask him to see Queen Mary
   - Riccio was boasting about his influence over Queen Mary
   - Riccio was foreign (Italian)
   - some thought that Riccio was really a spy sent by the Pope
   - some Scottish nobles wanted to create trouble between Queen Mary and Darnley.

Context 4: The Coming of the Civil War, 1603-1642

4. The candidate explains why Charles I was an unpopular monarch in England by 1640 by referring to evidence such as:
    *   he believed in the Divine Right of Kings which undermined Parliament
    *   his religious policies angered the Puritans and Parliament
    *   he used 'forced loans' to raise money for war against Spain
    *   he imposed the 'Ship Money' tax without Parliament's consent
    *   failures in foreign policy led to unpopularity eg the United Provinces
    *   policy of impressments was unpopular
    *   he collected 'tonnage and poundage' without Parliament's consent
    *   he introduced fines for people who had built on common land or in royal forests
    *   during the Period of Personal Rule (1629-1640) Charles ruled without consulting Parliament
    *   he was seen as a tyrant.

Context 5: "Ane End of Ane Auld Sang": Scotland and the Treaty of Union, 1690s-1715

5. The candidate explains why many Scots were disappointed by the Act of Union by 1715 by referring to evidence such as:
    *   Scotland had not become richer
    *   there was fear that English imports were ruining Scottish businesses
    *   there were new Customs and Excise taxes (eg Malt Tax)
    *   they disliked the changes in Scotland's weights, measures, money etc
    *   nobles and important politicians had left Edinburgh for London
    *   the House of Lords had allowed "patronage" in the Church of Scotland (Patronage Act)
    *   Episcopalians were allowed in Scotland (Toleration Act)
    *   they were now ruled by George of Hanover (rather than a Stuart)
    *   the Equivalent had not been paid.

Context 6: Immigrants and Exiles: Scotland, 1830s-1930s

6. The candidate explains why Irish immigrants were attracted to Scotland between 1830 and 1930 by referring to evidence such as:
    *   Scotland was close to Ireland
    *   travel was cheap
    *   there was work to be found in cotton/textile factories
    *   there was work in the coal mines
    *   many found work as navigators of the canals and railways
    *   there was work to be found on farms at harvest time
    *   the whole family could find employment
    *   work was more constant
    *   many Irish had already settled in Scotland which encouraged more to come
    *   Protestant Irish found it easy to settle into Scottish society.

Context 7: From the Cradle to the Grave? Social Welfare in Britain, 1890s-1951

7. The candidate explains why the Liberal government passed social welfare reforms between 1906 and 1914 by referring to evidence such as:
    *   changing attitudes towards the reasons for poverty
    *   inadequate provision by the Poor Law system and charitable organisations
    *   surveys of Booth and Rowntree showed the extent of poverty
    *   poor physical condition of recruits for the Boer War raised concerns about national security
    *   concerns about Britain's industrial strength/health of the workforce
    *   growth of the Labour Movement/spread of socialist ideas
    *   changing political ideology/emergence of 'New Liberalism'
    *   welfare reform had begun in other countries eg Germany.

Context 8: Campaigning for Change: Social Change in Scotland, 1900s-1979

8. The candidate explains why there was still a need to improve many women's lives after 1918 by referring to evidence such as:
    *   only women over 30 had the vote until 1928, so no political voice
    *   fewer than 20 women MP's by 1939
    *   many woman were forced to give up their jobs to returning soldiers, even when they were the family breadwinner
    *   a woman's place was still seen as being in the home eg women's magazines concentrated on recipes, knitting etc
    *   women were still excluded from top jobs eg in the Civil Service
    *   many employers, such as local authorities, imposed a marriage bar
    *   women's wages were still much less than men's – up to 50% lower for working class women
    *   Trades Unions still opposed employing women in many workplaces – argued they deprived men of jobs
    *   many women were widowed or remained unmarried as fiancés and husbands were killed in the war and there was a subsequent shortage of men
    *   many working class women could not afford the new labour saving devices which were being developed.

Context 9: A Time of Troubles: Ireland, 1900-1923

9. The candidate explains why the Anglo-Irish War broke out in 1919 by referring to evidence such as:
    *   Republicans refused to accept Home Rule
    *   Republicans would only agree to full independence
    *   73 Sinn Fein MPs refused to go to Westminster to take their seats
    *   Irish independence declared/Republican government formed
    *   Dail established in Dublin
    *   Sinn Fein challenged the authority of the British/established legal, financial and local government infrastructure
    *   Sinn Fein organised, trained and armed Irish Volunteers Force
    *   British used armed forces to try and stop the Irish taking control
    *   Irish Volunteers killed two members of the Royal Irish Constabulary, sparking violence.

European and World

Context 1: The Norman Conquest, 1060-1153

10. The candidate explains why knights were important in medieval society by referring to evidence such as:
    *   provided protection for other social groups eg churchmen
    *   maintained the control of Norman lords over their Saxon subjects
    *   knights were key figures in 11th century warfare
    *   made up King's chief fighting force in war
    *   highly trained warriors
    *   carried out duties such as castle-guard
    *   maintained order on their own land
    *   managed the economy of the land.

Context 2: The Cross and the Crescent: The First Crusade, 1096-1125

11. The candidate explains the reasons why the Crusaders were able to keep control of the Holy Land after 1097 by referring to evidence such as:

- the Crusaders appointed a king (Godfrey and later Baldwin) in Jerusalem ensuring law and order was maintained
- Hospitallers and Templars arrived from Europe specifically to protect Jerusalem
- the Crusaders traded with the Italian city states providing supplies for those in the east
- the Crusaders cooperated with Muslims in order to get them to tend the fields and grow crops
- the Crusaders built castles to protect the territory they had taken
- extra settlers from the east arrived, having been offered incentives to stay in Holy Land
- the feudal system was established in the east, organising the Crusaders.

Context 3: War, Death and Revolt in Medieval Europe, 1328-1436

12. The candidate explains why France was unsuccessful in the war against England between 1415 and 1422 by referring to evidence such as:
- French weakness due to the insanity of their King
- Dauphin was weak and mentally immature
- civil war between the Houses of Armagnac and Burgundy
- English alliance with the House of Burgundy
- effective leadership of Henry V eg tactics at Agincourt
- effectiveness of the English longbow
- disorganisation of the French armies eg divisions over tactics at Agincourt
- ruthlessness of Henry's tactics after Agincourt eg naval blockade, murder of captives, sieges of Rouen and Meaux.

Context 4: New Worlds: Europe in the Age of Expansion, 1480s-1530s

13. The candidate explains the reasons why the Spaniards were able to defeat **either** the Aztecs **or** the Incas by referring to evidence such as:
- they were deceitful in their dealing with the kings
- the religious beliefs of both Aztecs and Incas weakened them
- Spanish had horses and knew how to use them in battle
- Spanish had better weapons than the Aztecs or Incas
- Spanish had better (metal) armour
- Spanish captured the rulers of these states
- rulers underestimated Spanish greed/underestimated Spanish intentions
- both Aztecs and Incas had dominated/made enemies of their local neighbours
- Spanish made alliances with enemies of Aztecs/Inca Empire divided over succession
- Aztecs and Incas both unable to put up effective resistance (no steel, cannons).

Context 5: "Tea and Freedom": The American Revolution, 1763-1783

14. The candidate explains the reasons why the American War of Independence broke out in 1775 by referring to evidence such as:
- growing divide between the colonists and Britain
- colonists were angry at the continuing presence of British troops following the defeat of the French in 1763
- colonists were angry at George III's desire to exert greater control over colonies
- frustration over Britain's refusal to allow the colonies to expand westward
- growing anger over continuing taxation of colonies without direct representation in British parliament
- anger over the imposition of Sugar Act/Stamp Act/the Tea Act/Quartering Acts/Intolerable Acts

- events such as the Boston Massacre
- formation of the Continental Congress in 1774
- fighting at Lexington and Concord in April 1775 led to formation of Continental Army under leadership of George Washington in June 1775.

Context 6: "This Accursed Trade": The British Slave Trade and its Abolition, 1770–1807

15. The candidate explains the reasons why it took so long for Britain to abolish the slave trade by referring to evidence such as:
- there was a great deal of support for the slave trade from powerful people in business and parliament
- bribery used to ensure the continued support for the trade among some MPs
- many accepted the argument that the success of the British economy relied on the continuation of slavery
- fear of job losses in industries dependent on the slave trade
- fear of loss of tax revenue
- King George III supported the slave trade
- many towns such as Liverpool and Bristol benefited directly from the trade
- profits from the trade were essential to fund the war with France
- people believed the slave trade was a training ground for the British navy.

Context 7: Citizens! The French Revolution, 1789-1794

16. The candidate explains the reasons why the French people were unhappy with their government by 1789 by referring to evidence such as:
- Louis XVI was determined to rule the country alone/claimed 'Divine right of kings'
- people were listening to new political ideas saying that the people had a right to share power
- the middle class resented the political power of the nobility
- the Estates General had not been called for over a century
- the peasants resented the feudal power of the nobility to rule over them
- the French government was bankrupt and inefficient
- the peasants resented having to pay most of the taxes to the government
- the taxation system was seen as corrupt and wasteful
- the workers in the cities were suffering from poor wages and high food prices but the government did nothing to help them.

Context 8: Cavour, Garibaldi and the Making of Italy, 1815-1870

17. The candidate explains the reasons why Garibaldi's leadership was important to the unification of Italy by referring to evidence such as:
- brilliant military leader and commander
- initially supported aims of Mazzini's 'Young Italy' to unite states in a democratic republic
- defended Rome against the French in 1849 – respected by other nationalists
- reputation grew because he won victories over the Austrians eg Verese, Como
- was a member of the nationalist society from 1857
- popular with foreign powers eg Britain
- was hugely popular with the peasants
- used the peasant disturbances in Sicily to unite north and south
- led 'The Thousand' and sailed to Sicily in 1860
- conceded his conquests to Victor Emmanuel at Teano in 1860
- good oratorical skills.

Context 9: Iron and Blood? Bismarck and The Creation of the German Empire, 1815-1871

18. The candidate explains the reasons why the nationalist movement had failed to unite the German states by 1850 by referring to evidence such as:
    • liberalism/nationalism only affected the middle and upper classes
    • power/influence of Metternich/Austria eg German Confederation
    • desire for individual rulers to retain power/used armies to crush revolutionaries
    • lack of support for a united Germany from foreign powers eg Britain, Russia
    • student nationalist movements crushed eg Carlsbad Decrees 1819
    • failure of the 1848 revolutions
    • nationalists divided/'Kleindeutschland' or 'Grossdeutschland'
    • failure of the Frankfurt Parliament
    • Frederick William IV of Prussia refused crown of a united Germany
    • failure of the Erfurt Union.

Context 10: The Red Flag: Lenin and the Russian Revolution, 1894-1921

19. The candidate explains the reasons why the Tsar was able to remain in power following the 1905 revolution by referring to evidence such as:
    • the Tsar announced his October Manifesto, accepting cabinet government, free speech and a constitution for Russia, splitting his opposition
    • political parties became legal
    • a limited vote was extended to the peasants and industrial workers
    • many Liberals accepted these terms and ceased opposing the Tsar
    • right wing supporters of the Tsar began a wave of attacks on Jews and liberal intellectuals who continued their opposition
    • Witte was appointed Chairman of the Council of Ministers and arrested the entire St Petersburg soviet
    • the troops stayed loyal to the Tsar and crushed opposition in Moscow
    • the general strike came to an end as the middle classes withdrew their support
    • the government announced the end of redemption dues to placate the peasants
    • the Russo-Japanese War ended.

Context 11: Free at Last? Race Relations in the USA, 1918-1968

20. The candidate explains why the demand for civil rights continued to grow after 1945 by referring to evidence such as:
    • impact of the Second World War eg USA fighting against a violent racist regime abroad while violent racism flourished in the southern states
    • experience of black soldiers from the south who witnessed integration abroad
    • actions of early campaigners eg Phillip Randolph, Core (1942)
    • the existence of Jim Crow laws in the southern states
    • effects of segregation – eg schools, transport, restaurants
    • concern at other inequalities faced by Black Americans eg low wages, poor housing
    • refusal of State governments to desegregate following Brown v Topeka judgement
    • continuance of lynching
    • North/South divide became more obvious after 1945.

Context 12: The Road to War, 1933-1939

21. The candidate explains the reasons why Hitler's actions created problems in Europe between 1933 and 1939 by referring to evidence such as:
    • withdrawal from the Disarmament Conference/League of Nations was seen as a threat to rearm
    • Germany rebuilt her army, navy and airforce
    • Hitler declared that he wanted to regain territory lost at Versailles
    • Hitler wanted to take over Austria, an independent country
    • the policy of a greater Germany was a threat to countries with German minorities, especially Poland and Czechoslovakia
    • the policy of Lebensraum was a threat to countries in eastern Europe
    • the reoccupation of the Rhineland threatened the security of France and Belgium
    • Hitler was willing to break voluntary treaties eg the Locarno Pact, the Munich Settlement
    • Germany's involvement in the Spanish Civil War and the spread of Fascism.

Context 13: In the Shadow of the Bomb: The Cold War, 1945-1985

22. The candidate explains the reasons why America lost the war in Vietnam by referring to evidence such as:
    • American soldiers were poorly trained and equipped for jungle warfare
    • the draft system meant that there was a lack of experience among American forces
    • American soldiers had low morale and lacked respect for their officers – incidents of fragging
    • America was propping up South Vietnamese government that did not enjoy popular support among the South Vietnamese people
    • Vietcong benefited from experience of fighting the French
    • Vietcong were expert in conducting guerrilla warfare
    • failure of American tactics – strategic hamlets, carpet bombing, use of defoliants (Agent Orange)
    • American tactics alienated the civilian population of Vietnam and generated negative publicity at home
    • anti-war protests and lack of international support helped persuade American government to withdraw from Vietnam.

PART 2 HISTORICAL STUDY

Scottish and British

Context 1: Murder in the Cathedral: Crown, Church and People, 1154-1173

1. The candidate explains why castles were important in the twelfth century by referring to evidence such as:

   from the source:
   • castles were the key symbol of power
   • administrative centres of each town
   • base for local garrison
   • stored food, drink and other supplies.

   from recall:
   • used as a law court
   • used as a place of protection/to defend the Lord's land
   • used as a home
   • centre of entertainment eg feasts and banquets.

2. The candidate compares the sources by referring to evidence such as:

The sources agree completely

Source B	Source C
• 2 o'clock – monks woken for service	• service began in the middle of the night
• expected to pray at least 8 times a day	• expected to pray several times a day
• breakfast eaten in silence	• meal times, talking strictly forbidden

3. The candidate describes the murder of Archbishop Becket by referring to evidence such as:
   • four knights arrived at Canterbury and asked to see Becket
   • Becket refused to run away or hide/the knights were let into the cathedral
   • the knights attempted to arrest Becket/Becket refused to go with them
   • Becket stated he was willing to die a martyr for God
   • Edward Grim had his arm sliced during the ensuing struggle
   • the knights hit Becket on the head four times
   • one knight struck Becket with such force his sword was broken against his head and the paving stone
   • the crown of Becket's head was sliced off/his brains were extracted
   • the knights ran away.

Context 2: Wallace, Bruce and the Wars of Independence, 1286-1328

1. The candidate describes the events between 1286 and 1292 that led to Edward I becoming overlord of Scotland by referring to evidence such as:
   • death of Alexander III without sons
   • death of the Maid
   • rivalry between Bruce and Balliol/fear of a civil war in Scotland
   • Guardians asked Edward to decide who would be king
   • Edward asked the Guardians to agree he was overlord
   • Edward demanded that the (thirteen) Competitors recognise him as overlord
   • Competitors accepted Edward's demands
   • the Award of Berwick
   • Edward had an army with him
   • John Balliol did homage to King Edward.

2. The candidate explains why the leadership of William Wallace was important during the Wars of Independence by referring to evidence such as:

from the source:
   • he united people under his leadership as Guardian
   • he organised the army of Scotland
   • he sent Lamberton to Rome and Paris to plead Scotland's case there
   • he obtained iron from Germany for his army.

from recall:
   • he defeated the English at Stirling Bridge
   • he developed the idea of fighting in schiltrons
   • he made sure that Edward did not select the new Bishop of St. Andrews
   • he continued to resist Edward till he was executed.

3. The candidate compares the sources by referring to evidence such as:

The sources disagree

Source B	Source C
• all the Scots supported Bruce	• some Scots plotting against him
• had royal blood	• other nobles claimed to be more closely related to royalty
• his deeds had won him the support of the Scottish people	• he was a ruthless thug

Context 3: Mary, Queen of Scots and the Scottish Reformation, 1540s-1587

1. The candidate explains why Henry VIII of England ordered the invasions of Scotland after 1544 by referring to evidence such as:

from the source:
   • Henry wanted to break the Auld Alliance between Scotland and France
   • the Scots had agreed to marry Mary to Henry's son, Edward in the Treaty of Greenwich
   • the Scots resisted the demands of Henry VIII (encouraged by the French)
   • the Scots announced that the treaty was broken.

from recall:
   • the government of Scotland was moving towards favouring France eg Guise, Beaton
   • Henry disagreed that the Treaty of Greenwich was void because he failed to ratify it in time
   • the French had bribed Arran to change his mind about supporting the marriage
   • Henry intended to force the Scots into changing their mind.

2. The candidate describes the events leading up to the signing of the Treaty of Edinburgh in 1560 by referring to evidence such as:
   • Protestantism had spread within Scotland (encouraged by England)
   • Mary of Guise began to stamp down on Protestants eg executions
   • the Lords of the Congregation began to protest about this
   • Mary of Guise used French soldiers to help crush this rebellion
   • English help was sent to support the Protestants
   • while soldiers from the two nations faced each other Mary of Guise died
   • both sides agreed to withdraw their soldiers and leave the Scots to settle their own affairs.

3. The candidate compares the sources by referring to evidence such as:

The sources disagree

Source B	Source C
• she neglected its government	• she had been a successful ruler/established a successful government
• she left the running of the country to a group of nobles	• she defeated nobles who challenged her authority
• did not care about religion	• her religious policy was tolerant and ahead of its time

Context 4: The Coming of the Civil War, 1603-1642

1. The candidate compares the sources by referring to evidence such as:

The sources agree

Source A	Source B
• James VI and I was well educated and clever	• James VI and I was highly intelligent
• he thought kings were appointed by God and could do as they wished	• he believed in the Divine Right of Kings
• lost people's respect by giving money and power to favourites at court	• he gave gifts and pensions to courtiers

2. The candidate describes the methods used by James VI and I to raise money during his reign by referring to evidence such as:
   • he used forced loans
   • he raised customs duties/impositions
   • he used feudal dues
   • continued to use rights of wardship
   • crown lands were sold
   • he sold titles of honour/knighthoods, baronies, earldoms
   • patents of monopoly given
   • used purveyance to buy discounted goods for royal household
   • employed officials eg Cranfield to raise money for the Crown.

3. The candidate explains why Charles I faced opposition to his rule in Scotland by referring to evidence such as:

   from the source:
   • he tried to enforce his religious views
   • many Scots were Presbyterians and disliked change
   • Scots resented Charles because he was an absentee king/visited Scotland only once
   • Scotland was a poor country/many thought Charles did not care.

   from recall:
   • he introduced the Common Prayer Book in 1637
   • anger over the Prayer Book led to St Giles Riot
   • he tried to raise taxes from the Scots
   • King sent an army to the borders of Scotland/Bishops Wars began.

Context 5: "Ane End of Ane Auld Sang": Scotland and the Treaty of Union, 1690s-1715

1. The candidate describes what happened during the Worcester affair by referring to evidence such as:
   • the Company of Scotland's last ship "Speedy Return" had been lost
   • some of the crew of the Worcester hinted that they were responsible for its loss (pirates)
   • Captain Green and two of his crew were arrested and put on trial
   • Captain Green and two others were found guilty and sentenced to death
   • Queen Anne's government in England wanted her to pardon them
   • Queen Anne wanted her Scottish Government to pardon them
   • the Edinburgh mob ensured that the Scottish Government did not pardon them
   • Captain Green and the two crewmen were hanged.

2. The candidate explains why Queen Anne wanted a Treaty of Union between England and Scotland by referring to evidence such as:
   from the source:
   • the Scottish Parliament was difficult to control
   • the Scottish Parliament complained her policies were harming Scotland
   • the Scottish Parliament was threatening to break the Union of the Crowns
   • the problems with Scotland made it difficult to fight the war against France.
   from recall:
   • she wanted Scotland and England to have the same ruler
   • she wanted to ensure a Protestant succession
   • she was worried about the Jacobites trying to become rulers in Scotland
   • she was worried about French influence in Scotland.

3. The candidate compares the sources by referring to evidence such as:
   The sources disagree

Source B	Source C
• the Equivalent was money to help recover from Darien	• money paid to Scotland was to bribe rich and powerful men
• Scots thought they would have influence in a new powerful kingdom	• Scots feared they would have little influence over government decisions
• traders would benefit from access to English colonies	• business would suffer from competition from English imports.

Context 6: Immigrants and Exiles: Scotland, 1830s-1930s

1. The candidate compares the sources by referring to evidence such as:
   The sources agree

Source A	Source B
• disliked by native scots	• great deal of resentment against the immigrants
• Irish determination to keep their own culture was looked upon suspiciously	• Irish immigrants criticised for keeping their own language and religion
• Irish did not receive much credit for their contribution to the Scottish economy	• reluctance to admit that Irish labour was essential

2. The candidate explains why many poor Scots were able to emigrate during the nineteenth century by referring to evidence such as:
   from the source:
   • landlords paid travelling costs
   • rent arrears written off so that emigrants had money
   • buying cattle meant emigrants had capital
   • Edinburgh and Glasgow made a contribution towards their expenses in emigrating.
   from recall:
   • Highlands and Islands Emigration Society (HIES) gave assistance
   • charities eg Barnardos, helped orphans/young women to emigrate
   • countries such as Australia and Canada sent agents to advise on emigration

- family members living abroad gave encouragement and sent money for travel.

3. The candidate describes the ways Scots helped to improve the lands to which they emigrated by referring to evidence such as:
   - Scots brought farming skills to Canada
   - Scots developed sheep farming in Australia
   - tradesmen such as stone masons helped the building industry in USA
   - developed businesses, banks and trading companies
   - examples of contributions to economy and other aspects such as Andrew Carnegie (steel); Donald Mackay (Boston shipyards); Alan Pinkerton (detective agency); John Muir (national parks); example such as paper-making in New Zealand
   - Scots established education system eg Canada
   - Scots brought a tradition of hard work.

Context 7: From the Cradle to the Grave? Social Welfare in Britain, 1890s-1951

1. The candidate compares the sources by referring to evidence such as:

   The sources agree

Source A	Source B
• a pensioner with a yearly income of up to £21 received the full 25p a week	• it entitled people with an annual income of £21 to 25p a week
• pensions available to those who had been out of prison for ten years	• entitled to the pension provided they had avoided imprisonment in the previous ten years
• it was not a generous amount	• these payments were not meant to be a complete solution to the problem of poverty

2. The candidate describes the ways the Beveridge Report of 1942 suggested tackling the social problems facing Britain by referring to evidence such as:
   - recommended a welfare system which would look after people from 'the cradle to the grave'
   - recommended the setting up of a National Health Service to tackle disease
   - recommended the introduction of family allowances to tackle want
   - National Insurance contributions to be made by workers
   - benefits for the unemployed to be available for an indefinite period
   - advised the government to adopt a policy of full employment
   - recommended a comprehensive system of benefits including old age pensions, widow's pensions and maternity grants
   - advised benefits to be available without a means test.

3. The candidate explains why some people were disappointed with the Labour welfare reforms by 1951 by referring to evidence such as:

   from the source:
   - poor housing and homelessness were still serious problems
   - little done to enhance the educational opportunities for working class children/most left school at fifteen with no paper qualifications
   - still a shortage of hospitals and health centres
   - problems of poverty and deprivation not adequately solved.

   from recall:
   - not everyone covered by the National Insurance Act/safety net did not cover all
   - charges introduced in NHS eg prescriptions

- school building programme inadequate
- many new houses were only temporary eg prefabs.

Context 8: Campaigning for Change: Social Change in Scotland, 1900s-1979

1. The sources completely agree

Source A	Source B
• number of public houses decreased	• number of pubs fell if people voted for it
• tax on alcohol increased	• alcohol became more expensive when tax was raised by 34%
• people chose to spend money on goods and leisure activities	• there was a greater choice of things to do

2. The candidate describes the unrest on Red Clydeside between 1915 and 1919 by referring to evidence such as:
   - skilled engineers went on strike for more pay – 'tuppence an hour'
   - anger over importation of English and American workers, paid more than Scots workers
   - rent strikes when landlords raised rents and evicted female tenants whose husbands were away fighting
   - Clyde Workers Committee set up to protect munitions workers from compulsory long hours at low rates of pay under Munitions Act
   - Strike at Beardmore's Parkhead Steel Works over 'dilution' by unskilled labour
   - Clyde Workers' Committee organised strike demanding 40 hour week
   - 60,000 strikers gathered in George Square and raised Red Flag
   - police attacked crowd with truncheons and activists were arrested
   - English soldiers and tanks sent to Glasgow in case of further unrest.

3. The candidate explains why the development of North Sea Oil was so important for the economy of the north of Scotland by referring to evidence such as:

   from the source:
   - Aberdeen became oil capital of Europe/boom spread to north east towns
   - oil rig construction yards set up in Nigg and Ardersier
   - 3000 new jobs created in Shetland
   - many companies moved north to provide support and services.

   from recall:
   - construction yards also set up on west coast at Kishorn and at Arnish in Lewis
   - wide range of new, skilled jobs offered much higher wages
   - standard of living also raised by full employment eg good restaurants opened
   - increased demand for housing raised value of property, spreading prosperity.

Context 9: A Time of Troubles: Ireland, 1900-1923

1. The candidate compares the sources by referring to evidence such as:

   The sources completely disagree

Source A	Source B
• Irish people have benefited from the Union	• we have been the losers in the Union with Britain
• better wages for our work	• poor wages have made people desperate
• freedom and rights protected	• until Ireland has rights we still have no freedom

2. The candidate describes the actions taken by the Unionists against the Home Rule Bill by referring to evidence such as:
   - Unionists began to organise an effective campaign against Home Rule
   - organised meetings and rallies
   - gained support from important politicians
   - signed Ulster Covenant
   - Ulster Volunteers Force set up
   - UVF trained, organised and drilled like a real army
   - German rifles/ammunition brought in illegally to Ireland
   - gained support of British army eg "Curragh Mutiny".

3. The candidate explains why De Valera opposed the 1921 Treaty by referring to evidence such as:

   from the source:
   - De Valera had not been consulted about the terms of the Treaty
   - he refused to accept the six counties of Northern Ireland
   - he refused to take an oath of allegiance to the British King
   - he argued only full independence could bring peace.

   from recall:
   - De Valera would not agree to a boundary commission
   - De Valera refused to accept the British King being represented by a Governor-General in Ireland
   - De Valera insisted that Ireland should have full legal rights/would not accept the Irish Free State
   - De Valera wanted full control of Ireland's coasts
   - De Valera did not want the Royal Navy to use Ireland's ports.

PART 3 HISTORICAL STUDY

European and World

Context 1: The Norman Conquest, 1060-1153

1. The candidate explains why Harold lost the battle of Hastings by referring to evidence such as:

   from the source:
   - Normans had a large army including many horsemen and archers
   - Harold forced his exhausted army to march south immediately
   - Harold had lost many brave men in two previous battles
   - some of his soldiers deserted before the battle began.

   from recall:
   - Saxons had already had to fight a long and bloody battle at Stamford Bridge
   - Saxon army fought on foot
   - Saxons were tricked by William's feigned retreat
   - Harold was killed in the fighting.

2. The candidate evaluates **Source B** as evidence about William's attempts to control England after 1066 by referring to evidence such as:
   - primary source written while William was attempting to bring England under his control
   - written by William's priest so biased in favour of William
   - written to claim that William was fair to his enemies
   - says that he rewarded those who had fought for him by granting fiefs.

Maximum 1 mark for indicating content omission such as:

   - no mention of William's cruelty/military campaigns against the Saxons
   - no mention of the Harrying of the North.

3. The candidate describes the ways in which Scotland changed during the reign of David I by referring to evidence such as:
   - arrival of the Normans in Scotland
   - introduction of Feudalism on the Anglo-Norman model
   - appointment of King's sheriffs

   - increase in power of the king
   - development of castles across Scotland
   - creation and growth of burghs
   - expansion of monasticism
   - government by English style royal council.

Context 2: The Cross and the Crescent: The First Crusade, 1096-1125

1. The candidate explains why Pope Urban II called the First Crusade by referring to evidence such as:

   from the source:
   - Emperor Alexius asked for help
   - Turks were a threat to Christianity
   - wanted to stop western knights fighting among themselves
   - wanted to recapture Jerusalem.

   from recall:
   - wanted to help Christians in the East
   - wanted to reopen trade and pilgrim routes
   - wanted to protect Christian churches/shrines
   - wanted to show kings/emperors of Europe that he could raise an army
   - wanted to heal the schism (split in the church) and unite the Eastern and Western churches
   - wanted to place himself as overall ruler of a united church.

2. The candidate describes the siege and capture of Antioch by the First Crusade by referring to evidence such as:
   - Bohemond bribed a Muslim guard (Firouz) to let him into the city
   - the Crusaders used ladders and ropes to scale the wall
   - the Crusaders captured the three towers commanded by Firouz
   - once inside they opened the gate and let the rest of the army into the city
   - the inhabitants of the city were slaughtered
   - the Crusaders were then surrounded by a Muslim army (Kerbogha's)
   - the Holy Lance inspired the Crusaders to attack the Muslims
   - the Crusaders defeated the Muslim army/Kerbogha's men ran away.

3. The candidate evaluates the usefulness of **Source B** as evidence of the Crusaders' behaviour in the Holy Land by referring to evidence such as:
   - primary source written during the Crusades
   - author was an eyewitness/actually saw the events at Marrat au Numan
   - written to show his disgust at the Crusaders behaviour
   - says they cut their flesh into slices, cooked and ate them.

Maximum 1 mark for indicating content omission such as:

   - Crusaders slaughtered the inhabitants of Marrat au Numan
   - Crusaders spit roasted babies.

Context 3: War, Death and Revolt in Medieval Europe, 1328-1436

1. The candidate describes the succession problem to the French throne after 1328 by referring to evidence such as:
   - Charles IV died without a direct heir
   - Phillip of Valois seized the throne
   - Phillip claimed that he was the chosen heir of Charles IV
   - the English queen, Isabel claimed the throne of France as she was sister of Charles IV
   - English kings held lands in France
   - Edward claimed that he had a better claim to the throne than Phillip
   - Edward was willing to use his claim to the throne as a pretext for an attack on France.

2. The candidate evaluates the usefulness of **Source A** as evidence of the effects of the Battle of Poitiers on France by referring to evidence such as:
   - primary source written during this phase of the war/ secondary source recorded some years after the battle
   - written by Froissart an important and respected French chronicler
   - written to explain the impact of defeat on France
   - says that France was badly affected by the loss of so many fighting men.

Maximum 1 mark for indicating content omission such as:
   - does not mention the capture and holding to ransom of King John and his son.

3. The candidate explains why the King was able to crush the Peasants' Revolt by referring to evidence such as:

   from the source:
   - the King ordered the capture of the leaders of the revolt
   - gallows set up to put people off
   - many leaders of the revolt were hanged
   - pardons were granted on condition that there would be no future rising.

   from recall:
   - murder of the leader of the revolt, Watt Tyler
   - imprisonment and brutal execution of important figures eg John Ball and Jack Straw
   - King pacified the peasants in London by promising concessions.

Context 4: New Worlds: Europe in the Age of Expansion, 1480s-1530s

1. The candidate evaluates the usefulness of **Source A** as evidence of reasons for European exploration between 1480 and 1530 by referring to evidence such as:
   - primary source written at the time of European exploration and expansion
   - author an experienced sailor/a successful explorer
   - written to highlight his achievements – possible bias, one sided account praising his own actions – dismissive of native culture
   - says that his aim was to conquer the people/bring the land under Spain's rule/make Spain rich.

Maximum 1 mark for indicating content omission such as:
   - need to find new trade routes/desire to convert non-Christians.

2. The candidate describes the benefits Vasco da Gama's voyage brought to Europe by referring to evidence such as:
   - broke Venetian/Arab trade monopoly
   - established new trade route to India
   - established trading colonies at Goa and Ormuz
   - new sources of supply for spice trade found
   - cost of spices brought down
   - allowed Christianity/European influence to spread
   - encouraged further European expansion
   - enabled Empires to be built up
   - more immediate economic impact than New World discoveries.

3. The candidate explains why Magellan faced difficulties during his voyage round the world by referring to evidence such as:

   from the source:
   - he was a Portuguese commanding Spaniards so they did not like him
   - he kept the destination secret from his crew so they did not trust him

   - other captains plotted a mutiny against him
   - lost two ships in straits.

   from recall:
   - voyage took longer than planned – over two years
   - ran out of supplies leading to lowering of morale
   - disease broke out due to lack of supplies leading to death of crew
   - poor decision making – Magellan became involved in a local war in Philippines
   - lack of accurate charts/maps.

Context 5: "Tea and Freedom": The American Revolution, 1763-1783

1. The candidate describes the Boston Tea Party and the British government's response to it by referring to evidence such as:
   - colonists were angered by the passing of the Tea Act in 1773 which allowed the East India Company to undercut the colonial merchants and smugglers
   - Bostonians disguised themselves as Mohawk Indians and boarded the three tea ships
   - tea was emptied into the water of Boston harbour
   - some of the tea was stolen
   - King George III and Parliament were outraged when they heard of these events
   - Lord North rejected the offer of compensation from some of the colonial merchants
   - led to the passing of the 'Intolerable Acts'
   - Port of Boston closed/Massachusetts Act/Administration of Justice Act/Quartering Act/ Quebec Act.

2. The candidate evaluates the usefulness of **Source A** as evidence about what happened at Lexington and Concord in April 1775 by referring to evidence such as:
   - primary source written only a month after events at Lexington and Concord/written at the start of the year
   - author the leaders of the colonies, who would have detailed/first hand knowledge of what had taken place/possible bias
   - written to condemn/criticise the actions of the British army
   - describe attack as unprovoked/murdered colonists/cruelly slaughtered.

Maximum 1 mark for indicating content omission such as:
   - militia in Massachusetts had been training/ preparing for war
   - spies had warned of the British army's movements and counter-attack was launched at Concord.

3. The candidate explains why involvement of foreign countries caused difficulties for Britain in the War of Independence by referring to evidence such as:

   from the source:
   - the French attacked British colonies in the Caribbean and elsewhere which undermined Britain's control
   - the French harassed British shipping in the Atlantic interfering with trade
   - Britain lost control of the seas for the first time that century
   - Britain found it more difficult to reinforce and supply its forces in America.

   from recall:
   - France provided the colonies with finance
   - France provided the colonies with military assistance – soldiers, gunpowder
   - Spain distracted Britain by attacking Gibraltar
   - a Franco-Spanish force threatened Britain with invasion in 1779.

Context 6: "This Accursed Trade": The British Slave Trade and its Abolition, 1770–1807

1. The candidate describes the different stages of the triangular trade by referring to evidence such as:
   - ships sailed from Europe to Africa carrying manufactured goods
   - goods such as guns, alcohol, pots and pans were exchanged for slaves
   - slaves were held in slave factories on the west coast of Africa
   - slave ships left west Africa carrying slaves to the West Indies and the Americas
   - duration of the voyage was very long
   - slaves were usually sold by auction upon arrival in West Indies/America
   - ships carrying tobacco, sugar, molasses, cotton would sail back across the Atlantic
   - ships often departed from/arrived at British ports such as Bristol, Liverpool, Glasgow.

2. The candidate evaluates the usefulness of **Source A** as evidence of slave resistance in the West Indies by referring to evidence such as:
   - secondary source written years after the end of the slave trade
   - author a historian who is likely to have expertise on the subject/has carried out research
   - written to show that slave revolts were a big problem in the West Indies colonies
   - says that there were problems on a number of different islands/damage to property/problem was worse in Jamaica than in other colonies.

Maximum 1 mark for indicating content omission such as:
   - evidence of slave resistance eg dumb insolence, sabotage, running away.

3. The candidate explains why the slave trade was abolished by Britain in 1807 by referring to evidence such as:

   from the source:
   - people had begun to think of Africans as fellow human beings/regarded trade as unacceptable
   - trade with the West Indies was becoming less important to Britain
   - many merchants supported free trade
   - slavery began to be regarded as an inefficient way to produce goods.

   from recall:
   - influence of religious groups/the churches
   - national anti-slavery campaigns involving meetings, petitions, leaflets
   - growing support in parliament for abolition of slavery
   - first-hand accounts from former slaves such as Equiano influenced people
   - contribution of anti-slavery campaigners such as William Wilberforce, Thomas Clarkson.

Context 7: Citizens! The French Revolution, 1789-1794

1. The candidate evaluates the usefulness of **Source A** as evidence of the relationship between the Third Estate and the King in June 1789 by referring to evidence such as:
   - primary source from the period when the Third Estate was not allowed to meet at Versailles
   - part of the oath taken by members of the Third Estate
   - written to show that the Third Estate were determined to be the National Assembly
   - says that no one has the right to stop them from meeting where or when they want to.

Maximum 1 mark for indicating content omission such as:
   - Third Estate wanted to limit the power of the King.

2. The candidate explains why war broke out between France and her neighbours after 1791 by referring to evidence such as:

   from the source:
   - Austria and Prussia objected to the treatment of Marie Antoinette
   - Louis hoped that defeat would destroy the Revolution
   - the revolutionaries wanted to spread the Revolution
   - Britain joined to stop the French interfering in other countries.

   from recall:
   - Austria and Prussia wanted to stop the spread of the Revolution
   - Louis encouraged the Austrians to help him against the Revolution
   - Louis thought that the war would make him more popular
   - Britain feared that the French might interfere in Ireland.

3. The candidate describes the Reign of Terror by referring to evidence such as:
   - Robespierre became the head of the Committee for Public Safety
   - anyone disagreeing with the views of the Jacobins were labelled traitors
   - Committee of Public Safety could issue warrants of search and arrest
   - evidence often came only from informers
   - accusation was counted as evidence
   - Revolutionary Tribunals could order executions
   - death sentence was the only punishment available
   - up to 40,000 people were guillotined during this period
   - the Terror ended with the execution of Robespierre.

Context 8: Cavour, Garibaldi and the Making of Italy, 1815-1870

1. The candidate explains why the revolutions of 1848-1849 failed to unite Italy by referring to evidence such as:

   from the source:
   - nationalists failed to work together eg revolutionaries in Sicily and Naples
   - revolutionaries did not encourage mass participation
   - middle classes feared that democratic government would give power to the lower classes
   - revolutions were not supported by autocratic leaders eg Ferdinand of Sicily.

   from recall:
   - failure of 'Young Italy' to achieve aims
   - revolutionaries were easily suppressed by the Austrian army
   - lack of foreign support eg French sent soldiers to crush the Roman Republic
   - lack of enthusiasm of the peasantry.

2. The candidate describes the steps taken by Piedmont to bring about Italian unification up to 1860 by referring to evidence such as:
   - Piedmont's army sent to fight alongside Britain and France against Russia in the Crimean War (1854)
   - agreement reached between Cavour and Napoleon III at Plombieres (1858)
   - if Austria attacked Piedmont, France would assist Piedmont
   - promised France Savoy
   - Piedmont provoked Austria into declaring war on 19 April 1859 following mobilisation of Piedmont's army
   - Piedmont's alliance with France allowed success at Magenta and Solferino

- Piedmont encouraged French influence to inspire Parma, Tuscany and Romagna to demand unification with Piedmont
- Napoleon signed truce of Villafranca with Austria July 1859 ending war with Austria.

3. The candidate evaluates the usefulness of **Source B** as evidence of the skills of Cavour as a leader by referring to evidence such as:
   - primary source from the time of the unification of Italy/time Cavour was Prime Minister
   - author is a politician from Piedmont and may be biased in favour of Cavour/would know about Cavour's leadership style
   - written to highlight Cavour's talents as a leader
   - says Cavour has the talent to assess a situation/manipulate events.

Maximum 1 mark for indicating content omission such as:

- specific actions by Cavour as Prime Minister eg meeting with Napoleon at Plombieres provoking Austria into war in 1859.

Context 9: Iron and Blood? Bismarck and The Creation of the German Empire, 1815-1871

1. The candidate explains why Prussia was able to take the lead in German unification by 1862 by referring to evidence such as:

   from the source:
   - Prussia controlled the great rivers Rhine and Elbe – vital for communication and trade
   - other states hoped to benefit from industrial development in Prussia
   - Prussia took the lead in improving roads and railways
   - Frederick William IV of Prussia promised to work for a united Germany.

   from recall:
   - the Zollverein established Prussia as economic leader of the German states
   - Bismarck became Minister-President of Prussia in November 1862
   - his aim was to unite the German states by 'iron and blood'
   - military strength of Prussia.

2. The candidate evaluates the usefulness of **Source B** as evidence of the methods used by Bismarck to bring about the unification of the German states in 1871 by referring to evidence such as:
   - primary source from Bismarck's memoirs
   - written by Bismarck describing his own thoughts
   - to describe how he wanted to unify the German states
   - says he did not doubt a Franco-Prussian War must take place before a united Germany could be realised.

Maximum 1 mark for indicating content omission such as:

- details of methods used to provoke war eg Ems telegram.

3. The candidate describes the events that led to war between France and Prussia in 1870 by referring to evidence such as:
   - Prussia provoked France over Spanish succession issue
   - Hohenzollern candidate Prince Leopold, put forward by Prussia/relative of Prussian royal family
   - French felt threatened/sent Ambassador to Prussia to meet Prussian King
   - Prussian King agreed to withdraw Leopold as candidate but made no promises never to renew candidature
   - Bismarck edited the tone of the Ems Telegram to provoke the French
   - edited version of telegram released to French and German newspapers
   - French politicians were outranged by telegram
   - French reacted by declaring war on 19 July 1870.

Context 10: The Red Flag: Lenin and the Russian Revolution, 1894-1921

1. The candidate explains why national minorities disliked the policy of Russification by referring to evidence such as:

   from the source:
   - Non-Russians had to use the Russian language
   - Russian clothing and customs were to be used
   - Russian officials were put in to run regional governments
   - Poles were told to change and become Russian citizens.

   from recall:
   - Russians were the minority – only 44% of population
   - Catholic Poles and Asiatic Muslims were pressurised to convert to Russian Orthodoxy
   - Jews were persecuted for being 'anti-Russian'
   - Russian was used in schools and law courts.

2. The candidate evaluates the usefulness of **Source B** as evidence of the problems facing the Provisional Government by referring to evidence such as:
   - primary source from personal letter from period of great unrest/time when the Provisional Government was failing – so likely to be his real feelings about the situation
   - author the leader of the Provisional Government who knew well the extent of the problems in July 1917
   - written to warn the problems in Russia were getting worse/express his feelings about the level of unrest in Russia
   - says there will be chaos/famine/defeat at the front.

Maximum 1 mark for indicating content omission such as:

- failure of Brusilov offensive.

3. The candidate describes the ways the Civil War affected the Russian people by referring to evidence such as:
   - most of the Russian economy taken over by the state to supply Reds
   - foodstuffs were forcibly requisitioned from peasants by requisition squads
   - peasants were imprisoned or shot for hoarding grain
   - peasants ceased to produce surplus food in retaliation
   - famine resulted and millions died
   - cholera and typhus broke out killing thousands more
   - both Reds and Whites terrorised the peasants
   - food and fuel were rationed in the cities as supplies were inadequate/black market and bartering began
   - large enterprises were nationalized and strikes made illegal.

Context 11: Free at Last? Race Relations in the USA, 1918-1968

1. The candidate describes the problems facing European immigrants to the USA in the 1920s by referring to evidence such as:
   - often arrived with little wealth or possessions
   - faced discrimination on the grounds of culture/race/religion
   - faced discrimination in most areas of life and work simply because they were immigrants
   - did the poorest jobs with lowest pay
   - poor housing often in unsanitary slums
   - faced abuse from local politicians/lacked rights and representation
   - became stereotyped by public and media as a threat eg blamed for crime became stereotyped by public and media as a burden eg worsened housing shortages
   - blamed for political extremism eg Red Scare.

2. The candidate evaluates the usefulness of **Source A** as evidence of attitudes towards Black Americans in the southern states at the time of the Civil Rights movement by referring to evidence such as:

- primary source written at a time when the Civil Rights movement was beginning to become more active
- author is a Klan leader with extreme racist views and therefore biased
- speech made to warn them against northern influences/show the Klan in a positive light
- says that black people have nothing to fear from KKK provided they accept an inferior social position.

Maximum 1 mark for indicating content omission such as:

- Klan used violence against Black Americans

3. The candidate explains why Martin Luther King planned a Civil Rights protest in Selma, Alabama in 1965 by referring to evidence such as:

   from the source:
   - King wanted to put pressure on President Johnson to support new Civil Rights legislation
   - Sheriff Clark of Selma was a crude, violent racist
   - King thought he could stir up feeling against Clark in the same way as he had against Bull Connor
   - there was a march as part of the protest to Governor Wallace about police brutality and racism.

   from recall:
   - King wanted to win support for a new voting rights act
   - Black Americans were being prevented from registering to vote in Selma
   - very few Black Americans had succeeded in registering to vote in Selma
   - local Civil Rights campaigners had already begun organising protests in Selma
   - protests in Selma had been met with extreme violence from police/TV coverage.

Context 12: The Road to War, 1933-1939

1. The candidate describes the ways Britain appeased Germany between 1933 and 1936 by referring to evidence such as:
   - allowed Germany to break the Treaty of Versailles
   - allowed Germany to break the Locarno Treaty
   - British government and public opinion had revised their attitude to the Treaty of Versailles and agreed it was too harsh
   - Britain did not protest about the reintroduction of conscription
   - Britain took no action over the creation of a German air-force
   - the Anglo-German Naval Agreement allowed Germany to build a navy
   - the Anglo-German Naval Treaty allowed Germany to break Versailles
   - Britain accepted the reoccupation of the Rhineland/Lord Lothian 'Germany is only going into its own backyard'.

2. The candidate explains why Germany wanted Anschluss in 1938 by referring to evidence such as:

   from the source:
   - Austria was the key to south eastern Europe
   - Germany wanted Hungary as an ally
   - Anschluss would help to contain Czechoslovakia
   - political union with Austria was the next step.

   from recall:
   - the Austrians were fellow Germans/German speaking
   - Hitler was Austrian
   - Germany would take over the Austrian army
   - Germany would take over Austria's industry.

3. The candidate evaluates the usefulness of **Source B** as evidence of Britain's attitude to Czechoslovakia in 1938 by referring to evidence such as:
   - primary source from the period when the Czech/Sudeten crisis was developing
   - author was the British ambassador and reflects attitude of the government
   - written to show that the Czechs were to blame for the Sudeten crisis
   - says that Czechs can't be trusted/Czechs want war.

Maximum 1 mark for indicating content omission such as:

- British government put pressure on Czechoslovakia
- the result of this was the Munich Settlement.

Context 13: In the Shadow of the Bomb: The Cold War, 1945-1985

1. The candidate explains why the Cold War broke out after 1945 by referring to evidence such as:

   from the source:
   - Truman and Stalin did not trust each other
   - USA had gained an advantage over the Soviet Union by developing the atomic bomb
   - the Americans did not inform the Soviets of the development of the atomic bomb and did not consult over its use against Japan
   - after the Second World War the Americans and Soviets were no longer united by a common enemy.

   from recall:
   - differences between American system of capitalism and Soviet communism always caused tension/mistrust
   - the Soviet takeover of eastern Europe had angered the USA and its allies
   - Churchill's 'Iron Curtain' speech had antagonised the Soviets
   - the Marshall Plan contributed to divisions in Europe
   - arguments between East and West over the fate of Germany/Berlin in the years following the Second World War
   - Berlin Blockade, 1948-1949, deepened divisions between East and West.

2. The candidate describes the part played by the USSR in the Cuban Missile Crisis by referring to evidence such as:
   - the Soviet Union had developed an alliance with Cuba following Castro's seizure of power and the failure of the Bay of Pigs
   - with Castro's agreement, Soviet Union constructed missile launch sites on Cuba
   - Soviet cargo ships with missiles on board headed for Cuba, despite American protests
   - U2 spy plane shot down by Soviet missile over Cuba
   - Khrushchev thought he could take advantage of youth and inexperience of American President, Kennedy
   - Khrushchev eventually backed down in the face of American blockade/resolve
   - Soviet missiles were removed from Cuba in exchange for the removal of American missiles from Turkey.

3. The candidate evaluates the usefulness of **Source B** as evidence of why the process of détente had come to a halt by the early 1980s by referring to evidence such as:
   - primary source from 1983, a time when the process of détente had halted
   - author was the American President who was directing/influencing foreign policy at the time/possible bias, from an American perspective

- written to explain why he wants to strengthen American military power/end period of détente
- says there is a need to end freeze on building nuclear weapons.

Maximum 1 mark for indicating content omission such as:
- Soviet invasion of Afghanistan had contributed to end of the process of détente/American boycott of Moscow Olympics had strained relations further.

PART 1   THE SHORT ESSAY

Scottish and British

Context 1: Murder in the Cathedral: Crown, Church and People, 1154-1173

1. The candidate explains why Henry II and Archbishop Becket quarrelled so violently by referring to evidence such as:
   - Becket resigned as Chancellor/Henry felt betrayed
   - Becket defended the Church against the King
   - Criminous Clerks – Henry believed that all clergymen who committed a crime should be tried in the King's Court, whereas Becket believed that they should be tried in a Church Court
   - The Constitution of Clarendon – Becket refused to sign the document outlining the powers of the Church and agreeing to obey the king
   - Northampton Trial – Becket refused to attend court/Henry charged him with contempt of court
   - Becket fled to France before he could be sentenced/lived in exile for six years
   - Becket sought the protection of the Pope and Henry's enemy Louis VII against the King during peace talks in France, Henry refused Becket the royal kiss/Becket refused to accept the King's authority "Saving our order"
   - Becket excommunicated the Archbishop of York when he crowned the King's son
   - Becket excommunicated the bishops involved in the coronation when he returned to England
   - the personalities of the two men were very different.

Context 2: Wallace, Bruce and the Wars of Independence, 1286–1328

2. The candidate explains why some Scots were reluctant to accept the Maid of Norway as their ruler by referring to evidence such as:
   - she was a child – others would have to rule on her behalf and there could be disputes
   - she was a child and could possibly die – an adult ruler would be better
   - she was a girl – some people did not believe that a female could rule/give noblemen orders
   - she was a girl – some people did not think that a girl could lead an army into battle
   - she was in Norway – would she understand Scotland and be able to rule it?
   - she needed a husband – a Scottish husband could cause jealousy
     – a foreign husband could lead to Scotland being taken over
   - other nobles – Balliol and Bruce – had ambitions to rule
   - potential for civil war to break out
   - concern that Edward I might exploit the situation.

Context 3: Mary, Queen of Scots and the Scottish Reformation, 1540s-1587

3. The candidate explains why Mary, Queen of Scots, was forced to abdicate in 1567 by referring to evidence such as:
   - people thought she had been involved in the murder of her husband, Darnley
   - she had married her husband's murderer, Bothwell
   - people thought she was involved with Bothwell before the murder
   - she allowed Bothwell to prevent a fair inquiry into Darnley's death

- some people did not agree with a female ruling
- some people did not want to have a Roman Catholic as ruler
- some Roman Catholics were disappointed by her lack of support for their religion
- some nobles had plans to take over the government for themselves.

Context 4: The Coming of the Civil War, 1603-1642

4. The candidate explains why the reign of Charles I was opposed in Scotland by referring to evidence such as:
   - Charles demanded that Ministers accept and use the Prayer Book
   - resentment at the Act of Revocation whereby church or royal property which had been alienated since 1540 was taken back by the crown
   - resentment of Charles' coronation in Edinburgh eg High Church ceremony, employed Anglican forms
   - reaction/opposition to the introduction of Laud's Prayer Book, 1637/St Giles riots
   - reaction by the Scottish clergy on the requirement to wear gowns and surplices (Laud's Canons)
   - abolition of the Presbyteries/threat of dissolution
   - General Assembly not allowed to meet
   - Bishops were to be introduced into the Scottish Church
   - rejection of Canons included in the national covenant of 1638.

Context 5: "Ane End of Ane Auld Sang": Scotland and the Treaty of Union, 1690s-1715

5. The candidate explains why some people thought that Scotland would benefit from a Union with England in 1707 by referring to evidence such as:
   - a Union would end arguments about the Succession between England and Scotland
   - a Union would ensure the Protestant Succession and keep the Stuarts out of Scotland
   - a Union would stop the English and Scottish governments falling out with each other
   - a Union would prevent future wars between England and Scotland
   - a Union would open up English markets to Scottish businessmen
   - a Union would open the English Empire to Scots
   - a Union would ensure Scotland no longer suffered disproportionately when England went to war against France or Spain
   - the Equivalent would inject some much needed cash into Scotland
   - a Union would guarantee the Protestant Church in Scotland.

Context 6: Immigrants and Exiles: Scotland, 1830s-1930s

6. The candidate explains why life was difficult for many Irish immigrants to Scotland between 1830 and 1930 by referring to evidence such as:
   - Irish immigrants had to do the lowest paid work
   - many could not speak English
   - they lived in the slums of the industrial cities – details of overcrowding, poor sanitation, disease
   - immigrants were accused of keeping down wages or of stealing jobs
   - immigrants were accused of violence/causing crime
   - victims of discrimination, violence, press hostility
   - there was suspicion of the Catholic religion in a predominantly Protestant country
   - Irish immigrants felt that the education system was anti-Catholic
   - some Scots felt that Irish were unpatriotic eg during Great War.

Context 7: From the Cradle to the Grave? Social Welfare in Britain, 1890s-1951

7. The candidate explains why the Liberal Government reforms of 1906-1914 were important in improving the lives of children and the elderly by referring to evidence such as:
   - Education (Provision of Meals) Act provided free meals to the poorest children
   - by providing meals for the children they were able to concentrate better at school
   - Education Act 1907 – Medical inspections – allowed for the identification of health problems in school children
   - clinics were introduced into schools in 1912 to provide treatment for children with health problems
   - 1908 Children's Act (Children's Charter) provided legal protection for children eg protection from abuse
   - Children's Charter gave the abolition of the death sentence for children, segregation of child and adult prisoners
   - Children's Charter gave protection from smoking and drinking
   - 1908 Old Age Pensions Act provided pensions for those over 70, relieving the fear of ending their lives in the poorhouse/workhouse
   - pensions were to be paid for through general taxation, meaning the old people did not have to make contributions to qualify – especially helpful to women
   - pensions were paid through the Post Office relieving the stigma of the hated Poor Law – many more people claimed pensions as a result
   - Acts for children and the elderly showed that the government was taking responsibility for the most vulnerable in society.

Context 8: Campaigning for Change: Social Change in Scotland, 1900s-1979

8. The candidate explains why Scottish education in the 1930s was in need of reform by referring to evidence such as:
   - the school leaving age was 14/children left very young without qualifications
   - children could be physically punished/belted by teachers
   - maximum class size was 50 in state schools
   - pupils sat a 'qualifying' exam at 11 to determine their academic ability/which school they would go to/working class children largely disadvantaged by this
   - 3 year junior secondaries concentrated on practical subjects/pupils were prepared for the workplace/pupils gained no qualifications
   - 5 year secondary schools taught academic subjects for university entrance/exams
   - girls and boys followed different curricula – girls did domestic science, boys did technical subjects
   - schools were often poorly equipped/buildings were often old and inadequate but there was no money to improve them
   - there were very few grants to enable poorer students to go to university so many did not go/Carnegie Trust helped to fund 40% of students/37% were working class
   - there was no proper organised scheme of adult education because of lack of central funding.

Context 9: A Time of Troubles: Ireland, 1900-1923

9. The candidate explains why the Unionists were against the Home Rule Bill by referring to evidence such as:
   - Unionists considered themselves British not Irish and had an emotional attachment to Britain
   - Unionists believed it would end their way of life and that they would be less prosperous under Home Rule eg lower wages, poorer health care etc
   - feared the shipbuilding and linen industry based in Belfast would be damaged

- feared Ulster would have to bear the financial burden of the rest of Ireland which was poorer and dependent on the farming industry
- feared Ulster would be cut off from trading markets in Britain and the Empire
- feared the government in Dublin would be influenced by Roman Catholic Church
- feared the Protestant religion would be forced into decline
- feared Home Rule would eventually lead to full independence.

European and World

Context 1: The Norman Conquest, 1060-1153

10. The candidate explains why there was so little opposition to William I after 1066 by referring to evidence such as:
    - victory of William's forces at Hastings
    - death of Harold at Hastings
    - most Anglo-Saxon nobles died at Hastings
    - Anglo-Saxons lacked a native king
    - Anglo-Saxon opposition was weak and scattered
    - William's easy capture of London
    - brutal crushing of any opposition in the north (Harrying of the North)
    - building of castles across the kingdom as secure bases for his forces
    - development of the feudal system.

Context 2: The Cross and the Crescent: The First Crusade, 1096-1125

11. The candidate explains why people joined the First Crusade by referring to evidence such as:
    - the Pope was extremely influential and encouraged people to go on Crusade
    - many believed that it was their duty to recapture Jerusalem and help their Christian brothers
    - the promise that all sins would be forgiven was an attractive idea
    - preachers such as Peter the Hermit encouraged peasants to go on Crusade
    - peasants also went on Crusade because they hoped that they would have a better life in the East. "Milk and honey"
    - some knights were extremely religious and wanted to serve God eg Raymond of Toulouse
    - some knights saw an opportunity to gain land for themselves in the East eg Bohemond/Baldwin
    - some knights went on a crusade because they wanted to use their military skills in the East eg Tancred
    - some knights went on a crusade because of peer pressure/to represent the French royal family eg Hugh of Vermandois.

Context 3: War, Death and Revolt in Medieval Europe, 1328-1436

12. The candidate explains why the Black Death had serious consequences for England by referring to evidence such as:
    - one third of the population died
    - high casualty rate caused a shortage of labourers
    - some villages became derelict
    - disastrous effects on agriculture eg animals died, crops rotted in the fields
    - trade was interrupted
    - affected the attitudes of survivors eg less deferential towards the church
    - led peasants to demand higher wages
    - likely factor in the unrest which led up to the peasants revolt.

Context 4: New Worlds: Europe in the Age of Expansion, 1480s-1530s

13. The candidate explains why Christopher Columbus was important in European exploration by referring to evidence such as:
    - he used his wide sailing experience to support existing arguments about route to Japan
    - persevered for many years to find backers to undertake first voyage (8 years in Portugal, 7 years in Spain)
    - first to take a new route, sailing west to reach the east
    - he had excellent navigational skills (dead reckoning) to set and follow his course
    - voyage found/proved there was land to the west
    - founded the first Spanish settlements in the New World, in Hispaniola
    - claimed new territories for Spain/Spanish crown
    - made Spain (and subsequently Portugal) rich
    - made four voyages to the New World, discovering Caribbean Islands, Venezuelan Coast, Honduras
    - kept detailed accounts of voyages to add to knowledge of places and peoples.

Context 5: "Tea and Freedom": The American Revolution, 1763-1783

14. The candidate explains why the colonists were able to achieve victory in their war against the British by 1783 by referring to evidence such as:
    - poor leadership of British forces eg Howe, Cornwallis
    - tactical errors made by Britain eg Yorktown, Saratoga
    - British army was small in number/had to rely on mercenary forces
    - British soldiers were not properly trained/equipped to cope with terrain and conditions
    - colonial army was effectively led by George Washington
    - colonists had greater forces/able to call on minutemen when required
    - colonists benefited from assistance from foreign powers
    - attacks by French and Spanish weakened/distracted British forces
    - assistance from French and Spanish navies gave colonists control of the seas.

Context 6: "This Accursed Trade": The British Slave Trade and its Abolition, 1770–1807

15. The candidate explains why the Middle Passage was such a dreadful experience for slaves by referring to evidence such as:
    - slaves were held on board using tight pack/loose pack system
    - disease was common on ships – dysentery due to poor sanitary conditions
    - lack of fresh air – slaves held for long periods below deck
    - crew were often cruel towards slaves
    - female slaves often suffered sexual abuse from the crew
    - food was limited and bland/unfamiliar to slaves – some had to be force fed
    - slaves taken above deck and whipped to make them exercise
    - slaves would witness deaths of fellow slaves/evidence from the case of the Zong.

Context 7: Citizens! The French Revolution, 1789-1794

16. The candidate explains why so many people were frightened of the Committee of Public Safety in 1793 by referring to evidence such as:
    - opponents of the Jacobins were labelled as 'traitors' to France
    - Committee of Public Safety could issue warrants of search and arrest
    - Committee set up Revolutionary Tribunals – only they could order the death sentence

- evidence often came only from secret informers
- trials and executions were quick and uncontested/accused were not entitled to lawyers or right of appeal
- accusation meant the assumption of guilt in vast majority of cases
- many thousands of people were executed by guillotine or other means
- Committee enforced order in the Provinces with great brutality.

Context 8: Cavour, Garibaldi and the Making of Italy, 1815-1870

17. The candidate explains why the 1848-49 revolutions failed to bring about Italian unification by referring to evidence such as:
    - Charles Albert was initially reluctant to put himself forward as head of the nationalist movement
    - Austrian army was superior – due to the failure of the Austrian revolutions the Austrian army was re-enforced
    - Pope Pius XI abandoned the nationalist cause
    - peasants could not be relied upon to support the nationalist cause/nationalists lacked mass support
    - nationalists were divided and could not work together eg divisions between supporters of Mazzini, Charles Albert and the Pope
    - there was not enough foreign support to help the nationalist cause
    - Charles Albert was wrong to say that Italy could 'go it alone' (fara de se)
    - French intervention crushed the Roman Republic
    - Regionalism was strong
    - more organisation, planning and military strength would be needed to advance the nationalist cause
    - Italian nationalists now focused their attention on Piedmont as it held on to its constitution.

Context 9: Iron and Blood? Bismarck and The Creation of the German Empire, 1815-1871

18. The candidate explains why the 1848-49 revolutions failed to bring about German unification by referring to evidence such as:
    - the Frankfurt Parliament could not agree on the size of Germany – Kleindeutschland or Grossdeutschland
    - the Frankfurt Parliament lacked clear, agreed objectives and argued minority views at great lengths
    - King Frederick William of Prussia refused to take the crown of Germany
    - the Frankfurt Parliament was leaderless/lacked a strong leader
    - Austrians withdrew their delegates from the parliament after Frederick William's refusal and other states soon followed
    - the Parliament did not have an army to enforce its decisions
    - the old rulers of Germany still had control of their armies and used them to restore power
    - by 1849 Austria had recovered its political power and was willing to use its armies to destroy any further revolutions
    - Kings and other Heads of State did not see unification as being in their interest
    - by 1850 Austria had persuaded most of the old rulers to renew the German Confederation
    - after Erfurt, Austria was again dominant in Germany with a policy to keep Germany divided.

Context 10: The Red Flag: Lenin and the Russian Revolution, 1894-1921

19. The candidate explains why the Provisional Government had lost popular support by October 1917 by referring to evidence such as:
    - Provisional Government was not elected so lacked legitimacy/failed to hold elections
    - Provisional Government failed to end the war/war going badly/failure of June offensive
    - Provisional Government failed to give land to the peasants
    - Provisional Government failed to help unemployed or raise wages
    - Provisional Government failed to solve food shortages
    - Provisional Government could not govern without co-operation of Petrograd Soviet
    - Order Number One – soldiers should obey officers only if the orders did not contradict decrees of the Petrograd Soviet – weakened the Provisional Government's authority with the army
    - Lenin returned and proclaimed the 'April Theses' (peace, bread, land) refusing support for the Provisional Government
    - Provisional Government looked ineffective during Kornilov Revolt.

Context 11: Free at Last? Race Relations in the USA, 1918-1968

20. The candidate explains why the attitudes of Americans towards immigration changed after 1918 by referring to evidence such as:
    - growing fear of social unrest in aftermath of Russian Revolution
    - fear that Communism may spread to USA
    - worry about increasing numbers of immigrants from southern and eastern Europe
    - concern that immigrants would take jobs
    - concern that immigrants would depress wages
    - concern that immigrants would be used to break strikes
    - concern that immigrants would create pressure on scarce housing
    - feeling that new immigrants were inferior eg illiterate
    - feeling that USA could no longer take unrestricted numbers of immigrants
    - feeling that immigrants were involved in organised crime
    - influence of WASPs.

Context 12: The Road to War, 1933-1939

21. The candidate explains why Britain did not want to go to war with Germany in the 1930s by referring to evidence such as:
    - war was unpopular with the British people because of the losses of 1914-1918
    - there was a strong pacifist movement in Britain eg White Poppy campaign
    - there was fear that "the bomber will always get through" leading to huge losses
    - Germany had rearmed with powerful army, navy and air force
    - Britain had failed to modernise Armed Forces/was militarily weak
    - Chiefs of Staff warned that British forces could not deal with Germany, Italy and Japan
    - Britain had no reliable allies – USA neutral, France unstable and Russia communist
    - countries of the Empire warned that they might not support Britain in another European war
    - Fascism was seen as a barrier to the spread of Communism.

Context 13: In the Shadow of the Bomb: The Cold War, 1945-1985

22. The candidate explains why the USA and USSR had begun the process of détente by the 1970s by referring to evidence such as:
    - the experience of the Cuban crisis in the 1960s had shown how close the superpowers had come to nuclear war
    - the end of the Vietnam War had reduced tension between the USA and Soviet Union
    - there were concerns that the arms race could spiral out of control
    - America and the Soviet Union were experiencing economic difficulties
    - the superpowers were keen to focus on spending more money on domestic priorities
    - anti-nuclear protest movements were growing in many countries
    - there had been widespread criticism of the Soviet Union's action in Czechoslovakia
    - Brezhnev and Nixon had a desire to improve relations between the superpowers
    - the leaders of both countries wished to portray themselves as peacemakers.

PART 2 HISTORICAL STUDY

Scottish and British

Context 1: Murder in the Cathedral: Crown, Church and People, 1154-1173

1. The candidate describes the actions taken by Henry II to increase his power when he became king in 1154 by referring to evidence such as:
    - castles built without permission were seized or knocked down
    - barons who disobeyed the king were dealt with severely eg Earl of York had his title taken from him
    - mercenaries/private armies sent back to Flanders
    - Assize of Clarendon introduced to deal with serious crimes eg murder, theft/ensure the law was the same throughout the country
    - Assize of Northampton introduced to deal with arson, forgery
    - trial by ordeal introduced with sentencing/punishment
    - Novel Disseisin introduced to deal with land disputes
    - corrupt sheriffs sacked and replaced
    - barons no longer allowed to hold office of sheriff
    - key personnel introduced to enforce law and order eg Jury/Justices in Eyre.

2. The candidate evaluates the usefulness of the source by referring to evidence such as:
    - primary source written during the time the code of chivalry was followed
    - author was an eyewitness/poets wrote about knights and chivalry
    - to criticise the behaviour of knights
    - they steal from the church and rob pilgrims/show disrespect to children and the elderly.

    Maximum 1 mark for indicating content omission such as:
    - some knights upheld the Code of Chivalry eg fought for the Church on Crusade
    - some knights also enforced the law eg were members of a jury.

3. The candidate explains why priests were important to the twelfth century by referring to evidence such as:

    from the source:
    - offered support and hope that life after death would be better
    - taught people how to behave/fulfil their Christian duties
    - carried out key ceremonies eg baptism, marriage, funerals
    - taught local boys to read and write/prepared them for a career in the Church.

    from recall:
    - heard confessions/issued penance for sins committed
    - carried out ceremonies such as communion/confirmation/last rites
    - enforced Canon law at local level
    - kept part of their tithe (harvest) to give to the poor during times of need.

Context 2: Wallace, Bruce and the Wars of Independence, 1286-1328

1. The candidate evaluates the usefulness of the source by referring to evidence such as:
    - primary source written in 1298, at the time of the Battle of Falkirk
    - Walter of Guisborough is an English chronicler – possible bias
    - the chronicle is to describe what happened at Falkirk/celebrate English success and show Scots as cowards
    - it states that the Scots were in schiltrons/the Scots cavalry fled.

    Maximum 1 mark for indicating content omission such as:
    - Edward used his archers to break up the schiltrons
    - the Scots were defeated.

2. The candidate describes the events that led to the death of John Comyn at Dumfries in 1306 by referring to evidence such as:
    - Bruce arranged to meet with Comyn at Greyfriars in Dumfries
      or
      Bruce tricked Comyn to meet him at Greyfriars in Dumfries
    - Bruce accused Comyn of betraying him to King Edward
      or
      the two men began to argue about Comyn telling King Edward about Bruce
    - Bruce stabbed Comyn
      or
      Bruce hit Comyn with a sword
    - Bruce ran out of Greyfriars and told his companions what he had done
    - the monks carried Comyn to the altar
    - Comyn said that he would survive the wound
    - Bruce ordered his men to kill Comyn
      or
      some of Bruce's men killed Comyn
    - Comyn's blood spilled over the high altar.

3. The candidate explains why it took so long for Robert Bruce to be accepted as King of Scots by referring to evidence such as

    from the source:
    - he had to force many Scots to abandon King John Balliol
    - he had to force Scots to reject Edward II as overlord
    - Bruce was unable to force Edward II to change his mind
    - Bruce's efforts to spread the war to other parts of Britain were not successful.

    from recall:
    - it took a long time to drive the English out of their castles in Scotland
    - Bruce had been excommunicated so some people could not accept him as King

- the Comyns were long-standing rivals and the most powerful family in Scotland
- Bruce took several years to defeat the Comyns and their allies eg the MacDougalls
- Bruce's wars in Ireland had ended in failure at Dundalk
- Bruce's invasion of northern England had not forced Edward to accept him.

Context 3: Mary, Queen of Scots and the Scottish Reformation, 1540s-1587

1. The candidate evaluates the usefulness of the source by referring to evidence such as:
   - primary source written at the time the Treaty of Greenwich was broken
   - written by Knox, a Protestant leader/bias – says Arran "slipped away"/calls Cardinal Beaton "the Devil"
   - to describe how the Treaty of Greenwich was broken/to criticise Arran
   - tells that Arran changed his religion/broke the Treaty with England.

   Maximum 1 mark for indicating content omission such as:
   - some Scots were alarmed by the demands of Henry VIII and wanted to break the Treaty
   - Arran had been offered a duchy in France for changing sides – Chatelherault.

2. The candidate explains why the Scots rebelled against Mary of Guise in 1559 by referring to evidence such as:

   from the source:
   - she took stronger action against Protestants
   - she made more use of French officials
   - she had more French soldiers in key strongholds in Scotland
   - she wanted to introduce a new tax in Scotland.

   from recall:
   - Scottish Protestant Lords became more organised as "Lords of the Congregation" to challenge Mary
   - they wanted to challenge the Roman Catholic Church in Scotland eg Beggars' Summons
   - Knox returned and fuelled religious controversy – iconoclastic outrages in Perth
   - Scots feared that Frenchmen would be settled in Scotland and Scots sent to France
   - Scottish nobles resented Frenchmen taking Scottish jobs which they wanted.

3. The candidate describes the events that led to the execution of Mary, Queen of Scots in 1587 by referring to evidence such as:
   - 1580 the Pope's policy of encouraging plots against Elizabeth made English Protestants think Mary was a menace – especially since her son and heir was a Protestant
   - 1585 after several plots, the English government passed a law stating that Mary would be executed if she was actively involved in any plot against Elizabeth
   - 1585 Mary was moved to Chartley where English spies discovered how letters were smuggled
   - 1586 Babington contacted Mary to inform her of his plans to kill Elizabeth and help Mary to escape
   - Mary replied to Babington and agreed to Elizabeth's death
   - The incriminating letter was intercepted by Elizabeth's spies
   - Mary was arrested, put on trial and sentenced to death
   - Elizabeth hesitated to execute her cousin, the death warrant was concealed amongst a pile of letters and Elizabeth signed them all
   - 1587 February Mary was executed at Fotheringay.

Context 4: The Coming of the Civil War, 1603-1642

1. The candidate describes the changes in the way Scotland was governed after 1603 by referring to evidence such as:
   - Scotland was ruled by the Privy Council
   - Privy Council ensured that the King's will was followed in Scotland
   - Parliament was brought under strict Royal control
   - Parliament was run by a small committee called the Committee of Articles (Lords of the Articles)
   - Committee of Articles (Lords of the Articles) only could suggest new laws for Scotland
   - the King chose Lords and bishops to become part of the Committee of Articles (Lords of the Articles)
   - the King controlled the membership of the Committee of Articles (Lords of the Articles)
   - King was now based in London – 400 miles away and rarely visited.

2. The candidate explains why there was opposition to the methods used by Charles I to raise money by referring to evidence such as:

   from the source:
   - Charles raised money without reference to the Parliament
   - introduction of the forced loan 1626-27
   - imprisonment of knights without a fair trial for refusal to pay
   - ship money collected from counties without coastlines.

   from recall:
   - Hampden case. John Hampden was tried and found guilty for refusing to pay ship money
   - Charles sold monopolies and patents which meant the traders had to pay to take part in that trade or be forced out
   - forest fines charged people who lived on former royal forest land
   - collection of customs duties without Parliament's consent.

3. The candidate evaluates the usefulness of the source by referring to evidence such as:
   - primary source from 1642, the year the Civil War broke out
   - Thomas Wiseman was present in London at the time of the 'arrests'/possible bias as Wiseman appears to support the Houses of Parliament
   - to describe the events of the 'arrests', criticise the actions of the king
   - says Parliament has wrongly accused bishops of high treason/supports Parliament's right to be angered.

   Maximum 1 mark for indicating content omission such as:
   - Charles' abuse of Parliamentary privileges – not allowed into Parliament unless invited
   - reference to other reasons for outbreak of war eg Charles' grievances regarding the impeachment of Stafford and Laud, the Grand Remonstrance, Nineteen Propositions rejected by Charles in 1642.

Context 5: "Ane End of Ane Auld Sang": Scotland and the Treaty of Union, 1690s-1715

1. The candidate describes Scotland's economic problems in the years before the Union by referring to evidence such as:
   - farming in Scotland was very poor
   - the "Ill-years" had affected Scotland's harvests
   - people were unable to pay rents, landowners were short of money
   - Scotland did not produce many goods to trade with abroad
   - Scots were excluded from trading with England's colonies
   - the wars between England and France had reduced Scottish trade with France
   - Scotland never gained from peace treaties at the end of these wars

- Scotland had invested a lot of money in the Darien Scheme
- Scotland had lost all of this money when Darien failed.

2. The candidate explains why opponents of the Union were unable to stop it being passed in Scotland by referring to evidence such as:

from the source:
- they were not well organised (eg Squadrone Volante)
- they placed trust in Hamilton who was unreliable
- the government had sent secret agents to promote the Union
- the government offered money to people to support the Union.

from recall:
- the government threatened Scottish trade if the Union was not passed
- the government offered titles to people who supported the Union
- the government offered jobs to people who supported the Union
- the government made its officials support the Union or they would not be paid
- the government had soldiers in northern England and Ulster ready to go to Scotland
- the Equivalent made money available to Scotland.

3. The candidate evaluates the usefulness of the source by referring to evidence such as:
- primary source written a few years after the Union
- written by Daniel Defoe who had been an English spy and who was there at the time/possible bias
- to highlight the bad effects of the Union
- it describes how money and jobs are going to England/Scottish manufacturers are ruined.

Maximum 1 mark for indicating content omission such as:
- the Malt Tax and Customs and Excise were unpopular
- Scots were beginning to trade freely with English colonies.

Context 6: Immigrants and Exiles: Scotland, 1830s–1930s

1. The candidate evaluates the usefulness of the source by referring to evidence such as:
- primary source from the time of the potato famine/poverty/mass immigration
- a British magazine but showing an accurate/sympathetic image of conditions
- to show that there was poverty/starvation in Ireland
- women and children dressed in rags/very thin/bare-foot.

Maximum 1 mark for indicating content omission such as:
- many died at this time
- prospect of work in Scotland
- other factors eg push and pull.

2. The candidate explains why so many Highland Scots emigrated by referring to evidence such as:

from the source:
- landowners encouraged tenants to emigrate to gain greater profit from sheep
- farming was difficult due to poor soils and weather
- the failure of the potato crop
- Highlanders preferred foreign countries to Scottish cities.

from recall:
- the fishing industry was in decline
- kelp making was no longer profitable
- landowners cleared their tenants from the land
- cities such as Glasgow and Edinburgh funded Highlanders to emigrate.

3. The candidate describes the ways emigrants created Scottish communities in their new homelands by referring to evidence such as:
- Scots built communities in remote places
- they built schools as they valued education
- they built churches and stuck to their Presbyterian religion
- many went into business and industry
- they retained their culture eg Burns suppers, Highland games
- they created cultural societies eg Caledonian Society
- they gave Scottish place names such as Nova Scotia
- some continued to speak the Gaelic language.

Context 7: From the Cradle to the Grave? Social Welfare in Britain, 1890s–1951

1. The candidate evaluates the usefulness of the source by referring to evidence such as:
- primary source produced at a time of poverty
- Aberdeen organisation representative of an industrial city which would experience more poverty/possible bias because of attitudes shown eg only targeting the 'deserving poor' – sober and industrious
- to show their willingness to help the 'deserving poor'/sober and industrious who may become ill
- says drinking and laziness are causes of poverty/only those willing to work and stay sober are to be helped.

Maximum 1 mark for indicating content omission such as:
- other causes of poverty as the fault of the individual such as gambling
- some believed everybody should be helped/poverty was not always the fault of the individual (low wages/size of family/irregularity of work).

2. The candidate explains why the Second World War changed people's attitudes towards welfare reform by referring to evidence such as:

from the source:
- rationing helped encourage the idea of universal sharing of the nation's food supply
- the government were assisting all those suffering bomb damage – rich and poor
- classes were mixing in society who previously had little in common
- war highlighted problems that could be overcome by government action.

from recall:
- the poor health of some city children evacuated to the country highlighted the problems of poverty
- suffering of war caused a determination to create a better society once the war was over
- other reforms had been made by the government during the war such as free health care for war wounded and bomb victims, Emergency Milk and Meals scheme etc
- war raised awareness of continuing social problems (experience of evacuation), which many assumed had disappeared and that only the government could tackle
- Beveridge report, published in 1942, set out principles for government intervention and was very well received.

3. The candidate describes the limitations of the Labour Government reforms of 1945-1951 by referring to evidence such as:
- not everyone was covered by the National Insurance Act, only those with a certain level of contributions
- Social Security payments were felt to be inadequate by 1949/more people applied for national assistance
- the NHS became too expensive and prescription charges had to be introduced in 1951
- not enough new hospitals to meet the demands of a modern health service

- insufficient new housing to replace damaged housing and for the demobilisation of the 5 million service men and women
- quality of housing not a priority eg 37% of homes still had no fixed bath
- limitations of school building programme eg concentration on primary schools rather than secondary (only 250 by 1950s)
- limits of education provision eg 11+ was seen as unfair, affecting future job opportunities for those who failed to get into grammar schools.

Context 8: Campaigning for Change: Social Change in Scotland, 1900s-1979

1. The candidate evaluates the usefulness of the source by referring to evidence such as:
   - primary source produced in 1914 when militant suffragette activity was at its height/public disapproval of suffragette tactics at its height
   - produced by the British Museum which would be a potential target/had been attacked by suffragettes, so unsympathetic
   - to control behaviour of women visitors
   - states that women must be accompanied by men who will guarantee their good behaviour/states that unaccompanied women must bring a letter from a responsible person who will guarantee their good behaviour.

   Maximum 1 mark for indicating content omission such as:
   - references to other militant activities eg arson, attacking pillar boxes
   - other paintings were attacked in Glasgow and Birmingham
   - most women were not militants/many men supported suffragettes
   - Cat and Mouse Act.

2. The candidate describes the effects of the economic slump in Scotland in the 1920s and 1930s by referring to evidence such as:
   - the unemployment rate rose nationally to almost 15%
   - traditional industries/shipbuilding, iron and steel, coal mining, textiles went into severe decline
   - unemployment was worst in areas dependant on traditional industries eg 50% in Motherwell, Dundee in early 1930s
   - over 400,000 Scots emigrated in the 1920s
   - new political affiliations developed eg Communism, Nationalism
   - availability of cheap unskilled labour discouraged investment in new technology
   - Trades Unions organised a series of strikes and demonstrations protesting at job and wage cuts
   - unemployed workers went on hunger marches to Westminster
   - the Means Test was introduced/families were split up
   - central Scotland was made a 'Special Area' for government assistance in 1934

3. The candidate explains why more Scots used the countryside for recreation between the wars by referring to evidence such as:

   from the source:
   - new organisations such as youth hostels, cycling clubs set up
   - cheap motor bikes enabled access
   - the unemployed joined climbing clubs
   - Scottish Rights of Way and Recreation Society supported walkers' rights.

   from recall:
   - cheap cycles (£5) became easily available
   - second hand cars became easier to buy
   - cheap day trips to the countryside by coach increased
   - National Trust for Scotland (1931) opened up gardens and castles/estates for visitors
   - publicity/public information about outdoor recreation.

Context 9: A Time of Troubles: Ireland, 1900-1923

1. The candidate evaluates the usefulness of the source by referring to evidence such as:
   - primary source written at the time of the Easter Rising executions
   - author in position of authority in Ireland would be aware of public opinion – possible bias
   - to condemn the executions/warn of potential unrest
   - executing leaders has increased support and sympathy for rebels/people are angry at British reaction.

   Maximum 1 mark for indicating content omission such as:
   - support grew for Sinn Fein as a result of the executions
   - Unionists supported action taken by the British government.

2. The candidate describes the terms of the Anglo-Irish Treaty of 1922 by referring to evidence such as:
   - Ireland given same legal status within the Commonwealth as other countries such as Australia, Canada and New Zealand.
   - Ireland to be known as the Irish Free State
   - the British King was to be represented in Ireland by a Governor-General
   - all members of the Dail were to swear an oath of allegiance to the British King
   - Britain would still use Irish ports for the Royal Navy/to help with the defence of Britain and Ireland
   - Britain to look after Ireland's coast for the next five years
   - a Boundary Commission was to be set up to decide the exact boundary between Northern Ireland and the Irish Free State
   - a Council of Ireland was to be set up if and when Northern Ireland decided to join the Irish Free State.

3. The candidate explains why the Free State Army won the Irish Civil War in 1923 by referring to evidence such as:

   from the source:
   - used artillery supplied by the British to attack Republicans
   - won back Four Courts/other important buildings
   - Republican leaders captured and executed
   - support of the Catholic Church/public.

   from recall:
   - amnesty announced by Irish government, some Republicans surrendered
   - Republicans outnumbered
   - Republican leader Liam Lynch killed
   - De Valera surrendered and accepted partition.

PART 3   HISTORICAL STUDY

European and World

Context 1: The Norman Conquest, 1060-1153

1. The candidate explains why William became a successful leader of Normandy by referring to evidence such as:

   from the source:
   - William was a capable soldier from an early age
   - he was prepared to use ruthless methods when necessary
   - he recognised his need for allies
   - he married the daughter of the powerful Count of Flanders.

   from recall:
   - William defeated an attempted French invasion in 1054
   - he was a skilled tactician eg out manoeuvred King Henry at Mortemer
   - he increased the size of Normandy by taking over Maine
   - he arranged for his sister to marry the Count of Ponthieu.

2. The candidate compares the sources by referring to evidence such as:
The sources fully agree

Source B	Source C
• David was responsible for founding many abbeys	• he encouraged the work of Cistercian monks at Melrose and Kinloss
• David established a series of royal burghs	• David established many of Scotland's most important towns
• he put down a revolt against him in Moray – Anglo-Norman knights helped strengthen his rule	• he put down rebellions against his rule

3. The candidate describes the features of Norman government which were introduced to Scotland after 1124 by referring to evidence such as:
   • knight service eg members of the jury in law courts
   • sheriffs appointed to deal with administration, finance, military affairs and hold courts
   • government by royal council
   • creation of burghs to encourage trade through markets and fairs
   • royal officials appointed eg chancellor to look after royal records and keep great seal
   • law officers appointed who also introduced the Jury of Inquest
   • constable appointed as the King's military officer
   • encouraged Normans to settle in Scotland.

Context 2: The Cross and the Crescent: The First Crusade, 1096–1125

1. The candidate compares the sources by referring to evidence such as:
The sources agree completely

Source A	Source B
• stole food and possessions from Jews	• homes robbed and valuables stolen
• forced Jews to change religion and become Christian	• Jews forced to give up faith and become Christian
• slaughtered Jews	• attacked and killed Jewish men, women and children

2. The candidate explains why Emperor Alexius and the Crusaders had a poor relationship by referring to evidence such as:

from the source:
   • Emperor Alexius freed the Muslims inside Nicaea
   • Emperor Alexius insulted the Crusaders/did not let them plunder the city and take a share of the treasure
   • Crusaders no longer willing to keep oath of loyalty
   • Crusaders agree to keep any land captured for themselves.

from recall:
   • Crusaders blamed the Emperor for failure of the People's Crusade
   • Crusaders unhappy at their treatment at Constantinople eg Crusaders only allowed into city in small groups/forced to take oaths/supplies withheld
   • Baldwin kept Edessa and did not return it to Emperor Alexius
   • Bohemond kept Antioch and did not return it to the Emperor
   • Emperor Alexius did not help the Crusaders at Antioch.

3. The candidate describes the capture of Jerusalem in 1099 by referring to evidence such as:
   • Crusaders entered Jerusalem after nine days of fasting and praying
   • Crusaders used battering rams to weaken the city's defences
   • Crusaders used siege towers to climb the city's walls
   • Godfrey's men were the first inside the city
   • a Crusader called Letold killed the guards and let the other Crusaders in
   • the Crusaders killed everyone inside the city: men, women and children
   • the Jewish inhabitants of the city were burned in the synagogue
   • houses and temples were robbed
   • the bodies of the dead were searched for valuables and burned.

Context 3: War, Death and Revolt in Medieval Europe, 1328–1436

1. The candidate explains why the French were defeated at Crecy by referring to evidence such as:

from the source:
   • the French army was forced to fight uphill
   • French crossbows took time to reload
   • French cavalry were forced back by a hail of arrows
   • French foot-soldiers were trampled by their own men.

from recall:
   • the English longbow was superior to the French crossbow
   • speed and accuracy of longbow men
   • effective leadership of Edward III
   • bravery of the Black Prince during the battle

2. The candidate describes the Jacquerie risings in France 1358 by referring to evidence such as:
   • uprisings began near Beauvais in May 1358
   • uprisings spread through north eastern France (Valois, Amiens)
   • peasants sacked and burned castles
   • French nobles were killed
   • the rising was put down by Charles of Navarre
   • the peasant army was defeated near Meaux in June 1358
   • savage reprisals were taken against the peasants
   • caused nobles to accept the authority of the French King in order to support and maintain their position.

3. The candidate compares the sources by referring to evidence such as:
The sources mainly disagree

Source B	Source C
• chateaux and churches across north-west France were sacked	• recovery of French lands had not been destructive
• Charles VII worried about a new English attack	• Charles was worried at first but built strong defences and encouraged attacks in the channel
• English still controlled Calais	• English had to pour resources into defending Calais

Context 4: New Worlds: Europe in the Age of Expansion, 1480s–1530s

1. The candidate describes the improvements in technology which made the voyages of discovery possible by referring to evidence such as:
   - development of new ship types eg nao, caravel
   - new sail arrangements – lateen sails
   - the new mast arrangements – mizzen
   - improvements to compass
   - development of navigation equipment – astrolabe, quadrant, cross staff, log line
   - improved cartography
   - portolano charts
   - more detailed rutters.

2. The candidate explains why Vasco da Gama's voyage was important for European trade by referring to evidence such as:

   from the source:
   - crossed the Indian Ocean to Calicut
   - brought back a cargo of spices
   - increased profits – 60 times cost of voyage
   - enabled trade to many lands – Ethiopia, Arabia, Persia, India.

   from recall:
   - broke Arab-Venetian monopoly of the spice trade
   - costs were brought down – middlemen cut out
   - discovered new coast, ports
   - enabled Portuguese to set up a base in Goa for trade further east.

3. The candidate compares the sources by referring to evidence such as:
   The sources agree completely

Source B	Source C
• their culture their religion and their civilisations were destroyed by the Conquistadors	• their existing religions were harshly dealt with/discouraged
• Kings who had gold and wealth were held captive and their people forced to pay ransoms in gold	• Europeans took gold and riches from New World peoples by any means, fair or unfair
• Europeans brought them new diseases which wiped them out in hundreds of thousands	• smallpox and measles spread rapidly and whole populations had no resistance and died

Context 5: "Tea and Freedom": The American Revolution, 1763–1783

1. The candidate describes what happened during the Gaspée incident in 1772 by referring to evidence such as:
   - the British had been patrolling the seas to prevent smuggling/impose customs
   - the British vessel Gaspée ran aground off the coast of Rhode Island
   - the vessel was attacked by a crowd of local men
   - the commander of the Gaspée was wounded by a musket shot
   - the British government launched an investigation into the incident
   - the inhabitants of Rhode Island refused to cooperate with the British investigation.

2. The candidate explains why many colonists had turned against British rule by 1776 by referring to evidence such as:

   from the source:
   - people were persuaded by Paine that the British government were abusing the rights of the American people
   - Paine's ideas were very popular/150,000 pamphlets were sold
   - the King had rejected the Olive Branch Petition
   - the British were using mercenary soldiers to help them run the colonies.

   from recall:
   - anger at unfair taxation – Sugar Tax, Stamp Act etc
   - colonists felt that actions of the British government were damaging trade
   - anger among the colonists about the growing number of British soldiers in the colonies
   - acts of violence by the British eg Boston Massacre
   - lack of representation in the British parliament.

3. The candidate compares the sources by referring to evidence such as:
   The sources agree to a considerable degree

Source B	Source C
• Cornwallis' position at Yorktown was deteriorating fast	• Yorktown ended up being in a poor position
• American forces prevented Cornwallis' forces from moving inland	• American troops moved in quickly to contain Cornwallis
• the French defeated the British fleet in Chesapeake Bay	• the French defeated the British fleet in a naval battle near Yorktown

Context 6: "This Accursed Trade": The British Slave Trade and its Abolition, 1770–1807

1. The candidate explains why resistance was difficult for slaves on the plantations by referring to evidence such as:

   from the source:
   - slaves were controlled by strict laws or codes
   - slaves who escaped were hunted down
   - slave risings lacked effective leadership
   - slave resistance was crushed by the better armed and organised whites.

   from recall:
   - plantation owners often used black overseers to help them maintain authority
   - punishments for escaping were very severe and acted as a deterrent
   - slaves lived in fear of being sold off/separated from their families if they broke the rules
   - slaves had little or no education and could be brainwashed into accepting plantation life
   - many islands were small and it was difficult for slaves to evade capture.

2. The candidate compares the sources by referring to evidence such as:

There is agreement between the sources

Source B	Source C
• the slave trade had many powerful supporters	• plantation owners had the support of important groups who promoted slavery
• British ports relied on the trade	• dozens of British ports, and surrounding areas relied on the slave trade
• many people believed that the trade had helped to make Britain wealthy and prosperous	• slave trade seemed vital to the continuing prosperity of Britain and the Caribbean Islands

3. The candidate describes the ways the Abolitionists tried to win support for their cause by referring to evidence such as:
   • Abolitionists formed the Society for the Abolition of the Slave Trade in 1778
   • published pamphlets/posters in support of their cause
   • mounted press campaigns
   • Josiah Wedgewood designed a range of goods to promote the cause
   • published accounts of former slaves, such as Equiano
   • lobbied Parliament and persuaded MPs (led by Wilberforce) to support legislation to end the slave trade
   • encouraged people to sign petitions
   • held public meetings
   • Clarkson – collected evidence of the barbarities of the trade
   • tried to persuade Christians that the slave trade was against the teachings of the Bible.

Context 7: Citizens! The French Revolution, 1789–1794

1. The candidate describes the complaints of the French peasants in 1789 by referring to evidence such as:
   • lack of support to overcome bad harvests and food shortages in the 1790s/famine in 1789
   • prices of goods rose very rapidly
   • peasants had to pay taxes such as the taille, vingtieme, gabelle
   • the landowners/nobles did not pay taxes
   • peasants had to pay money to the Church
   • peasants were subject to feudal services eg the corvee forced them to work on road building/repairs without pay
   • peasants were forced into long periods of military service
   • no political power – peasants made up a large percentage of the population.

2. The candidate compares the sources by referring to evidence such as:

The sources disagree

Source A	Source B
• honest reward for work	• wanted to get as much as they could for as little effort as possible
• lived only for wife and children	• cared only about themselves
• quiet and humble/wished only to live in peace	• violent and arrogant

3. The candidate explains why many French people were unhappy with the treatment of the Catholic Church during the French Revolution by referring to evidence such as:

from the source:
   • the Catholic Church was to be brought under state control
   • Church lands were sold but the government kept the money
   • priests became state servants rather than Church servants
   • Protestants would be allowed to vote for Catholic Bishops/Bishops to be elected

from recall:
   • Catholic religion was no longer the official religion
   • the Pope's authority was being undermined
   • Catholic clergy were made to swear an oath of loyalty to the Assembly
   • Robespierre introduced a new official state religion.

Context 8: Cavour, Garibaldi and the Making of Italy, 1815–1870

1. The candidate describes why Napoleon Bonaparte had an important influence on Italian unification by referring to evidence such as:

from the source:
   • he created a kingdom in Italy in the North
   • he abolished internal customs barriers
   • he built roads across the Alps which brought Italians together
   • he encouraged the Italian language and literature

from recall:
   • he created a national army
   • he appointed people of talent rather than social standing to high office which changed the way Italy was governed
   • trade became quicker and easier between the regions under his system of single weights, measures and currency
   • some were united in their opposition to his demands for tax, recruits for war and robbery of art treasures.

2. The candidate describes the events between 1850 and 1871 which led to the unification of Italy by referring to evidence such as:
   • involvement of Piedmont in Crimea War on side of Britain and France won support
   • Pact of Plombieres
   • War of Italian Independence – April-July 1859 defeated Austria
   • Battles of Magenta and Solferino and conquest of Lombardy
   • Peace of Villafranca
   • annexation of central Italian states
   • Garibaldi and thousand – expedition to Kingdom of the Two Sicilies
   • Garibaldi's handing over of conquests to Victor Emmanuel
   • alliance with Prussia and gift of Venetia, 1866
   • Franco-Prussian War 1870-71 and entry into Rome
   • money was raised through subscriptions and donations to help Garibaldi's Sicilian expedition.

3. The candidate compares the sources by referring to evidence such as:

The sources disagree

Source B	Source C
• Cavour was not always a supporter of a united Italy	• Cavour's ambition was always to unite Italy
• Cavour took advantage of opportunities rather than plan them	• Cavour was a great diplomat and brilliant planner
• Cavour acted to stop Garibaldi	• Cavour allowed Garibaldi to win the South

Context 9: Iron and Blood? Bismarck and The Creation of the German Empire, 1815–1871

1. The candidate describes the ways German national feeling grew before 1848 by referring to evidence such as:
    - the German Confederation encouraged the growth of national feeling
    - students held meetings to promote the ideas of nationalism and unity eg Karl von Hase
    - Carlsbad decrees united students to the cause of nationalism
    - the popularity of German artists, musicians and writers helped create a common identity/cultural nationalism eg Grimm Brothers, Beethoven
    - the Zollverein brought economic co-operation between the states
    - the Zollverein allowed good roads and railways to be built linking the states together and allowing ideas of common identity to spread through travel between the states
    - economic growth in Germany strengthened the political position of the German states
    - Prussia's dominance over the Zollverein/Austria's exclusion from the Zollverein strengthened Prussia's influence over the German states.

2. The candidate describes why Austria had lost her leading position in Germany by 1860 by referring to evidence such as:

    from the source:
    - Austria unable to replace skilful Metternich
    - Austria lost an important ally in Russia
    - defeat by France destroyed Austria's strong military reputation
    - industrialisation in Prussia had increased her economic growth and strengthened her position

    from recall:
    - Austria's attempt to replace the Zollverein failed
    - Austria was behind Prussia in industrial output/Prussia produced more than any country except Britain
    - the railway network improved Prussia's military efficiency
    - Prussia's economic strength increased as head of the Zollverein (Custom's Union)

3. The candidate compares the sources by referring to evidence such as:
    The sources agree

Source B	Source C
his first task was going to be the re-organisation of the army to strengthen Prussia's position in Germany	it was Bismarck's decision to reform the army which made Prussia dominant in Germany
Bismarck wanted to seize an excuse to create war against Austria	Bismarck planned to force Austria to go to war with Prussia
Bismarck wanted to control the smaller states and unite Germany under Prussian leadership	Bismarck aimed to extend Prussian power over the other German states to unite them with Prussia at the head

Context 10: The Red Flag: Lenin and the Russian Revolution, 1894–1921

1. The candidate describes the hardships faced by industrial workers in Russia before 1914 by referring to evidence such as:
    - wages were low and working conditions were poor
    - working hours were very long/12 hour shifts
    - high number of deaths from accidents and work related health problems/poor diet
    - poor living conditions/shared rooms in tenement blocks/barrack style buildings next to factories
    - no privacy or private space/shared beds occupied in shifts/curtains in place of walls
    - under surveillance by Okhrana/police spies infiltrated the unions
    - did not have full voting rights
    - strikes/protests often put down by police or government troops eg Bloody Sunday, Lena Goldfields
    - food shortages.

2. The candidate describes why the Russian Royal Family had become increasingly unpopular by 1917 by referring to evidence such as:

    from the source:
    - Nicholas and Alexandra were unwilling to give up autocratic rule
    - Tsar did not let Duma run the country/largely ignored it
    - Tsar left Alexandra in charge of the government which was disastrous
    - Alexandra was influenced by Rasputin to sack ministers.

    from recall:
    - Tsar took personal charge at the Front so was personally blamed for the heavy losses/general impact of war
    - Alexandra was German and was thought by some to be a spy
    - Rasputin was thought to be Alexandra's lover and this brought Royal Family into disrepute
    - Alexandra ignored the growing problems faced by the workers.

3. The candidate compares the sources by referring to evidence such as:
    The sources disagree

Source B	Source C
he made rousing speeches and raised morale/ensured the Red Army was well fed and properly armed	he ordered the execution of one in every ten men in the regiment, as a warning to the rest
he was an inspirational leader and was dedicated to the cause	he was a ruthless leader who used strict discipline
over 5 million men joined the Red Army of their own free will	he forced people to join the Red Army to raise the number of troops

Context 11: Free at Last? Race Relations in the USA, 1918–1968

1. The candidate describes the activities of the Ku Klux Klan in the 1920s and 1930s by referring to evidence such as:
    - campaigned against immigration in the 1920s especially Jews and Roman Catholics
    - acted anonymously eg wore robes and hoods/activities took place at night
    - used violence against opponents eg whippings/beatings/tar and featherings
    - used intimidation of black Americans eg fiery crosses/house burnings
    - lynching of black Americans ie murder of black Americans accused of committing crimes
    - infiltrated government eg 16 senators gained election in 1920s with KKK help
    - infiltrated state officials and police – especially in the Deep South and Oklahoma, Indiana and Texas
    - large peaceful demonstrations eg 1928 March down Pennsylvania Avenue, Washington DC

- KKK was less active after 1925 as membership fell following allegations of corruption amongst Klan leadership
- attempted to disrupt trade unions which admitted black members eg CIO.

2. The candidate compares the sources by referring to evidence such as:
The sources agree

Source A	Source B
• King's first step towards becoming the leading figure in the civil rights movement	• King became a leader of the civil rights movement
• Courts decided that segregation on Montgomery's buses was illegal	• US Supreme Court announced Alabama's bus segregation laws were illegal
• Montgomery remained a segregated town – white only theatres, pool rooms, restaurants	• most other services in Montgomery remained segregated

3. The candidate describes why Malcolm X was opposed to non-violent protest by referring to evidence such as:

from the source:
- Malcolm's mistreatment in his youth gave him different attitudes towards Whites from Martin Luther King
- he became influenced by the ideas of Elijah Mohammed who preached hatred of white people
- he believed that support of non-violence was a sign that Black people were still living in mental slavery
- he believed violent language and threats would frighten the authorities into action.

from recall:
- Malcolm X claimed that even Whites who appeared friendly were 'wolves in sheep's clothing'
- he believed that non-violence deprived Black people of their right to self-defence
- he claimed that peaceful protest gained little for most Black people
- he didn't think non-violent campaigns tackled the problems for Blacks in northern cities.

Context 12: The Road to War, 1933-193

1. The candidate explains why Hitler wanted to rearm Germany in the 1930s by referring to evidence such as:

from the source:
- Germany was defenceless
- surrounded by hostile countries
- strong Germany would restore balance of power
- to defend Europe from the threat from the east.

from recall:
- France had built the Maginot Line
- Communism/Russia was a threat to Germany/Europe
- an army would be to unite all Germans/create Greater Germany/gain Lebensraum
- an army would be necessary to regain territory lost at Versailles
- gain popularity and economic growth for Germany.

2. The candidate compares the sources by referring to evidence such as:
The sources disagree

Source B	Source C
• Sudeten German should return to Germany	• Sudetenland had never been part of Germany
• Sudeten Germans resented being part of Czechoslovakia since 1919	• Sudeten German unrest originated in early 1930s
• persecuted as ethnic minority	• treated with respect

3. The candidate describes events in 1939 that led to the outbreak of war between Britain and Germany by referring to evidence such as:
- Germany invaded Czechoslovakia in March 1939 breaking the Munich Agreement
- Great Britain sped up her rearmaments programme/led to conscription
- Hitler demanded the return of Danzig from Poland
- Germany demanded permission to build a road and railway line through Poland
- Britain promised to defend Poland if she were attacked
- August 1939 Germany and Russia signed the Nazi-Soviet Non-Aggression Pact which left Hitler free to attack Poland
- September Germany invaded Poland
- Britain declared war on Germany.

Context 13: In the Shadow of the Bomb: The Cold War, 1945–1985

1. The candidate describes the events which led to the formation of the Warsaw Pact in 1955 by referring to evidence such as:
- the Soviet take-over of Eastern European countries had increased tension between East and West
- Soviet Union felt threatened by the West's actions – Churchill's Iron Curtain speech/offer of Marshall aid to all European countries
- Berlin airlift had increased tension between East and West
- Allies merged their zones to form West Germany, formalising the division of Germany, increasing tension
- NATO was formed in 1949
- NATO expanded in 1951 to include Greece and Turkey
- USA forms SEATO in 1954
- USA forms CENTO in 1955
- West Germany joined NATO in 1955
- Soviet Union felt increasingly surrounded
- Soviet Union saw the Warsaw Pact as a means of exerting its control over Eastern Europe.

2. The candidate compares the sources by referring to evidence such as:
The sources disagree

Source A	Source B
• the Soviet Union had the idea of installing a small number of nuclear missiles on Cuba	• Americans believed that the Soviets planned to place a large number of their missiles in Cuba
• Khrushchev did not want to start a war	• Americans regarded Soviet action as a warlike act
• purpose of missiles was just to defend Cuba from American attack	• missiles had an offensive purpose – pointed directly at major American cities

3. The candidate explains why American became involved in a full scale war in Vietnam by 1964 by referring to evidence such as:

from the source:
- France asked America for assistance in Vietnam
- America feared that Vietnam would become communist
- they believed that they could establish a friendly government in South Vietnam, under the leadership of President Diem
- America feared that a civil war was developing in South Vietnam.

from recall:
- America was increasingly concerned about the influence of China in south-east Asia
- there was a widespread belief in the Domino Theory
- there was a fear that other countries eg Thailand, Laos, Burma, Cambodia even New Zealand and Australia could fall to communism
- there was a general concern that America was falling behind in the Cold War at this time and needed to make a stand against communism
- 'advisors' had been in Vietnam to support the government of Diem since the early 1960s
- Gulf of Tonkin incident led America to become involved in a full scale war in Vietnam.

HISTORY INTERMEDIATE 2 2012

PART 1 THE SHORT ESSAY

Scottish and British

Context 1: Murder in the Cathedral: Crown, Church and People, 1154–1173

1. The candidate explains the importance of monasteries in the twelfth century by referring to evidence such as:
   - monasteries were a place of worship/monks prayed for the souls of those who had died
   - monasteries had infirmaries, used to look after the sick
   - monastic gardens were used to grow herbs for medicine
   - monasteries were used as a place to stay by pilgrims
   - monasteries were centres of learning/had vast libraries and chronicles
   - monasteries were a place of education, used to prepare boys for a career in the Church
   - monastic land was used to rear sheep and was an important part of the wool industry
   - monasteries were part of the feudal system, providing land in return for service.

Context 2: Wallace, Bruce and the Wars of Independence, 1286–1328

2. The candidate explains why the Scots won the Battle of Stirling Bridge by referring to evidence such as:
   - the English were over-confident and were not careful about what they did
   - the English were led by the Earl of Surrey who had relinquished command to Cressingham who was not an experienced military commander
   - the English did not have their best men who were fighting in France
   - the English wasted time on the morning of the battle by holding a knighting ceremony
   - the English re-called men who had crossed the bridge several times and so gave away their plan
   - the English delayed even longer by trying to start negotiations with the Scots
   - the English argued about using the bridge or a nearby ford and wasted more time
   - Cressingham rejected good advice in his haste to win the battle
   - the bridge was narrow and created a bottleneck
   - the ground on the Scottish side of the bridge did not suit the English way of fighting
   - the Scots (Wallace and Murray) timed their attack perfectly
   - the Scots captured the end of the bridge and blocked English attempts at reinforcement and/or retreat
   - the Scots drove the English into wet ground where they could be massacred
   - the English archers could not fire arrows in case they killed their own men.

Context 3: Mary, Queen of Scots and the Scottish Reformation, 1540s–1587

3. The candidate explains why Queen Elizabeth kept Mary, Queen of Scots, in prison for so long by referring to evidence such as:
   - Elizabeth did not want to set Mary free in case she returned to Scotland where she could cause trouble for Elizabeth by making it a base for French and Roman Catholic activities
   - Elizabeth was supporting the Protestants who were ruling Scotland
   - Mary was Elizabeth's heir and she did not trust her

- Elizabeth knew that there were plots to kill her and to make Mary Queen of England
- Mary was a Roman Catholic and Elizabeth wanted England to remain Protestant
- Mary had strong French connections and Elizabeth was an enemy of France
- Elizabeth was worried about executing Mary because it could cause trouble internationally
- Elizabeth did not want to execute a queen in case it gave the idea that queens could be killed
- Elizabeth did not want to execute her closest relation.

Context 4: The Coming of the Civil War, 1603–1642

4. The candidate explains why James VI and I faced serious problems over religion by referring to evidence such as:
   - demands of moderate Puritans for changes to the Church
   - the Millenary petition 1603 was presented to James requesting changes to practices in the Church, most were rejected
   - demands of Presbyterians for removal of Bishops
   - Archbishop Bancroft's Canons stated that the clergy had to subscribe to 39 articles and the Prayer Book. James licensed the Canons which provoked the clergy
   - Roman Catholic demands for more lenient treatment
   - activities of Catholic extremists – the Gunpowder Plot
   - reaction to the 'Spanish Match' – negotiations for a marriage between Charles, James's son and the Spanish Infanta, Maria, went on for almost a decade and led to distrust amongst English Protestants
   - Direction of Preachers issued by James in 1622 gave Bishops more control which worried Puritans
   - many in Parliament were offended at James's belief in the Divine Right of Kings.

Context 5: "Ane End of Ane Auld Sang": Scotland and the Treaty of Union, 1690s–1715

5. The candidate explains why support for the Jacobites grew between 1707 and 1715 by referring to evidence such as:
   - Queen Anne (d.1714) was to be followed by the Hanoverians
   - Hanoverians were seen as "foreign" compared to the "Scottish" Stuarts
   - the Hanoverian succession alarmed Roman Catholics
   - James Stuart (James VIII, the Old Pretender) was old enough to rule/lead a campaign
   - many Scots regretted the loss of their Parliament in 1707
   - the Union had not brought the expected benefits
   - the Equivalent had not been paid promptly nor in cash
   - new taxes in Scotland were resented
   - Scottish measures, currency etc had been replaced with English ones.

Context 6: Immigrants and Exiles: Scotland, 1830s–1930s

6. The candidate explains why so many Scots emigrated between 1830 and 1900 by referring to evidence such as:
   - the Highland Clearances
   - potato famine in the 1840s
   - the decline of herring, kelp and whisky industries
   - further clearances due to deer estates and sporting activities
   - changes in lowland farming such as mechanisation
   - rising cost of farmland in Scotland/cheap land overseas
   - industrial revolution led to less demand for skilled labour
   - activities of emigration societies/assisted passages
   - use of agents/posters to encourage emigration
   - letters from relatives
   - higher wages overseas eg servants.

Context 7: From the Cradle to the Grave? Social Welfare in Britain, 1890s–1951

7. The candidate explains why the Labour Government reforms of 1945-1951 were important in creating a welfare state by referring to evidence such as:
   - welfare state involved care from the "cradle to the grave" which was encouraged by Beveridge and followed by Labour
   - National Insurance Act offered comprehensive coverage
   - National Assistance Act would cover those left out
   - National Health Service was offered free to everyone
   - National Health Service offered many services eg hospitals, dentistry, opticians, prescriptions
   - attempts to build more houses eg 200,000 a year between 1945 and 1951
   - new towns led to a healthier environment
   - secondary education for all was offered, leaving age raised to 15, massive school building programme started
   - Labour extended on previous Liberal and wartime reforms
   - significant progress was made in dealing with the problems identified in the Beveridge Report.

Context 8: Campaigning for Change: Social Change in Scotland, 1900s–1979

8. The candidate explains why Scots had improved access to leisure opportunities by 1939 by referring to evidence such as:
   - hours of work were restricted by law/most workers had at least half day holidays/people had more time for leisure
   - people had more money to spend as wages improved/economy recovered
   - purpose built cinemas attracted huge audiences so more were built/104 in Glasgow alone/cinema entry very cheap for children/use of jam jars
   - hire purchase schemes enabled most households to buy a radio
   - cheaper/increased availability of transport enabled people to take day trips to the countryside or travel to support a team/go hostelling, camping, etc
   - new large football stadiums allowed thousands to attend matches/support their teams
   - town councils built libraries and museums/sports facilities such as ice rinks and golf courses which were cheap to use
   - Scottish comics for children such as the Beano and Dandy became available/more women's magazines produced/cheap paperbacks became available
   - many dance halls/ice cream parlours/cafés opened as meeting places, especially for young people.

Context 9: A Time of Troubles: Ireland, 1900–1923

9. The candidate explains why a civil war broke out in Ireland in 1922 by referring to evidence such as:
   - legacy/impact of pre-war Home Rule Bill – many Irish people expected Home Rule Bill to be implemented when war ended
   - the terms of the Anglo-Irish Treaty split the Nationalists
   - the pro-Treaty group eg Collins and Griffith accepted partition
   - the anti-Treaty group eg De Valera wanted Ireland to be completely independent
   - the anti-Treaty group took over the Four Courts and other buildings in Dublin
   - they refused to obey the provisional government
   - they did not accept the election results which showed support for the Treaty
   - the pro-Treaty group demanded the Four Courts be returned
   - when the Four Courts was not returned, the pro-Treaty group opened fire.

European and World

Context 1: The Norman Conquest, 1060–1153

10. The candidate explains why Duke William won the Battle of Hastings in 1066 by referring to evidence such as:
    - Normans had a larger army which included many horsemen and archers
    - Saxon army fought only on foot with axes and swords
    - Saxons had already had to fight a long and bloody battle at Stamford Bridge
    - Harold had lost many of his best men
    - Harold had little time to prepare for the battle having marched straight from the north
    - Saxon army tired from marching long distance
    - morale was poor in Harold's army and some of his soldiers deserted before the battle began
    - Saxons believed that the Normans were retreating and broke ranks to pursue them
    - William lifted his helmet to dispel the rumour that he had been killed
    - Norman knights turned to attack the disorganised Saxons
    - Harold was killed in the fighting.

Context 2: The Cross and the Crescent: The First Crusade, 1096–1125

11. The candidate explains the reasons why the People's Crusade failed to capture Jerusalem by referring to evidence such as:
    - the peasant Crusaders were not trained soldiers/their army included women and children
    - the Crusaders had limited supplies and very few weapons
    - Peter the Hermit was not a good military leader/lacked experience
    - their poor reputation across Europe meant people were unwilling to help them
    - the Crusaders fought the Byzantine army at Nis and many Crusaders were killed
    - the Crusaders lost their supplies and money
    - the Crusaders ignored Emperor Alexius' advice to wait for the knights
    - the Crusaders argued amongst one another and split into different groups
    - the Crusaders were defeated by the Turks.

Context 3: War, Death and Revolt in Medieval Europe, 1328–1436

12. The candidate explains why Joan of Arc was burnt at the stake in 1431 by referring to evidence such as:
    - she had contributed to the revival of French spirits in the Hundred Years War
    - she had shown open defiance towards the English eg sent messages telling them to leave France or be defeated
    - she claimed that God had called her to drive the English out of France
    - she played a major role in bringing about the coronation of the Dauphin at Reims
    - she had contributed to the war effort eg she raised the siege of Orleans
    - she was captured at Compiegne and handed over to Bishop Cauchon
    - Charles VII refused to ransom Joan or save her
    - she was put on trial by a religious court
    - she was accused of wearing men's clothes
    - she was accused of inventing visions
    - she refused to deny that she had been an instrument of God
    - she was condemned as a heretic.

Context 4: New Worlds: Europe in the Age of Expansion, 1480s–1530s

13. The candidate explains the reasons why European monarchs encouraged voyages of exploration by referring to evidence such as:
    - their personal prestige would be enhanced by successful voyages
    - they would achieve lasting fame beyond their deaths
    - they and their countries would become more wealthy
    - they would increase their territory and influence
    - they would have new sources of natural resources and mineral wealth/slaves and workers
    - they would have new trade opportunities
    - they would be able to spread Christianity/save souls
    - they would add to the world's knowledge
    - they would keep up with European rivals, eg Portugal v Spain, France v England
    - personal interest/curiosity of monarchs such as Henry of Portugal, Isabella of Spain, Francis I of France.

Context 5: "Tea and Freedom": The American Revolution, 1763–1783

14. The candidate explains the reasons why many colonists were unhappy with British rule by 1775 by referring to evidence such as:
    - the colonists were unhappy with the imposition of laws and taxes which were seen as unjust
    - the passing of the Stamp Act and the Townshend Act 1760s had been very unpopular measures
    - details of specific points of these acts explaining unhappiness
    - they resented being taxed without representation
    - events such as the Boston Massacre and the Boston Tea Party led to an increase in anti-British feeling among colonists/unhappiness at high handed actions of British government
    - the colonists were angered by the passing of the Intolerable Acts
    - the colonists were unhappy with the continuing presence of British soldiers in the colonies
    - the colonists were further angered by the passing of the Quartering Act
    - some colonists were frustrated that the British were stopping them from moving further west
    - some colonists felt that the policies of the British government were damaging trade.

Context 6: "This Accursed Trade": The British Slave Trade and its Abolition, 1770–1807

15. The candidate explains the reasons why so many people in Britain continued to defend the slave trade by referring to evidence such as:
    - the slave trade brought wealth to Britain
    - the slave trade brought employment to Britain in areas such as shipbuilding, ports, mills
    - cities such as Bristol, Liverpool and Glasgow relied on the slave trade
    - the products of the slave trade – cotton, tobacco, sugar – were in great demand
    - involvement in the slave trade helped Britain to remain a world power
    - the slave trade was seen as a valuable training ground for the Royal Navy
    - some MPs were slave owners and could influence other MPs
    - many MPs were being bribed to ensure that they continued to give their support for the continuation of the slave trade
    - the slave trade still enjoyed the support of the King.

Context 7: Citizens! The French Revolution, 1789–1794

16. The candidate explains the reasons why Louis XVI was sentenced to death in 1792 by referring to evidence such as:
    - unpopularity of the monarchy due to the flight from Varennes
    - Louis was against the constitution and would not co-operate with the new government
    - Louis was accused of wanting France to lose the war
    - Brunswick Manifesto worked against the French monarchy
    - Louis was found guilty of supporting France's enemies and of "spilling French blood"
    - victories at Valmy and Verdun weakened Louis' position
    - Jacobins, supported by the mob, demanded the death of the King
    - allowing the King to live might encourage French royalists or Prussia and Austria
    - the Convention voted for the death by a large majority.

Context 8: Cavour, Garibaldi and the Making of Italy, 1815–1870

17. The candidate explains the reasons why Italian nationalism grew between 1815 and 1848 by referring to evidence such as:
    - the impact of the ideas of the French Revolution on Italian intellectuals ie the idea of being a citizen of a united country with its own flag, language, etc
    - the impact of Napoleon Bonaparte's rule on Italy eg abolition of internal customs barriers and the cultivation of national language and literature
    - reaction against the Vienna settlement of 1815 and the increased influence of Austria over Italy
    - Austrian domination in Italian military, legal and cultural aspects united many Italians against Austria
    - activities of the secret societies such as the Carbonari and Adelfi
    - the impact of the Romantic movement to stir nationalist feeling eg poets, composers and writers such as Leopardi, Verdi and Pellico
    - activities of Young Italy led by Mazzini
    - ideas of philosophers such as Gioberti and Balbo who came up with moderate ideas for a united Italy
    - the ambitions of the business classes who demanded unity through a customs league similar to the German Zollverein.

Context 9: Iron and Blood? Bismarck and the Creation of the German Empire, 1815–1871

18. The candidate explains the reasons why Prussia was successful in the wars of unification by referring to evidence such as:
    - Prussian army reforms of 1863 helped strengthen the army
    - resources for war were strengthened due to industrial and economic growth aided by the Zollverein
    - development of a modern railway network in Prussia allowed for ease of troop movements
    - Bismarck ensured the neutrality of Russia when Prussia went to war with Austria
    - French neutrality in the Austrian war was ensured when Bismarck promised Napoleon III territorial gains
    - Italy was promised land in Venetia in return for assisting Prussia in the war with Austria
    - the leniency towards Austria in the Treaty of Vienna ensured Austria would not seek revenge and ally with France
    - Prussian army was strengthened with the acquisition of the armies of the North German Confederation after 1867
    - Prussia was able to use troops, railways and resources of the southern German states when France attacked Prussia
    - Prussian army weapons, tactics and leadership (eg von Moltke, Von Roon) were superior
    - weaknesses of opponents.

Context 10: The Red Flag: Lenin and the Russian Revolution, 1894–1921

19. The candidate explains the reasons why the Russian people were so discontented by February 1917 by referring to evidence such as:
    - the war was going badly; millions had died/soldiers were reluctant to fight
    - peasants became angry about the conscription/loss of so many young men
    - shortages of workers on the land meant food was in short supply, especially in the cities
    - poor organisation of transport stopped fuel and materials getting to the towns
    - inflation was very high; 300% increase in cost of living
    - many people were working long hours for the war effort BUT many people were out of work as factories ran out of materials
    - the winter was very cold and people were freezing because of lack of food and fuel
    - middle classes wanted more say in running the government
    - the Tsar and Tsarina were blamed for the failure to win, people had no faith in their rulers
    - suspicion over Tsarina's German nationality
    - concern at the influence of Rasputin on Tsarina.

Context 11: Free at Last? Race Relations in the USA, 1918–1968

20. The candidate explains why the Ku Klux Klan was so powerful in the South in the 1920s by referring to evidence such as:
    - huge organisation – estimated to have 3 million members in 1924
    - it was surrounded in secrecy which made it difficult to oppose
    - it had effective methods of intimidation – eg fiery cross
    - it was a terrorist organisation which supported the use of violence to achieve its aims
    - they kidnapped, whipped, mutilated people if they did not do what the Klan wanted
    - the Klan lynched many Black Americans to show their supremacy
    - important members of the community such as police, judges and politicians were members of the Klan
    - the Klan held great marches in cities such as Washington to show their strength
    - the Klan was deeply rooted in the South, eg origins went back to the Civil War
    - the Klan was supported by many Americans in the South who shared its views.

Context 12: The Road to War, 1933–1939

21. The candidate explains the reasons why Hitler wanted to break the Treaty of Versailles in the 1930s by referring to evidence such as:
    - the Germans hated the Treaty
    - Hitler wanted to show that he was a strong leader
    - he wanted revenge for the humiliation of the Treaty
    - he wanted Germany to be treated fairly/equal to other countries
    - he wanted to build up the German armed forces
    - he wanted to take back the land that Germany had lost, eg Poland/Polish Corridor
    - he wanted to remilitarize the Rhineland
    - he wanted Germany to join with Austria
    - he had promised to destroy the Treaty in "Mein Kampf".

Context 13: In the Shadow of the Bomb: The Cold War, 1945–1985

22. The candidate explains the reasons why the Cold War had broken out between 1945 and 1950 by referring to evidence such as:
    - there were deep ideological differences between the USA (capitalist) and the Soviet Union (communist)
    - American President Truman and the Soviet leader Stalin did not trust each other
    - the distrust between the USA and the Soviet Union intensified when the Americans developed the atomic bomb without informing the Soviets
    - after the Second World War the Americans and Soviets were no longer united by a common enemy
    - the Soviet takeover of Eastern Europe had angered America and its allies
    - Churchill's 'Iron Curtain' speech had angered the Soviets
    - the Marshall Plan contributed to the divisions in Europe
    - there were arguments between East and West over the fate of Germany/ Berlin in the years after the Second World War
    - Berlin Blockade, 1948-1949, deepened the divisions between East and West
    - the establishment of NATO by America and its allies in 1949 caused further division.

PART 2 HISTORICAL STUDY

Scottish and British

Context 1: Murder in the Cathedral: Crown, Church and People, 1154–1173

1. The candidate explains why Henry II had problems when he became king in 1154 by referring to evidence such as:

    from the source:
    - barons had increased their wealth and power
    - barons had private armies/were stealing land and valuables
    - barons had refused to pay taxes
    - barons rebelled against the king.

    from recall:
    - barons had built illegal castles
    - sheriffs were corrupt and had been keeping fines which belonged to the king
    - there was no common law within the empire
    - there was no common language within the empire
    - the Church had increased its authority/Church courts had become powerful.

2. The candidate describes the duties of a medieval baron by referring to evidence such as:
    - barons took an oath of fealty/promised to be loyal and serve the king
    - barons provided knights for the king's army
    - barons paid higher taxes during times of war
    - barons were an important part of the feudal system and provided land for knights/peasants
    - barons protected those who lived on their land
    - barons were members of the king's council and offered advice on how to govern the country
    - barons enforced the king's law at local level
    - trusted barons became sheriffs and collected fines and taxes for the king.

3. The candidate compares the sources by referring to evidence such as:
   The sources fully agree

Source B	Source C
• the knights dragged Becket away and told him he was under arrest	• the knights told Becket he was the king's prisoner and forced him from the altar
• Becket knelt down and said he was ready to die for God	• Becket said he was willing to be a martyr and began to pray
• the knights drew their swords and in the scuffle injured Edward Grim.	• Edward Grim tried to protect Becket but he was attacked and his arm was badly cut.

Context 2: Wallace, Bruce and the Wars of Independence, 1286–1328

1. The candidate compares the sources by referring to evidence such as:
   The sources disagree

Source A	Source B
• Balliol claimed he was descended from the eldest line of the family of David, Earl of Huntingdon	• it did not matter that Balliol was descended from the eldest of Earl David's daughters
• it did not matter that he was a generation younger than Bruce	• Bruce was one generation closer to royalty than Balliol
• feudal law of primogeniture always supported the eldest line of a family.	• the feudal law of primogeniture did not apply to kingdoms.

2. The candidate explains why Balliol was a failure as King of Scots by referring to evidence such as:

    from the source:
    - King Edward had stripped him of his title publicly
    - the Bruces had never supported him
    - the Scottish nobles felt the need to appoint twelve men to help Balliol
    - Balliol was unable to stop Edward interfering in the government of Scotland.

    from recall:
    - King Edward was determined to act as overlord of Scotland/ Balliol had already accepted Edward as his overlord
    - King Edward heard legal appeals from Scotland
    - Balliol had been defeated at the Battle of Dunbar
    - King Edward took Balliol away as a prisoner.

3. The candidate describes how Robert Bruce made all the Scots accept him as king by referring to evidence such as:
    - he murdered Comyn
    - he ruined the Comyns by destroying their lands
    - he destroyed the power of the Comyns' friends/allies/connections eg the MacDougalls
    - he captured the castles of his rivals
    - he captured the castles of the English so rivals found themselves without English support
    - he defeated Edward II at Bannockburn removing any hope of further English support
    - he forced nobles to accept him formally as king eg in the Declaration of Arbroath
    - he forced nobles to become either Scottish or English (Treaty of Edinburgh/Northampton).

Context 3: Mary, Queen of Scots and the Scottish Reformation, 1540s–1587

1. The candidate explains why King Henry VIII interfered in Scotland after 1542 by referring to evidence such as:

    from the source:
    *   Henry VIII wanted Mary to marry his son, Edward
    *   Henry VIII wanted to reduce French influence in Scotland
    *   Scotland and England had often been at war
    *   Henry VIII wanted to spread Protestantism.

    from recall:
    *   Mary had become queen in 1542 and she would need a husband
    *   the Scots had broken their agreement to this marriage (Treaty of Greenwich)
    *   Henry VIII tried to enforce the Treaty of Greenwich by invading Scotland
    *   Scottish Protestants wanted/needed the support of England.

2. The candidate describes the problems Mary, Queen of Scots faced when she arrived in Scotland in 1561 by referring to evidence such as:
    *   she was a woman and many Scots (eg Knox) did not think a female could rule
    *   she was young and lacked experience
    *   she was Roman Catholic and Scotland had only recently become a Protestant country
    *   Protestants worried that she would restore Catholicism/Roman Catholics hoped she would restore Catholicism
    *   she had been brought up in France and many feared a return of French influence (Huntley's rebellion)
    *   nobles had been running the country and they might not want to take orders
    *   nobles feared they would lose their jobs to rivals or Frenchmen
    *   there would be problems finding a husband for her – could arouse rivalries
    *   Elizabeth of England was wary because Mary was her closest living relative and claimed to be Queen of England.

3. The candidate compares the sources by referring to evidence such as:
    The sources agree

Source B	Source C
• Mary's supporters fought for several years	• Mary's supporters did not give up until 1573
• death of Moray and Lennox	• two regents were killed
• capture of Edinburgh Castle 1573.	• Edinburgh Castle forced to surrender 1573.

Context 4: The Coming of the Civil War, 1603–1642

1. The candidate explains why there were difficulties between James VI and I and the English Parliament between 1603 and 1625 by referring to evidence such as:

    from the source:
    *   James viewed Parliament as argumentative and unco-operative
    *   Parliament regarded James to be stubborn and thought he spent too much money
    *   James angered the 1610 Parliament by dismissing them
    *   James again dismissed Parliament in 1614 and angered the nobility by bringing in favourites to find ways of raising money.

    from recall:
    *   Parliament was suspicious of James' perceived Catholic sympathies
    *   James' belief in the Divine Right of Kings offended the House of Commons
    *   James ruled without Parliament from 1614 to 1621
    *   James was criticised for neglecting the business of government in favour of leisure pursuits.

2. The candidate describes the reaction in Scotland to the introduction of the new Prayer Book in 1637 by referring to evidence such as:
    *   riot in St Giles Cathedral: men and women assaulted the Dean of St Giles whilst he was reading from the new Prayer Book
    *   violence provoked elsewhere eg Bishop of Brechin threatened his congregation with two loaded pistols while he read the new service
    *   emergency body known as 'The Tables' was formed to organise opposition, chosen from the Scottish Parliament
    *   petitions sent to Charles 1637-1638
    *   National Covenant for the Defence of True Religion was drawn up in 1638 and circulated for signature
    *   General Assembly of the Kirk abolished Scotland's bishops completely in November 1638
    *   General Assembly of the Kirk banned the Prayer Book, November 1638
    *   Charles' decision to use force in 1638 was met with opposition and resulted in the First Bishops War.

3. The candidate compares the sources by referring to evidence such as:
    The sources fully agree

Source B	Source C
• Strafford accused of High Treason, impeached and later executed	• Parliament accused Strafford of High Treason and pressured Charles to sign his death warrant
• Triennial Act meant new Parliaments every three years, whether the King liked it or not	• an Act ensured regular Parliaments without the King's consent
• Parliament made Ship Money illegal.	• Charles was compelled to agree to the Ship Money Act.

Context 5: "Ane End of Ane Auld Sang": Scotland and the Treaty of Union, 1690s–1715

1. The candidate explains why the Scots invested in the Darien scheme by referring to evidence such as:

    from the source:
    *   prosperity depended on farming which suffered from bad weather and poor soil
    *   Scottish overseas trade was limited
    *   Scots thought that England's prosperity came from its overseas trade based on colonies
    *   Paterson promised them a colony where "trade will increase and money will make money".

    from recall:
    *   the Ill years made Scotland poorer
    *   Scots had seen huge profits made by the East India Company
    *   Scotland did not have any colonies
    *   they were told Darien was in a key location on the Isthmus of Panama between two oceans.

2. The candidate compares the sources by referring to evidence such as:
    The sources agree

Source B	Source C
• some Scots believed trading with England's colonies would make Scotland a richer country	• angry that they could not make money by trading with England's colonies
• Scotland's trade (with France) was badly affected by England's frequent wars	• they wanted to reduce the bad effects of England's war on Scotland's trade (Wine Act)
• The Act of Security offered a shared monarch in return for access to England's colonies.	• they demanded access to England's colonies in return for sharing a monarch.

3. The candidate describes how Queen Anne's government won support for the Act of Union by referring to evidence such as:
    • it promised "the Equivalent"
    • it paid arrears of wages etc only to those who supported the Union
    • it insisted that government officers etc supported the Union
    • it sent Argyll and then Queensberry to organise support for the Union
    • it offered titles to nobles who supported the Union
    • it paid bribes to others to secure their support
    • it offered government jobs (civil service/army) only to those who supported the Union
    • it sent spies and agents (eg Defoe) to work for the Union
    • it made it clear that it had military forces in northern England and Ireland ready to take action.

Context 6: Immigrants and Exiles: Scotland, 1830s–1930s

1. The candidate describes the "pull" factors which attracted Irish immigrants to Scotland by referring to evidence such as:
    • work was available on farms especially at harvest time
    • there was work to be found in cotton/textile factories
    • there was work in building canals and railways
    • there was work for the whole family
    • there was work in the coal and iron ore mines
    • wages were higher in Scotland
    • housing was available in growing towns and cities
    • many Irish had already settled in Scotland which encouraged more to come/ letters home from Ireland
    • Scotland was close and fares were cheap.

2. The candidate explains why the Catholic Church was important to many Irish immigrants in the nineteenth century by referring to evidence such as:

    from the source:
    • the church gave them a place to worship/sense of security
    • they could be baptised, married and buried
    • priests would listen to problems
    • church was the centre of social life/chance to meet fellow countrymen.

    from recall:
    • priests could write letters and read letters from home
    • priests could help with jobs and housing
    • Catholic church could provide charity for the poorest immigrants
    • provided social events – dances, lectures, football clubs.
    • built schools to provide education.

3. The candidate compares the sources by referring to evidence such as:
    The sources completely disagree

Source B	Source C
• land is of poor quality and always will be	• has prepared good land and preparing more
• area is remote/he is lonely	• community is doing well/fellow immigrants have already built a church and a school-house
• wants to return to Scotland.	• this is the best place in the world.

Context 7: From the Cradle to the Grave? Social Welfare in Britain, 1890s–1951

1. The candidate describes the problems facing the poor between 1890-1905 by referring to evidence such as:
    • low wages and irregular work/earnings
    • unable to afford medical attention
    • poverty led to poor housing and overcrowding
    • poor diet/children often malnourished
    • relied on charities to provide help
    • elderly and the destitute were forced into the workhouse/poorhouse
    • education suffered as children were needed to work and earn money for the family
    • attitude towards the poor was that they had to help themselves/they got no help from the government.

2. The candidate compares the sources by referring to evidence such as:
    The sources agree fully

Source A	Source B
• medical care was provided for the workers, not wives and children	• health insurance benefits did not extend to the worker's family
• pensions only covered people over 70	• pensions were only available to those over 70
• benefits only lasted a short time and the amounts paid were small.	• benefits were often not enough to live on.

3. The candidate explains why the Beveridge Report was popular with so many people by referring to evidence such as:

    from the source:
    • the system was open to everyone regardless of their wealth
    • there would be no return to the hated Means Test
    • the government would ensure that everyone had a reasonable standard of living
    • the National Health Service would be free to everyone meaning that poor people could receive good medical attention.

    from recall:
    • proposed a fair insurance scheme where everyone would pay the same contribution to receive the same benefits
    • proposed to simplify insurance benefits
    • took away the stigma of receiving state help
    • promised every family an allowance for every child.

Context 8: Campaigning for Change: Social Change in Scotland, 1900s–1979

1. The candidate describes the peaceful activities of women campaigning for the vote by referring to evidence such as:
   • held public meetings
   • door to door canvassing
   • organised letters/petitions to MPs and Parliament
   • arranged meetings with MPs and Cabinet ministers
   • organised fund raising events eg bazaars
   • recruited women at the workplace/spoke at trade union meetings
   • published newspapers and pamphlets
   • took part in peaceful demonstrations eg Coronation March, Women's Pilgrimage.

2. The candidate compares the sources by referring to evidence such as:
   The sources agree fully

Source A	Source B
• decline of shipbuilding had a knock on effect on the iron and steel industries	• disastrous effect on shipbuilding hurt coal, iron and steel industries
• Scotland's manufacturers failed to invest in new technology	• better technology made foreign goods cheaper
• overseas markets were lost during the war.	• customers overseas had been lost.

3. The candidate explains why there were more employment opportunities for women after the Second World War by referring to evidence such as:

   from the source:
   • women seemed suited to work in the developing light industries, such as making cash registers and typewriters
   • non-unionised women workers popular as not expected to cause trouble over wages or hours
   • government created jobs in the new NHS and welfare agencies which were attractive to women
   • expanding service industries also created further jobs open to women.

   from recall:
   • no requirement to pay women equally so cheaper to employ
   • more part-time jobs which attracted women
   • changing social attitudes enabled more married women to go out to work
   • better educational opportunities enabled women to enter a wider range of jobs.

Context 9: A Time of Troubles: Ireland, 1900–1923

1. The candidate compares the sources by referring to evidence such as:
   The sources agree fully

Source A	Source B
• fifty eight officers threatened to resign if sent to fight	• officers based in Dublin said they would rather leave the army than serve in Ulster
• the soldiers could not be punished as they had the support and sympathy of the army	• the Mutiny was very popular and as a result the officers could not be disciplined
• the government was forced to accept defeat.	• The government had no choice but to give in to the soliders' demands.

2. The candidate describes the events of the 1916 Easter Rising by referring to evidence such as:
   • rebels captured a number of buildings in the centre of Dublin
   • Tricolour flag flown from the GPO building
   • extra soldiers/artillery brought in to help the British
   • rising lasted for a week
   • majority of Dubliners did not support the rebels
   • rebels cut off/surrounded by British
   • British brought in 12,000 extra soldiers to fight
   • British used gunboat to shell the rebels' position
   • soldiers on both sides were injured or killed
   • rebels surrendered
   • leaders executed.

3. The candidate explains why the Anglo-Irish War began in 1919 by referring to evidence such as:

   from the source:
   • Sinn Fein declared independence/established the Dáil
   • Sinn Fein refused to acknowledge British laws and officials/set up their own administrative system
   • Sinn Fein too dangerous to ignore
   • the Dáil was recognised as the official government and its influence grew.

   from recall:
   • Sinn Fein organised, trained and armed Irish Volunteers
   • 28 Unionist MPs refused to go to Dáil/wanted Irish assembly closed
   • British used armed force to try to stop the Irish
   • Irish Volunteers killed two members of the Royal Irish Constabulary, sparking violence.

PART 3 HISTORICAL STUDY

European and World

Context 1: The Norman Conquest, 1060-1153

1. The candidate evaluates the usefulness of the source by referring to evidence such as:
   • primary source written during the time of the Norman conquest
   • written by a Norman priest who is clearly biased in favour of Duke William
   • written to show that William was Edward's chosen successor
   • says that Edward promised that William would become the next king.

Maximum 1 mark for commenting on content omission such as:
- Harold was the choice of the English nobles
- Harold claimed that Edward had appointed him as successor in 1066.

2. The candidate explains why King David was deeply influenced by Norman England by referring to evidence such as:

from the source:
- King David was brought up in the court of William Rufus
- William prepared David to become a Norman knight
- he became friends with wealthy Normans
- he became one of the largest landowners in England.

from recall:
- he was brother-in-law to King Henry
- he became Earl of Huntingdon
- he became a close friend of King Henry
- he acted as a royal judge for King Henry.

3. The candidate describes the ways in which King David supported the Church in Scotland by referring to evidence such as:
- he poured wealth derived from trade into the building of abbeys and monasteries
- he gave charters providing land for the church
- he encouraged his nobles to grant land and money to the church
- he brought craftsmen from Europe to help build abbeys and monasteries
- he encouraged new monastic orders to come to Scotland
- he Normanised the Celtic church eg appointed Normans to Celtic bishoprics of St Andrews, Dunkeld and Moray
- he set up or revived bishoprics of Glasgow, Galloway and Dunblane
- he founded great monasteries and abbeys in Scotland such as Melrose, Newbattle and Kinloss
- he appointed churchmen to important positions in his government.

Context 2: The Cross and the Crescent: The First Crusade, 1096–1125

1. The candidate explains why the First Crusade found Antioch difficult to capture by referring to evidence such as:

from the source:
- Antioch had twenty five miles of wall/nearly four hundred towers
- siege machines would be of no use
- the wall around the city had been reinforced
- each tower was well defended by Muslim guards.

from recall:
- Antioch was surrounded by mountains and a river
- Antioch could not be completely blockaded/Muslims could not be starved into surrendering
- the Muslim governor had expelled all Christians from the city in case of treachery
- the Crusaders were low in spirit/many wanted to return home.

2. The candidate evaluates the usefulness of the source by referring to evidence such as:
- primary source written during the First Crusade
- author was an eyewitness/actually saw the events at Antioch
- written to show his happiness at the discovery of the lance/to show that God helped the Crusaders
- says Peter Bartholomew found the Holy Lance/says there was joy and celebration in Antioch.

Maximum of 1 mark for commenting on content omission such as:
- many Crusaders did not believe the Holy Lance was genuine
- Peter Bartholomew was forced to walk over hot coals to prove his innocence.

3. The candidate describes the problems faced by the Crusaders after they captured Jerusalem in 1099 by referring to evidence such as:
- many Crusaders had returned home/there were not enough Crusaders to defend the Crusader states/Latin states
- the Crusader states were far apart and not easy to defend
- the land was infertile/there was a lack of settlers
- the Crusaders lacked supplies eg timber, cotton
- there were no peasants left to farm the land
- the Crusaders were surrounded and outnumbered by Muslims
- the Crusaders needed boats to help them capture the coastline
- the Crusaders often fought among themselves
- the Crusaders needed the help of Italian merchants.

Context 3: War, Death and Revolt in Medieval Europe, 1328–1436

1. The candidate explains why war broke out between England and France in 1337 by referring to evidence such as:

from the source:
- Philip declared that Edward was a disobedient vassal
- Philip took Aquitaine from Edward
- Edward challenged Philip's legitimacy
- Edward decided to press his claim using force.

from recall:
- Edward claimed that he was the rightful king of France
- Philip claimed overlordship of English lands in France
- French attacks had taken place on English merchant shipping in the channel
- Philip invaded Gascony.

2. The candidate describes the events leading up to the Peasants' Revolt in 1381 by referring to evidence such as:
- in the 1360s-1370s English armies suffered humiliating defeats in France
- 1366 – popular preacher John Ball was excommunicated
- 1377 – peasants presented a petition to parliament demanding an end to serfdom
- 1377 – the strong and popular King Edward III was replaced by Richard II who was only 10 years old
- 1377 – imposition of the first Poll Tax to be paid by everyone over 14
- 1380 – new Poll Tax 3 times higher than 1377 tax
- 1381 – Richard Waldegrave made a speech criticising the monarchy
- 1381 – peasants in south east refuse to pay Poll Tax and attack tax collectors
- riots took place in Essex and Kent.

3. The candidate evaluates the usefulness of the source by referring to evidence such as:
- primary source written by someone who is writing about contemporary events
- written by a French chronicler who shows signs of bias against Henry
- written to describe the cruelty of Henry V after the battle
- says that French survivors of the battle were killed on Henry's orders.

Maximum 1 mark for indicating content omission such as:
- wounded French nobles who survived the battle were taken prisoner rather than being killed.

Context 4: New Worlds: Europe in the Age of Expansion, 1480s–1530s

1. The candidate evaluates the usefulness of the source by referring to evidence such as:
   - secondary source written in 1984, a long time after da Gama's voyage
   - author a historian so would have researched the issue/unlikely to be biased
   - to demonstrate da Gama's cruelty to native people
   - burned pilgrims for lack of respect/mutilated innocent fishermen to frighten the king.

   Maximum 1 mark for commenting on content omission such as:
   - da Gama traded successfully with native people – value of spice cargo
   - other explorers also cruel/exploited native people eg Columbus taking slaves.

2. The candidate describes the ways the native people of the Americas were unable to resist the Conquistadors by referring to evidence such as:
   - they had no guns or gunpowder
   - they had no iron weapons or armour
   - they had no horses so only infantry
   - they had no wheeled transport
   - they had fatalistic religions which emphasised death
   - they were divided in the face of a common enemy (other Mexican tribes disliked Aztecs/Incas in succession dispute)
   - their kings did not inspire personal loyalty/tradition of passive obedience to authority
   - their rulers were naïve in trusting the promises of Cortes/Pizarro.

3. The candidate explains why Jacques Cartier was a successful explorer by referring to evidence such as:

   from the source:
   - he made three voyages to unknown waters without losing a ship
   - land he found became the basis for the French colony of Canada
   - he formed friendships with the native people
   - he was trusted to take Donnacona's sons to meet the French king in Paris.

   from recall:
   - explored the Gulf of St Lawrence and sailed up the St Lawrence River
   - kept a detailed record of the people, animals and places he saw
   - journeyed far inland from the Atlantic
   - survived dreadful winter conditions and illness among his crew.

Context 5: "Tea and Freedom": The American Revolution, 1763–1783

1. The candidate evaluates the usefulness of the source by referring to evidence such as:
   - primary source from the trial conducted shortly after the Boston Massacre had taken place
   - evidence from an officer/leader of the British forces who was actually involved in the confrontation with the colonists/possible bias
   - to explain that he was not responsible for the British soldiers firing on colonists/to explain how the British were acting in self defence
   - states there was a general attack on his men/lives were in imminent danger/ he gave no order to fire.

Maximum of 1 mark for commenting on content omission such as:
- the colonists in Boston were furious about the system of taxation imposed upon them by the British and this had caused great tension.

2. The candidate explains why some colonists remained loyal to Britain during the War of Independence by referring to evidence such as:

   from the source:
   - most colonists were of British descent
   - many colonists were becoming wealthy through trade with Britain
   - some loyalists felt that the conflict was the colonists' fault
   - some colonists had a great loyalty to the King.

   from recall:
   - some colonists feared law and order would break down if British rule were overthrown
   - some colonists feared the spread of revolutionary ideas
   - some colonists sought to win favour with the British government
   - individuals like Flora McDonald encouraged Scots colonists to remain loyal to Britain.

3. The candidate describes the ways in which foreign countries helped the colonists in the war against the British by referring to evidence such as:
   - France provided the colonies with finance
   - France provided the colonies with military assistance – soldiers, gunpowder etc
   - the French attacked British colonies in the Caribbean and elsewhere
   - the French harassed British shipping in the Atlantic
   - foreign intervention caused Britain to lose its control of the seas
   - foreign intervention made it more difficult for Britain to reinforce and supply its forces in America
   - Spain distracted Britain by attacking Gibraltar
   - a Franco-Spanish force threatened Britain with invasion in 1779.

Context 6: "This Accursed Trade": The British Slave Trade and its Abolition, 1770–1807

1. The candidate describes the way slave factories operated on the West African coast by referring to evidence such as:
   - slaves were captured by African chiefs to be traded for manufactured goods
   - slaves were held in factories/prisons, often for weeks at a time
   - factories were often heavily fortified to protect them from attack
   - hundreds, sometimes thousands of slaves were imprisoned together
   - slaves were held in chains, they were often beaten and whipped by their captors
   - slaves were examined by surgeons and placed in different categories
   - slave ships sailed to factories to barter/buy slaves
   - preparation for sale to ships' captains
   - slaves were often branded
   - slaves would eventually be transferred onto slave ships for transportation across the Atlantic to America/West Indies.

2. The candidate evaluates the usefulness of the source by referring to evidence such as:
   - secondary source written many years after the end of the slave trade
   - author a historian who is likely to have expertise on the subject/has carried out research

- to show the cruel treatment of the slaves on the middle passage
- slaves were chained/whipped/desperate slaves tried to jump overboard.

Maximum of 1 mark for commenting on content omission such as:
- female slaves were often subject to sexual abuse
- diseased slaves thrown overboard.

3. The candidate explains why William Wilberforce was an important figure in the campaign for the abolition of the slave trade by referring to evidence such as:

from the source:
- Wilberforce became leader of the Society for the Abolition of the Slave Trade
- Wilberforce used evidence gathered by abolitionists to try to persuade Parliament to end the slave trade
- Wilberforce regularly introduced anti-slavery bills in Parliament
- after his failure to win majority support he published even more horrific accounts of the slave trade.

from recall:
- Wilberforce was able to use his influence with Prime Minister Pitt to win support
- Wilberforce's speeches brought great publicity to the cause of the abolition of the slave trade
- Wilberforce helped to convince fellow Christians of the evils of the slave trade
- Wilberforce succeeded in persuading Parliament to end the slave trade in 1807.

Context 7: Citizens! The French Revolution, 1789–1794

1. The candidate describes the problems faced by Louis XVI in 1789 by referring to evidence such as:
- the French government was bankrupt and inefficient
- the taxation system was seen as corrupt and wasteful
- supporting the American War of Independence had been very expensive
- the peasants blamed the King for having to pay most of the taxes
- the workers in the cities blamed the King for poor wages and high food prices
- people were suspicious of Marie Antoinette's nationality
- Marie Antoinette was blamed for spending too much money on luxuries
- the peasants and middle class wanted more power for the Estates General
- there was a spread of new ideas questioning the power of the monarchy.

2. The candidate explains why the Declaration of the Rights of Man was important to the French people by referring to evidence such as:

from the source:
- the Declaration stated that all men were free and equal
- everyone had the right to own property
- people were to do only what the law told them to do
- all people had to obey the law no matter what their status.

from recall:
- governments must be chosen by the people
- only the people had the right to make the laws
- there was to be freedom of speech, press, religion etc
- no one could be arrested unless they had broken a law.

3. The candidate evaluates the usefulness of the source by referring to evidence such as:
- secondary source written long after the events of the Reign of Terror

- written by a British historian who would have conducted research
- to show that Danton was a brave man/to show that the Terror killed good people
- says that Danton held his head high/he will live in the memory of men.

Maximum of 1 mark for commenting on content omission such as:
- a large number of people were killed in the Terror
- Danton had turned against the Terror.

Context 8: Cavour, Garibaldi and the Making of Italy, 1815–1870

1. The candidate describes the events of the 1848-1849 revolutions in Italy by referring to evidence such as:
- January 1848 the first serious disturbances took place in Palermo and other Sicilian towns
- March 1848 smoking riots broke out in Milan after the news of the fall of Metternich
- March 1848 revolution in Venice led to the surrender of the Austrian authorities there
- March 1848 Charles Albert of Piedmont declares war on Austria to rid them from northern Italy
- April 1848 Pope Pius condemns the war against Austria and in May King Ferdinand recalled his troops sent to help Charles Albert
- July 1848 Austrian army defeats the Piedmontese and their allies at the Battle of Custozza
- November 1848 crowds march on the Pope's palace, Pius leaves Rome in secret
- Roman Republic declared in February 1849
- March 1849 Charles Albert renews his war with Austria, is defeated and abdicates
- July 1849 fall of the Roman Republic at the hands of the French
- August 1849 fall of the Venetian Republic at the hands of the Austrians.

2. The candidate explains why Piedmont became the dominant state in Italy after 1850 by referring to evidence such as:

from the source:
- the economy of Piedmont had been modernised and its trade trebled within ten years
- roads and railways were built, meaning raw materials and machinery could be brought in to develop industry
- the port of Genoa had been modernised to help improve trade
- Piedmont became the centre of Italian nationalist thought in the 1850s because of its liberal constitution.

from recall:
- the strength of its army was highly regarded and developed due to industry
- the Sicardi Laws of 1850 controlled the power of the Church and asserted the dominance of the state over the Church
- Cavour helped forge trade treaties with Britain and France
- The Connubio (1851-1852) forged a parliamentary agreement between Cavour and Ratazzi which strengthened Parliament in relation to the crown.

3. The candidate evaluates the usefulness of the source by referring to evidence such as:
- primary source from an eyewitness who knew Garibaldi well
- author was Garibaldi's secretary possible bias
- to show the importance of Garibaldi's leadership/show his contribution to unification
- Garibaldi's strong leadership united Italy.

Maximum of 1 mark for commenting on content omission such as:

- he was a successful military leader who inspired the Red Shirts to victories
- conquest of Sicily and the Southern Campaign.

Context 9: Iron and Blood? Bismarck and the Creation of the German Empire, 1815–1871

1. The candidate evaluates the usefulness of the source by referring to evidence such as:
   - primary source written at the time when nationalist feeling more widespread
   - written by a German living in the Rhineland
   - to show feelings of belonging to the German nation
   - sees Germany as a whole, speaking the same language/united in hatred towards the French.

   Maximum of 1 mark for commenting on content omission such as:
   - growth of economic nationalism eg Zollverein and trade
   - growth of political ideas of liberalism.

2. The candidate explains why the Frankfurt Parliament failed by referring to evidence such as:

   from the source:
   - suffered from a lack of agreed objectives which made decision making difficult
   - took nearly a year to decide on a constitution
   - took nine months to decide on the rights of the German people
   - King Frederick William refused to accept Parliament's offer of the crown.

   from recall:
   - Parliament had no armed forces of its own to enforce decisions
   - Princes refused to accept the resolutions of the Parliament
   - Parliamentarians would not lead a popular revolt against the Princes
   - by 1849 the German princes had regained control.

3. The candidate describes the events of the Franco-Prussian war of 1870-1871 by referring to evidence such as:
   - Bismarck provoked France into war eg the Ems telegram
   - war was declared by France on the North German Confederation in July 1870
   - German armies mobilised quickly and were gathered on the French frontier in eighteen days
   - German army invaded France whilst the French were still mobilising
   - French defeated at Worth and Spichern and forced to retreat
   - by September a French army was trapped at Metz
   - the French army at Sedan, including Napoleon III, were forced to surrender, Napoleon's government was overthrown and the new government decided to fight on
   - 27 October 1870, the French army at Metz were forced to surrender
   - January 1871, the siege of Paris finished with the French surrender
   - peace treaty signed at Frankfurt 10 May 1871.

Context 10: The Red Flag: Lenin and the Russian Revolution, 1894–1921

1. The candidate evaluates the usefulness of the source by referring to evidence such as:
   - secondary source written some years after the revolution OR primary source by a prominent revolutionary who lived under Tsar's regime
   - written by an important Bolshevik who did not know the Tsar personally/likely to be biased against the Tsar
   - to criticise the Tsar/to justify his removal
   - Tsar was unreliable/Tsar was stupid.

Maximum of 1 mark for commenting on content omission such as:

- Tsar had been brought up to be an autocrat
- Tsar was dedicated to his family.

2. The candidate describes the events of Bloody Sunday in January 1905 by referring to evidence such as:
   - striking factory workers in St Petersburg marched to the Winter Palace
   - the march was led by Father Gapon, a police spy
   - the police had asked the marchers to go home/not to march
   - the workers wanted to petition the Tsar about their working conditions/long hours and low pay
   - the crowd was large (200,000) but peaceful and included women and children
   - marchers wore their Sunday clothes, sang hymns and carried icons and pictures of the Tsar
   - the Tsar was not there but the palace and the streets round it were guarded by troops
   - mounted Cossacks at the front charged the marchers
   - soldiers panicked and opened fire, killing and injuring many (between 100 and 1000 depending on source).

3. The candidate explains why the Bolsheviks were able to stay in power in Russia in 1917-1918 by referring to evidence such as:

   from the source:
   - the Congress of Soviets pleased the peasants by declaring that landlords' rights to property were abolished so that the land could be redistributed
   - Sovnarkom was set up and given authority to pass new laws
   - the Bolsheviks allowed the long-awaited elections to the Constitutional Assembly to be held
   - they created a new secret police, the Cheka, to wipe out any counter-revolutionary activity.

   from recall:
   - signed an armistice with Germany and negotiated an end to the war
   - closed down the Constituent Assembly after one meeting as Social Revolutionaries won the majority
   - censored or banned all non-Bolshevik newspapers
   - banned other political parties
   - may also refer to organising Red Army and fighting the civil war.

Context 11: Free at Last? Race Relations in the USA, 1918–1968

1. The candidate describes the ways the Civil Rights Movement improved the lives of black Americans by referring to evidence such as:
   - campaign over Brown v Board of Education, Topeka led the Supreme Court to state that 'Separate but Equal' in education was unconstitutional
   - the Montgomery Bus Boycott led to the end of segregation on city buses
   - the movement helped bring about the Civil Rights Act 1957 which gave some legal support to black Americans seeking to register to vote
   - sit-ins led to the end of segregation at lunch counters
   - freedom rides contributed to the end of segregation on inter-state buses
   - the movement helped bring about the Civil Rights Act 1964 banned segregation in public areas/education/employment
   - Voting Rights Act 1965 banned obstacles to voter registration
   - Civil Rights Act 1968 provided protection for civil rights workers helping black people in the South.

2. The candidate evaluates the usefulness of the source by referring to evidence such as:

- a primary source said in 1963 during the Birmingham Civil Rights campaign
- said by John F Kennedy who was leader of the USA
- the President gives his view that something has to be done
- he says that the protest damaged the reputation of Birmingham and the USA/ highlights the need for equal treatment for all citizens.

Maximum of 1 mark for commenting on content omission such as:
- does not mention public sympathy for Civil Rights movement brought about by the events in Birmingham
- does not mention the mistreatment of black protesters
- television coverage became available.

3. The candidate explains why Stokely Carmichael opposed non-violent protest by referring to evidence such as:

from the source:
- non-violent movement could not relate to young blacks in the ghettos
- non-violence did nothing about the black people who had been killed or mistreated
- non-violence meant that black people had to accept being beaten again
- non-violence said that black people would get power by accepting mistreatment.

from recall:
- Carmichael wanted black people to stand up for/take pride in themselves
- he felt that black people had the right to defend themselves
- he felt non-violent protest was not bringing about change quickly enough
- he had been involved in the non-violent campaign but got fed up of being arrested and mistreated
- he felt that the non-violent protest had benefited the South but had little impact on the plight of poor black Americans in the North.

Context 12: The Road to War, 1933–1939

1. The candidate evaluates the usefulness of the source by referring to evidence such as:
- primary source from the period when the Nazis were in power
- from a school book intended to influence/school book introduced by the Nazis – likely to be biased
- to show that the Aryan race was superior/show that other races were inferior
- German blood defended Europe/spread German culture.

Maximum of 1 mark for commenting on content omission such as:
- Jews were also the target of Nazi racial policy
- others also targeted.

2. The candidate explains why Britain and France were worried about Germany's actions by 1936 by referring to evidence such as:

from the source:
- Germany withdrew from the Disarmament Conference
- Germany withdrew from the League of Nations
- German treaty with Poland meant that France lost an ally
- Germany announced the creation of an air force and navy.

from recall:
- Hitler announced the introduction of conscription
- Army to rise to 500,000 men
- Hitler tried to take over Austria in 1934
- Germany remilitarized the Rhineland in 1936.

3. The candidate describes the events that led to the takeover of Czechoslovakia by referring to evidence such as:
- Hitler ordered an attack on Czechoslovakia in May 1938 (Operation Green)
- Britain and France nearly declared war on Germany – the 'May Crisis'
- Nazi agitation in Sudetenland organised by Henlein
- the Runciman mission was sent to persuade Czechoslovakia to surrender the Sudetenland to Germany, but failed
- Hitler made a very anti-Czech speech in September
- first meeting: Hitler and Chamberlain met after a further threat to attack Czechoslovakia
- second meeting: agreement for Germany to gain Sudetenland was reached, but war became likely after further demands – 'Black Wednesday'
- third meeting: UK, France, Germany and Italy at Munich and Munich Settlement was reached
- in March 1939 Germany broke the settlement terms by invading the Czech areas
- Slovakia split away to form a separate 'puppet state'
- parts taken by Hungary and Romania.

Context 13: In the Shadow of the Bomb: The Cold War, 1945–1985

1. The candidate explains why there was a crisis in Berlin in 1961 by referring to evidence such as:

from the source:
- a new labour law preventing strikes had caused unrest in the factories
- there were shortages of food and higher prices
- there had been a massive increase of refugees fleeing to the West
- in the six months up to June 1961, 103,000 East Germans had fled through Berlin.

from recall:
- many people living in East Berlin saw that West Berlin was wealthier and had a more democratic society
- many East Germans were unhappy at being separated from friends and family in the West
- it was felt that Berlin was a centre for western spies
- the East German government took the decision to close the border between East and West Berlin and build a wall.

2. The candidate describes the ways people showed their opposition to the war in Vietnam by referring to evidence such as:
- many of those conscripted avoided enlisting by draft dodging
- many protestors burned their draft cards to demonstrate their opposition to the war
- students protested against President Johnson – slogans such as "Hey! Hey! LBJ. How many kids did you kill today?"
- large demonstrations against the war – often leading to violent clashes
- students held protests in many universities across the USA eg Kent State – often students occupied universities
- prominent figures such as Mohammed Ali, Martin Luther King spoke out against the war
- many musicians of the time wrote and performed anti-Vietnam songs
- Vietnam veterans spoke out against the war
- the media presented evidence of cruelty by American soldiers, war crimes such as the My Lai massacre, tactics of defoliation.

3. The candidate evaluates the usefulness of the source by referring to evidence such as:
   - primary source from 1976, at a time when the Soviet Union and the USA were involved in the process of détente
   - from a speech by Brezhnev, who was responsible for Soviet foreign policy/ relations with the USA at this time/likely to be biased
   - to show the Soviet Union was in favour of peace/was peace loving
   - states that we want peaceful co-existence/want to bring about lasting peace.

Maximum of 1 mark for commenting on content omission such as:
- the policy of détente came about as a response to economic problems in the Soviet Union
- Brezhnev's private stance was not consistent with public statements.

HISTORY INTERMEDIATE 2 2013

PART 1   THE SHORT ESSAY

Scottish and British

Context 1: Murder in the Cathedral: Crown, Church and People, 1154-1173

1. The candidate explains why the church was important in the twelfth century by referring to evidence such as:
   - the Church was a place of worship
   - the Church offered spiritual guidance on how to be a good Christian
   - the Church carried out important rituals eg baptism/ marriage/funerals
   - the Church had political power eg excommunication/ interdict
   - the Church had an impact on daily life eg decided holidays/no red meat on Fridays
   - the Church held its own court and enforced Canon Law
   - the Church was a place of education and was used to train boys who wished to become priests
   - the Church had economic significance and owned vast amounts of land

Context 2: Wallace, Bruce and the Wars of Independence, 1286-1328

2. The candidate explains why Scots had accepted Bruce as their king by 1328 by referring to evidence such as:
   - some Scots had always agreed he was their king/he had royal blood
   - he had driven the English out of Scotland
   - he had murdered the leading opponent – Comyn
   - he had the support of leading Scottish churchmen eg Wishart, Hamberton
   - early victories – Loudon Hill, Glentrool, Pass of Brander
   - captured castles – Linlithgow, Perth, Roxburgh,Edinburgh
   - he had won a great victory at Bannockburn
   - military success showed that God was on his side
   - he had made a peace treaty with England/gained recognition from England
   - he had destroyed the power/position of the Scottish enemies (eg herschips)
   - he had driven his Scottish enemies out of Scotland (the Disinherited)
   - he had forced other Scots to recognise his authority (eg the Earl of Ross)
   - he allowed former enemies to change their minds and even gave them their land back
   - he had gained international recognition as king – the Pope, the King of France etc

Context 3: Mary, Queen of Scots and the Scottish reformation. 1540s-1587

3. The candidate explains why Mary's marriage to Darnley led to her downfall in 1567 by referring to evidence such as:
   - Darnley was unpopular with many Scots whose advice against him she ignored
   - Most of Mary's trusted officials resigned and rebelled in protest against him (chaseabout Raid) which weakened her Government
   - Darnley showed himself to be lazy by not doing any government work (Mary used a stamp to replace him) which discredited Mary
   - Darnley made his discontent public (drinking/staying out) which discredited Mary

- Mary made use of new officials who were also unpopular (Riccio/ Bothwell) with other Scottish nobles
- Darnley became involved in the murder of Riccio – started a downward spiral of events
- Darnley refused to attend his son's baptism – raised further embarrassing issues
- Mary discussed divorce or alternatives to disposing of Darnley
- Darnley was murdered and Mary was assumed to be complicit
- Mary married Bothwell who was assumed to be the murderer which made her a co-conspirator
- Mary was blamed for having a relationship with Bothwell before Darnley's murder – made her morally unacceptable as a ruler

Context 4: The Coming of the Civil War, 1603-1642

4. The candidate explains why the reign of King James VI and I caused problems with the English Parliament between 1603 and 1625 by referring to evidence such as:
   - James was viewed by some as overgenerous to his favourites eg James gave between £60,000 and £80,000 on gifts to courtiers in the first ten years of his reign
   - James was viewed as extravagant by Parliament eg coronation cost £20,000
   - James was criticised for neglecting Parliament in favour of leisure pursuits
   - James' belief in the Divine Right of Kings offended some members of Parliament
   - arguments over finances between James and Parliament led to the failure of the Great Contract of 1610 and the dismissal of Parliament
   - the 'Addled Parliament' objected to impositions, which led to Parliament being dismissed again in 1614
   - quarrels over the sale of monopolies by the Crown
   - MPs anxious to ensure that the King understood the rights of the Commons presented James with the 'Apology to the House of Commons' in 1606, which asserted that their privileges were under threat
   - the Millenary petition of 1603 was presented to James requesting changes to practices in the Church of England, most were rejected
   - Archbishop Bancroft's Canons stated that the clergy had to subscribe to 39 articles and the Prayer Book. James licensed the Canons which provoked the clergy

Context 5: "Ane End of Ane Auld Sang": Scotland and the Treaty of Union, 1690s-1715

5. The candidate explains why support for the Jacobites had risen by 1715 by referring to evidence such as:
   - many Scots, loyal to the House of Stewart, felt that King James was their rightful King
   - Jacobites were anti-Union
   - there was resentment of new taxes – excise, malt tax
   - there was no immediate benefit from the Union eg. trade
   - Scots did not like the change of currency/measurements etc.
   - the Equivalent had not been paid as the Scots had expected
   - some felt that Mary/Anne had usurped their father's position and wanted to right that wrong
   - some did not like the new Hanoverian ruler/the "German lairdie"
   - some felt slighted by the new Government eg the Earl of Mar, "Bobbing John"

Context 6: Immigrants and Exiles: Scotland, 1830s-1930s

6. The candidate explains why many Scots who emigrated became successful in their new homelands by referring to evidence such as:
   - Scottish emigrants usually had a good level of education

- most Scots spoke English which helped them settle in the USA and countries of the Empire
- many Scots brought capital with them to start farms and businesses
- Scottish farmers were skilled at working more difficult land
- Scots had a reputation for hard work
- Scots founded many industries eg paper-making in New Zealand (credit examples such as wool/brewing/steel)
- money from Scottish banks was skilfully invested in business and industry
- Scottish emigrants helped each other by providing work and housing
- credit examples of successful Scots – Carnegie/Fisher etc.

Context 7: From the Cradle to the Grave? Social Welfare in Britain, 1890s-1951

7. The candidate explains why the Second World War changed attitudes towards government involvement in the welfare of its people by referring to evidence such as:
   - bombing destroyed rich/poor homes and the Government intervened to find shelter for the victims
   - bombing broke down barriers between middle and working classes eg bomb shelters, war work and people began to have more sympathy for each other
   - government assistance was no longer seen as shameful
   - evacuation exposed continuing poverty in cities and created desire for government action
   - rationing administered by Ministry of Food/supply was to ensure healthy diets for all
   - government took more responsibility for the nation's health eg free milk and vitamins/free immunisations against diphtheria (1941)
   - free medical care for those who were victims of war
   - local authorities were encouraged to provide school meals for all children of working mothers, not just the poor
   - the Government was interfering more in people's lives eg conscription, direction of labour
   - Beveridge Report produced in 1942 was well received by the public and encouraged government involvement in solving the problems of society
   - changing expectations of government involvement in easing the problems of society since everyone was suffering hardship

Context 8: Campaigning for Change: Social Change in Scotland, 1900s-1979

8. The candidate explains why standards of living fell for many Scots in the 1930s by referring to evidence such as:
   - high levels of unemployment (up to 50%)
   - overseas markets disappeared after the Wall Street Crash/Scotland depended on exporting its goods
   - collapse of traditional industries such as steel making/shipbuilding
   - many forced to leave Scotland to find work/factories relocated to England
   - Means Test/families split up
   - poor Scots economy could not provide market for new goods so few new factories opened
   - government action limited eg assistance limited to 'special areas'
   - few educational opportunities for working class children so little social mobility
   - poor/insufficient housing in cities/ overcrowded slums
   - poor/non-existent health care
   - poor standard of living/lack of progress for women

Context 9: A Time of Troubles: Ireland, 1900-1923

9. The candidate explains why the Easter Rising of 1916 failed by referring to evidence such as:
   - the rebels had a small army/few of their leaders were trained soldiers
   - the rebels were outnumbered by the British
   - the rebels failed to take over the city centre or capture Dublin Castle
   - the rebels were cut off/surrounded by the British
   - extra artillery was brought in by the British
   - the British drafted in 12,000 soldiers to fight
   - the British used a gunboat to shell the rebels' position
   - the majority of Dubliners did not know what was happening/did not support the rebels
   - many rebels were killed
   - Easter Rising leaders were executed

EUROPEAN AND WORLD

Context 1: The Norman Conquest, 1060-1153

10. The candidate explains why David I's reign has been described as the "Normanisation" of Scotland by referring to evidence such as:
    - Scotland was ruled by the Royal Council
    - knight service was introduced eg castle-guard
    - a feudal baronage was established in Scotland
    - introduction of sheriffs
    - influx of Norman families – eg the Bruces
    - use of knights in the royal army
    - building of castles
    - founding of monasteries
    - introduction of coinage
    - David gave land to his Norman friends
    - marriage between Normans and Scottish women

Context 2: The Cross and the Crescent: The First Crusade, 1096-1125

11. The candidate explains why the relationship between Emperor Alexius and the Crusaders was difficult by referring to evidence such as:
    - Bohemond and Alexius were suspicious of each other
    - Emperor Alexius and the Crusaders did not trust one another
    - Byzantine officers attacked the People's Crusade
    - the Crusaders believe Alexius was to blame for the failure of the People's Crusade
    - Alexius made the Crusaders wait outside Constantinople/would only allow them into the city in small numbers
    - Alexius made the Crusaders take an oath of loyalty eg made them promise to return any Byzantine land captured
    - Alexius let the Muslims inside Nicaea go free
    - Alexius did not let the Crusaders plunder Nicaea/kept the city for himself
    - Alexius did not help the Crusaders when they were surrounded at Antioch
    - the Crusaders did not keep their oath of loyalty eg Baldwin took Edessa/Bohemond took Antioch

Context 3: War, Death and Revolt in Medieval Europe, 1328-1436

12. The candidate explains why war broke out between England and France in 1337 by referring to evidence such as:
    - Edward III was an ambitious king with an eye on foreign conquest
    - the success of Edward's rule at home led him to seek success abroad

- French kings claimed overlordship of English possessions in France
- English had economic interests in France – wine/wool/grain
- English resented the continuing French alliance with Scotland
- English kings claimed the throne of France
- a dispute arose over the succession following the death of Charles IV in 1328
- French attacks were reported against English and Flemish merchants in the channel
- King Philip IV declared Edward III's lands in France forfeit
- King Philip IV's invasion of Gascony

Context 4: New Worlds: Europe in the Age of Expansion, 1480s-1530s

13. The candidate explains why the lives of Native Peoples in the New World were changed by the voyages of discovery by referring to evidence such as:
    - European diseases introduced/no immunity to European diseases which proved so deadly
    - whole populations wiped out eg in Hispaniola
    - defeated in battle/overthrow of native kings and leaders/new system of government by foreign rulers set up
    - native people no longer held positions of power or authority
    - enslavement of peoples by Spaniards/introduction of slaves from Africa by Portuguese
    - destruction of major cities/new European style cities developed eg Lima/Mexico City
    - native religions stamped out/forcible conversions to Christianity
    - riches/wealth of country taken overseas
    - native animals destroyed or driven away/new species eg sheep and horses introduced
    - traditional farming techniques abandoned/new crops/practices introduced
    - overthrow of native civilisations/ native traditions forgotten/ ignored eg calendar

Context 5: "Tea and Freedom": The American Revolution, 1763-1783

14. The candidate explains why the British had lost the war against the Americans by 1783 by referring to evidence such as:
    - the British forces were poorly led
    - tactical errors by Britain eg Yorktown/Saratoga
    - British army was small in number/had to rely on mercenary forces
    - British soldiers were not properly trained/equipped to cope with terrain and conditions
    - colonial army was led effectively by George Washington
    - British generals underestimated the bravery of the Americans
    - rebels tactics also made life very difficult/often used guerrilla tactics against the British
    - colonists had greater forces/able to call on Minutemen when required
    - fighting a war so far from home made it difficult to supply British forces
    - attacks by French and Spanish weakened/distracted British forces
    - assistance from French and Spanish Navies gave colonists control of the seas

Context 6: "This Accursed Trade": The British Slave Trade and its Abolition, 1770-1807

15. The candidate explains why the British Parliament voted to end the slave trade in 1807 by referring to evidence such as:
    - William Wilberforce had campaigned successfully inside Parliament
    - Wilberforce had won the support of influential people, such as former Prime Minister William Pitt
    - the Society for the Abolition of the Slave Trade had campaigned, with growing support for the previous 20 years
    - Thomas Clarkson had toured Britain, collecting evidence of the barbarities of the trade and shared his findings and evidence at public meetings
    - former slave Olaudah Equiano published an account of his experience as a slave
    - tactics such as petitions, public meetings, pamphlets, posters, Wedgwood's anti-slavery memorabilia won publicity and support among public and politicians
    - merchants, increasingly, regarded slavery as an inefficient way to produce goods
    - goods such as sugar could be produced more cheaply, without slaves, in places such as India
    - the industrial revolution meant that the slave trade was seen as less important to the British economy
    - Christians increasingly regarded the slave trade as evil
    - abolition could help Britain in its Naval War against France

Context 7: Citizens! The French Revolution, 1789-1794

16. The candidate explains why French peasants were angry before the revolution in 1789 by referring to evidence such as:
    - peasants had suffered from bad harvests and food shortages especially 1788
    - the price of food rose much faster than wages
    - peasants had to pay taxes such as the taille, vingtieme, gabelle
    - resented the nobility's exemption from most taxes
    - peasants resented the nobles' ownership of the land
    - peasants disliked having to use landowners mills and being under tight control
    - peasants had to pay a tithe to the church/resented church ownership of land
    - peasants were subject to the corvee – forced labour on road building/ repairs
    - peasants were forced to serve long periods in the army
    - the peasants had no political rights and felt the government was not helping them

Context 8: Cavour, Garibaldi and the Making of Italy, 1815-1870

17. The candidate explains why Italy had failed to become a united country before 1848 by referring to evidence such as:
    - 1815 Congress of Vienna had restored autocratic leaders of the Italian states
    - Italian states in the north were under Austrian domination
    - Metternich's role in controlling ideas of nationalism and liberalism eg suppression of 1821 and 1831 revolutions
    - strict censorship and secret police in most of the states stopped the spread of ideas
    - secret organisations such as the Carbonari were ineffective eg unclear in aims
    - Carbonari lacked mass support in the revolutions of 1821 and 1831
    - lack of clear objectives among the nationalist groups eg divisions over how a united Italy should be organised
    - much of the peasant populations of the Italian states were largely indifferent to nationalism
    - support for the nationalist cause was largely confined to the minority eg wealthy and educated classes
    - nationalist revolutionary groups were mostly parochial

Context 9: Iron and Blood? Bismarck and the Creation of the German Empire, 1815-1871

18. The candidate explains why the German states were united by 1871 by referring to evidence such as:
    - growth of cultural nationalism allowed the states to recognise similarities such as language, traditions and culture eg Grimm Brothers and Beethoven
    - growth of the Zollverein (customs union) between the German states allowed the states to prosper
    - growth of the Zollverein allowed Prussia to become economically dominant in Europe
    - growth of ideas such as liberalism and nationalism throughout the German states
    - restructuring of the Prussian army following reforms
    - annexation of Schleswig in 1865
    - Bismarck's diplomacy ensured French and Russian neutrality in the Austro-Prussian war of 1866
    - disputes over Schleswig and Holstein gave Prussia an opportunity to wage war on Austria for dominance over the German states
    - North German Confederation was formed after the Austro-Prussian war (Treaty of Prague) uniting the northern German states and creating a Kleindeutschland/little Germany
    - Bismarck used the Hohenzollern Candidature and the Ems telegram to provoke France into declaring war on Prussia
    - defeat of France united the Southern German states with the North

Context 10: The Red Flag: Lenin and the Russian Revolution, 1894-1921

19. The candidate explains why the First World War was important in causing the downfall of the Tsar by referring to evidence such as:
    - Tsar decided to take personal control of the army so was seen as responsible for defeats
    - heavy losses demoralised the army and soldiers became reluctant to fight for the Tsar/rising numbers of deserters
    - shortage of weapons and ammunition during World War One further demoralised troops
    - generals lost faith in the Tsar and encouraged him to abdicate
    - soldiers feared being sent to the front/took the side of the workers
    - Tsar went to the front and left the Tsarina in charge – she was not competent to take charge
    - peasants resented the loss of their sons in the fighting/loss of their animals to the army
    - poor medical treatment of the wounded caused bitterness
    - war effort devastated the economy leading to high inflation and unemployment
    - shortages of food and fuel in cities led to great discontent
    - workers demonstrated about shortages and working conditions
    - Tsarina allowed Rasputin to influence her decision making and sacked competent ministers
    - Tsarina was German and many people thought she was not fully loyal/she was a spy
    - Tsar wrongly believed Tsarina's reports rather than those of his government ministers
    - middle classes saw the government and the Tsar as incompetent

Context 11: Free at Last? Race Relations in the USA, 1918-1968

20. The candidate explains why there was a growing demand for civil rights between 1945 and 1965 by referring to evidence such as:
    * the groundwork for a civil rights movement had been laid by early reformers such as du Bois, Garvey and Washington
    * the experience of Black American servicemen during WWII had made them aware of non-segregated societies
    * during WWII, all Americans were called upon to fight for freedom and democracy, but Black Americans felt that they were denied their basic rights in their own country
    * success of Philip Randolph and the 'Double V' campaign
    * successes of early civil rights organisations such as CORE and NAACP
    * black people in the south living under a system of segregation
    * black people in the south were subjected to violent persecution – lynching
    * the KKK was still active in the southern states
    * success of non-violent protests – eg Montgomery Bus Boycott/ Birmingham march
    * inspirational leadership of black leaders such as Martin Luther King
    * successes of non-violent movement encouraged black people to demand more

Context 12: The Road to War, 1933-1939

21. The candidate explains why the events of 1939 caused the Second World War to break out by referring to evidence such as:
    * in March 1939, Germany invaded most of Czechoslovakia, breaking the Munich settlement of 1938
    * Slovakia broke away and became a pro-German 'puppet state'
    * Chamberlain/Great Britain and France decided to abandon the policy of appeasement (however, did not defend Czechoslovakia)
    * Hitler's demands to build a railway through the Polish corridor and the return of Danzig increased tension with Poland
    * Britain and France promised to defend Poland if she were attacked by Germany
    * Soviet Union/Russia attempted to reach an agreement with Britain to defend Poland but Britain refused
    * August 1939, Germany and Russia signed the Nazi-Soviet Non-Aggression Pact, agreeing not to go to war with each other so Germany was safe in the east
    * Soviet Union/Russia and Germany agreed to divide Poland between them
    * September 1, Germany invaded Poland and Britain gave Germany an ultimatum to stop the attack
    * Germany ignored the ultimatum and Britain and France declared war on her

Context 13: In the Shadow of the Bomb: The Cold War, 1945-1985

22. The candidate explains why a crisis had broken out over Cuba by 1962 by referring to evidence such as:
    * Castro had angered American businesses by nationalising key industries
    * Kennedy was looking for an opportunity to take revenge against Castro after the failure of the Bay of Pigs incident
    * Castro had angered America by forming an alliance with the Soviet Union
    * Castro agreed to site Soviet missiles on Cuba
    * US spy planes took photographs of missile bases being constructed on Cuba
    * Cuba was only a short distance from the American mainland
    * the Soviets refused to remove their missiles from Cuba
    * Soviet ships were sailing towards the American blockade around Cuba with additional missiles
    * President Kennedy was under huge pressure to stand up to communist aggression
    * American public opinion would not accept the presence of Soviet missiles on Cuba

Part 2 HISTORICAL STUDY

Scottish snd British

Context 1: Murder in the Cathedral: Crown, Church and People, 1154-1173

1. The candidate evaluates the usefulness of the source by referring to evidence such as:
   * primary source written during the reign of Henry II
   * official document issued by Henry II himself
   * to inform people about the laws/to frighten people
   * says accused will have to face the ordeal of water/if guilty will lose right hand and foot

   A maximum of one mark will be awarded for indicating content omission such as:
   * Henry introduced the Assize of Clarendon to deal with murder, robbery and theft
   * Henry introduced land laws eg the Assize of Recent Disposition/Mort d'Ancester

2. The candidate describes the use of castles in the twelfth century by referring to evidence such as:
   * castles used as a home by a lord/king
   * castles used as fortress/place of protection from attack
   * castles were symbols of power/status
   * castles used as barracks for knights performing guard duty
   * castles were administrative centres/headquarters of a village
   * castles were used as a court where local law was enforced
   * castles were used as a place of entertainment eg feasts
   * castles were used as a place to keep criminals/prisoners

3. The candidate explains why Henry II and Archbishop Becket quarrelled by referring to evidence such as:

   from the source:
   * Becket failed to appear at the Northampton trial
   * Henry humiliated Becket and confiscated his lands/Henry accused him of fraud/Henry charged him with contempt of court
   * Becket fled to France without Henry's permission
   * Becket appealed to the Pope/continued to defend the rights of the Church

   from recall:
   * Henry felt betrayed by the behaviour of his former close friend eg Becket resigned as Chancellor
   * Becket disagreed with Henry over the issue of Criminous Clerks
   * Becket refused to sign the Constitution of Clarendon
   * Henry asked the Archbishop of York to crown his son
   * Becket excommunicated the Archbishop of York and the bishops involved in the young Henry's coronation

Context 2: Wallace, Bruce and the Wars of Independence, 1286-1328

1. The candidate describes the events which allowed Edward I to interfere in Scotland between 1286-1292 by referring to evidence such as:
   * death of King Alexander III
   * the succession of Edward's great-niece, Margaret, the Maid of Norway

- the Guardians turned to Edward to strengthen their authority
- in the Treaty of Salisbury, Eric of Norway let Edward act to protect the Maid
- in the Treaty of Birgham, the marriage between the Maid and Edward's son was agreed
- the death of the Maid left Scotland without a clear heir
- Edward agreed to settle the succession
- Edward obliged the Scots to recognise him as overlord at Norham
- Edward was given direct control over Scotland at Norham
- Edward made King John Balliol do homage to him as his overlord
- Edward brought an army with him to Norham
- several nobles (Bruce, Balliol, Competitors) claimed the throne
- nobles began to gather armies
- Bishop Fraser wrote to Edward for help
- Bruce wrote to Edward for help

2. The candidate evaluates the usefulness of the source by referring to evidence such as:
- secondary source written many years after Bruce's reign
- written by a Scottish poet – likely to be biased – pro-Bruce/anti-Balliol
- to show Balliol should not have been chosen as king/was incompetent
- tells Balliol was made king because he agreed to obey Edward/how Balliol lost his crown

A maximum of one mark will be awarded for indicating content omission such as:
- King John Balliol was called "toom tabard"/sent to the Tower of London
- Bruce had also promised to obey Edward

3. The candidate explains why William Wallace resigned after the Battle of Falkirk by referring to evidence such as:

from the source:
- Wallace's victory at Stirling Bridge was the only reason he made it to the top/was made Guardian
- nobles resented him for stealing their traditional position of leadership
- Wallace had chosen a bad location to fight Edward
- jealousy/snobbery led them to withdraw from Falkirk

from recall:
- it was rare for a low-born person to rise up the ranks
- Wallace was a younger son of an obscure knight
- without the nobles (cavalry), Wallace was easier to defeat at Falkirk
- Wallace's use of schiltrons contributed to his defeat
- Wallace was thoroughly defeated at Falkirk and could not justify his position as Guardian

Context 3: Mary, Queen of Scots and the Scottish Reformation, 1540s-1587

1. The candidate explains why Cardinal Beaton was unpopular with Scottish Protestants by 1545 by referring to evidence such as:

from the source:
- he had persuaded Arran to give up Protestantism and return to the Catholic Church
- he had increased French influence in Scotland
- he had influenced Scots to cancel the Treaty of Greenwich
- he had helped confirm the Auld Alliance with France

from recall:
- he failed to protect Scotland from Henry VIII's invasion
- he persecuted Protestants in Scotland eg Wishart

- he upset Protestants by using church money to provide for his family
- he upset Protestants by being a pluralist (holding several jobs at once)

2. The candidate describes the events which led to Scotland becoming a Protestant country in 1560 by referring to evidence such as:
- Mary of Guise had clamped down on Protestants in Scotland
- Mary of Guise wanted to introduce a new tax in Scotland to pay for its government
- the Lords of the Congregation rebelled against Mary of Guise
- John Knox returned to Scotland and began preaching
- iconoclastic outrages took place eg in Perth
- there were disturbances on "Flitting Friday"/the date given by the Beggars' Summons
- French soldiers were called to Scotland
- English soldiers were sent to help the Lords of the Congregation
- during the peace conference, Mary of Guise died
- the Scottish Parliament was called and it made Scotland a Protestant country

3. The candidate evaluates the usefulness of the source by referring to evidence such as:
- secondary source written by a modern historian many years after Mary's reign
- the author will have researched his information
- to show that Mary's protestant critics had very strict religious views/disapproved of her frivolity
- it criticises Mary for dancing

A maximum one mark will be awarded for indicating content omission such as:
- Mary was criticised for keeping her Roman Catholic religion
- concern at possible French influence eg French nobles coming to Scotland

Context 4: The Coming of the Civil War, 1603-1642

1. The candidate describes the attempts made by Charles I to raise money between 1629 and 1640 by referring to evidence such as:
- selling monopolies
- extending the traditional ship's tax (previously levied only on coastal towns) to the whole countryside
- collection of tonnage and poundage without Parliament's consent
- forced loans
- sale of offices
- sale of royal lands
- forest fines, by which anyone living inside the fourteenth century boundaries of a royal forest was fined
- fining people if they did not accept knighthoods (as Knights had to provide loans to the crown)

2. The candidate explains why the religious policies of Charles I caused resentment in England and Scotland by referring to evidence such as:

from the source:
- decorative changes to services were opposed by Puritans who believed in simple services
- Puritans opposed stained-glass windows and Priests wearing decorated robes
- Puritans thought Laud's changes made the Church of England look too Catholic
- harsh treatment of a Puritan critic (William Prynne) gained more opposition for Charles

from recall:
- opposition to Charles' demands to the use of the New Prayer Book/riot in Edinburgh when it was introduced in 1637
- resentment at the Act of Revocation which demanded the return of church land taken since 1540
- resentment of Charles' coronation in Scotland which employed Anglican forms
- opposition to the introduction of Bishops into the Scottish Church

3. The candidate evaluates the usefulness of the source by referring to evidence such as:
- primary source written at the time of the Long Parliament
- part of the list of demands by MPs themselves/by those in opposition to the King
- to persuade Charles to make changes to the way he controlled Parliament
- MPs wanted advisers removed and put on trial/want Charles to stop dismissing parliament whenever he wants

A maximum of one mark will be awarded for indicating content omission such as:
- want Charles to get rid of Court of Star Chamber which he was using to lock up his opponents
- the hated Church of England reforms were to be reversed

Context 5: "Ane End of Ane Auld Sang": Scotland and the Treaty of Union 1690s-1715

1. The candidate evaluates the usefulness of the source by referring to evidence such as:
- secondary source written long after events
- the source would have been researched and should be accurate
- to explain why the Scottish economy was very weak at that time
- Scotland lost its money at Darien/ harvests were very poor

A maximum of one mark will be awarded for indicating content omission such as:
- Scotland's trade with Europe was being hampered by England's wars with France

2. The candidate describes the Succession Problem which Queen Anne wanted to solve before her death by referring to evidence such as:
- Queen Anne's children had all died/there was no direct heir
- only a Protestant heir would be acceptable for England and Scotland
- Queen Anne did not have any close Protestant relatives to succeed her
- Queen Anne's closest relative, her Catholic half-brother James (the Old Pretender), was not acceptable for religious reasons
- Queen Anne's closest Protestant relative was her second cousin, George, Elector of Hanover
- some people were wary of having someone so distantly related and unfamiliar with Britain as ruler
- Scots were threatening to choose a different Protestant heir for Scotland to end the "Union of the Crowns"
- Queen Anne was determined not to split her inheritance
- the Scots had no realistic alternative to the Hanoverians except, perhaps, the Duke of Hamilton

3. The candidate explains why there was so much opposition to the Union in Scottish burghs by referring to evidence such as:

from the source:
- surrender of Scotland's honour/auld animosity to England
- loss of wine trade with France
- fear of loss of custom from MPs and Lords after parliament moved to London

- Church of Scotland ministers feared for its future/preached against it

from recall:
- frightened of cheap English competition
- fears about new taxes on Scotland
- worried about the changes of money/weights, measures etc.
- fear for the survival of Scots law

Context 6: Immigrants and Exiles: Scotland, 1830s-1930s

1. The candidate describes the work done by Irish immigrants in Scotland by referring to evidence such as:
- Irish found seasonal employment on farms
- the cotton and textile factories of Lanarkshire provided employment
- linen and jute factories in Dundee provided work
- Irishmen worked on canal and railway building
- coal and iron ore mines in Lanarkshire, Ayrshire and Central Scotland
- there were jobs such as unskilled labouring and cart driving
- some Irish immigrants became street sellers or opened shops in the cities
- some opened pubs

2. The candidate explains why many Scots resented Irish immigrants by referring to evidence such as:

from the source:
- newspapers described Irish as being violent
- drunken navvies took control of Hamilton and terrified people
- blamed for taking most of the money available to the poor
- blamed for theft and burglary

from recall:
- most Irish immigrants were Catholic, most Scots were Protestant
- blamed for taking Scots jobs/depressing wages
- blamed for creating overcrowding in housing
- blamed for not fitting in to Scottish society

3. The candidate evaluates the usefulness of the source by referring to evidence such as:
- primary source from a time of large scale emigration from the Highlands
- the writer is reporting from personal experience – likely to be accurate
- to show that the landlord was helpful and generous/that people wanted to emigrate
- they let the landlord know what they needed in order to emigrate/their way was eased

A maximum of one mark will be awarded for indicating content omission such as:
- only a one-sided view – many landlords forced their tenants to leave
- the Clearances involved a great deal of cruelty

Context 7: From the Cradle to the Grave? Social Welfare in Britain, 1890s-1951

1. The candidate evaluates the usefulness of the source by referring to evidence such as:
- primary source produced at a time of extensive poverty in Britain
- Rowntree investigated the extent of poverty and published his findings
- to show the extent of the problem of poverty in the town of York
- there were overcrowded conditions/this affected standards of health

A maximum of one mark will be awarded for indicating content omission such as:
- low rates of pay/death of breadwinner
- large families/poor diets
- study only covered one industrial town, York/Booth studied poverty in London

2. The candidate describes the ways the Liberal government reforms of 1906-1914 failed to meet the needs of the people by referring to evidence such as:
- not all local authorities introduced free school meals at first
- medical inspections did not provide treatment (until school clinics in 1912)
- amount of old age pensions was not enough to prevent poverty
- pension age was set too high at 70
- health insurance only covered the worker and not their families/lasted only 13 weeks (at 10s, 5s weekly for next 13 weeks)
- unemployment insurance only covered certain industries
- no attempts were made to tackle poor housing
- no attempts to improve the education of the poor

3. The candidate explains why the Labour reforms of 1945-1951 were considered by many to be a success by referring to evidence such as:

from the source:
- there would be one single insurance payment/government improved the National Insurance system
- unemployment and sickness benefits helped the workers
- maternity and widows' benefits ensured that families were also covered
- National Assistance Act to help those not covered by the National Insurance scheme

from recall:
- 200,000 homes a year were built between 1945 and 1951
- prefabs were built/new towns were built
- unemployment was reduced to 2.5% by 1946
- free medical care was given to all resulting in a significant fall in the death rate
- the school leaving age was raised to 15, which made secondary education a reality for all

Context 8: Campaigning for Change: Social Change in Scotland, 1900s-1979

1. The candidate explains why Suffragette actions were important in getting women the vote by referring to evidence such as:

from the source:
- Suffragettes kept the campaign for votes for women in the news every other day
- put their own lives in danger so women could win the right to vote
- the dramatic death of Emily Davison had given the movement its first martyr and left no doubt about the Suffragettes' dedication
- their courage in prison continued to win them sympathy and admiration

from recall:
- publicity they attracted prevented the issue being ignored (despite importance of other situations eg Ireland/Germany)
- won support of many men eg dockers provided a bodyguard for Mrs Pankhurst in 1914
- won sympathy by enduring force feeding/forced the government to pass the Cat and Mouse Act to quieten public outrage

- agreed to stop the campaign to help the war effort, winning government support
- force feeding persuaded some women to join the WSPU

2. The candidate describes the ways job opportunities changed in Scotland after the Second World War by referring to evidence such as:
- development of new primary industries eg North Sea Oil/North Sea Gas/Nuclear power at Dounreay
- introduction of new light industries eg IBM/TVs/typewriters etc.
- expansion of public sector eg NHS/DHSS
- expansion of service sector eg banking/finance in Edinburgh/hospitality industry/ retail
- expansion of communications sector eg telecommunications/broadcasting
- increased opportunities for women workers/more part-time jobs available
- greater investment in Scotland enabled factories to set up
- new towns attracted electronics/research and development/NEL in East Kilbride
- improved transport/car ownership enabled commuting to work
- opening of car plant at Linwood/trucks at Bathgate
- fewer jobs in traditional industries/contraction of shipbuilding/steel/deep coal mining

3. The candidate evaluates the usefulness of the source by referring to evidence such as:
- primary source produced in 1935 when Scottish seaside holidays and day trips were popular
- postcard so taken by professional photographer – possible bias as form of advertising
- to show that Portobello is an attractive pleasure beach/place to holiday
- shows lots of holidaymakers enjoying the sea/shows funfair in the background as added attraction

A maximum of one mark will be awarded for indicating content omission such as:
- does not show the popularity of indoor activities such as cinema/ dancing/radio

Context 9: A Time of Troubles: Ireland, 1900-1923

1. The candidate explains why Unionists campaigned against Home Rule before 1914 by referring to evidence such as:

from the source:
- Home Rule threatened the Protestant way of life
- Unionists believed the Bill was part of a Catholic plot to take over Belfast
- Home Rule would lead to full independence for Ireland/separation from the United Kingdom
- Unionists wanted to keep Ireland part of the British Empire

from recall:
- believed that Home Rule meant Rome Rule
- feared interference from Dublin in business affairs
- feared the shipbuilding/linen industry would suffer
- feared loss of trade with Britain/Empire
- believed Ulster's prosperity would be lost when tied to poor rural Ireland
- believed Ulster would be isolated in Europe

2. The candidate describes the actions of both sides during the Anglo-Irish War of 1919-1921 by referring to evidence such as:
- IRA ambushed and killed police eg Soloheadbeg/Tipperary
- British Government banned Dail Eireann/Sinn Fein
- Ireland placed under curfew

- IRA used guerrilla tactics eg attacked isolated RIC barracks/stole weapons
- Black and Tans used stop and search tactics
- Lord Mayor of Cork murdered by RIC
- IRA set up spy network called "The Squad" who killed informers/detectives
- Bloody Sunday: IRA killed 11 government agents
- Black and Tans killed 12 civilians at Croke Park
- IRA massacred an Auxiliary unit near Cork
- Auxiliary unit burned Cork city centre

3. The candidate evaluates the usefulness of the source by referring to evidence such as:
   - primary source spoken at the end of the Civil War
   - Eamon De Valera was the leader of the Republican army and so would have taken the decision to end the war
   - to inform Republicans that the war had ended/to offer hope that they would one day fight again
   - says our army has been overrun/many of our soldiers are in prison or have been executed

   A maximum of one mark will be awarded for indicating content omission such as:
   - an amnesty was announced allowing Republicans to go free if they stopped fighting
   - Republican hard-line leader Liam Lynch was killed

European and World

Context 1: The Norman Conquest, 1060-1153

1. The candidate describes the methods William used to crush opposition to his rule in England by referring to evidence such as:
   - Saxon army was crushed at Hastings
   - building of castles across southern England as a base from which to crush rebellion
   - Tower of London built to deal with unrest in London
   - military expeditions – eg to the Godwinson strongholds in South west England
   - destruction of Saxon and Danish army at York 1069
   - William remained in occupation of the north through the winter of 1069
   - destruction of villages and farmland north of the Humber as a punishment for rebellion (Harrying of the North)
   - attack on rebel forces in South east England in 1070/Hereward the Wake's rebellion was crushed

2. The candidate compares the sources by referring to evidence such as:
   The sources fully agree

   Source A
   - William was able to extend his influence throughout England
   - people were made to swear an oath of loyalty to William
   - peasants were assumed to be too unimportant

   Source B
   - William was able to tighten his control over England
   - the baron would kneel before him and swear to be his man
   - the peasants were rated lowest in the feudal system

3. The candidate explains why David I encouraged the development of burghs in Scotland by referring to evidence such as:

   from the source:
   - the King shared in wealth from tolls and market dues
   - trade in the burghs helped the local economies
   - burghs also attracted foreign merchants to Scotland
   - annual fairs brought in more tolls

from recall:
- burghs encouraged trade in Scottish produce such as wool, skins and grain
- trade encouraged better relations with other countries
- justice was dispensed through burgh courts
- burgh walls provided a defence for the local population

Context 2: The Cross and the Crescent: The First Crusade, 1096-1125

1. The candidate compares the sources by referring to evidence such as:
   The sources fully agree

   Source A
   - Pope Urban II said Jerusalem must be recaptured
   - the Pope wanted to stop Christian churches from being destroyed
   - the Pope wanted to stop knights fighting amongst themselves

   Source B
   - the Pope encouraged Christians to reclaim Jerusalem any way they could
   - the Pope said he would not rest until every Christian church in the East was protected
   - the Pope told knights they must end their bad behaviour

2. The candidate describes the problems faced by the People's Crusade on their journey to Jerusalem by referring to evidence such as:
   - the People's Crusade had little military experience/few weapons/was ill-disciplined
   - Peter the Hermit was a good spiritual leader but a poor military one
   - the People's Crusade was unprepared and quickly ran out of food and money
   - attacks on local people and the Jewish community earned them a poor reputation/made people unwilling to help them
   - the People's Crusade attacked the local people in Belgrade/some Crusaders were killed in the fighting
   - the Byzantine army attacked the People's Crusade at Nish/heavy casualties/Peter the Hermit's supplies lost
   - the People's Crusade argued amongst themselves and divided into separate groups/Peter the Hermit was no longer the recognised leader
   - the People's Crusade was massacred at Civetot by the Turks

3. The candidate explains why the Crusaders were able to keep control of the Latin States after 1099 by referring to evidence such as:

   from the source:
   - Godfrey of Bouillon was a strong and able Crusader/re-organised the army and prepared them for battle
   - the Crusaders defeated the advancing Muslim army
   - they extended their territory in the East/were able to push their enemies back
   - Godfrey built castles to protect the land

   from recall:
   - the Crusaders recruited specialised knights to help them defend the Latin States eg Knights Templars/Hospitallers
   - the Crusaders negotiated with Muslim peasants ensuring that there was a supply of crops for the Latin States
   - the Crusaders established the feudal system in the East ensuring each knight fulfilled his duty to fight/carry out castle guard
   - the Crusaders established trade links with Italian cities ensuring a supply of material and resources was sent East
   - Italians set up trading stations/paid taxes to Crusaders

Context 3: War, Death and Revolt in Medieval Europe, 1328-1436

1. The candidate explains why the English were successful at the Battle of Poitiers by referring to evidence such as:

   from the source:
   - effectiveness of English archers firing from cover
   - led to panic in the French army/caused many to flee
   - skill of the Black Prince in keeping reinforcements/stopping King John's attempt to outflank him
   - Black Prince cut King John off from rest of his army

   from recall:
   - the French delayed their attack for a day to attempt to negotiate a truce allowing the English to consolidate their position
   - the English army positioned itself on high ground
   - the French were lured into the first attack due to feint by English knights
   - English archers had 'bodkin' arrows which could pierce plate armour
   - King John was forced to surrender

2. The candidate describes the effects of the Black Death on England by referring to evidence such as:
   - terror caused by the spread of a mysterious illness with no reliable cure
   - around one third of the population died
   - entire villages left deserted
   - severe disruption caused to agriculture due to labour shortages
   - labour shortages led to a rise in wages
   - worsening relations between peasants and landowners
   - rising crime
   - some peasants left the land that they were previously tied to
   - people began to question the teachings of the Church

3. The candidate compares the sources by referring to evidence such as:
   The sources fully agree

   Source B
   - Joan of Arc led the French armies to victory
   - the end of their long and bitter civil war meant that the French now had greater unity
   - French leaders adopted new methods of fighting

   Source C
   - Joan of Arc played a vital role by inspiring the army to victory
   - the Burgundians made peace with the French King ending the feud which had divided France
   - the French built a more efficient, tactical army

Context 4: New Worlds: Europe in the Age of Expansion, 1480s-1530s

1. The candidate explains why explorers went on voyages of discovery by referring to evidence such as:

   from the source:
   - some wanted to become famous
   - there was a great desire to know more about the world
   - some believed it was their Christian duty to spread their faith
   - explorers could become very rich

   from recall:
   - find new sources of spices and luxury goods
   - find and claim new lands for their country
   - find new trade routes avoiding Arab taxes
   - rising population in Europe – looking for opportunities elsewhere
   - improved naval technology/improved navigation techniques enabled longer voyages

2. The candidate compares the sources by referring to evidence such as:
   The sources agree

   Source B
   - crews threatened mutiny
   - Columbus pretended they had travelled a shorter distance than they had to reassure them
   - the Pinta set off on its own and the Santa Maria ran aground

   Source C
   - a mutiny broke out
   - Magellan did not tell the fleet their destination as he knew this long journey would terrify them
   - one ship sank and another disobeyed and returned to Spain

3. The candidate describes the voyage of Vasco da Gama in 1497 by referring to evidence such as:
   - sailed from Lisbon with four ships
   - sailed into South Atlantic out of sight of land/towards the coast of Brazil
   - rounded Cape of Good Hope using Dias's route
   - sailed up east coast of Africa
   - landed in Malindi and took on an experienced pilot
   - sailed to Calicut in India
   - traded and acquired a cargo of spices for gold
   - lost two ships and half his men
   - successfully found the sea route to India
   - voyage made a huge profit (6,000%)
   - underestimated the sophistication of the king/civilisation in Calicut/ thought the Hindus were Christians/treated native peoples harshly/soured relations
   - Portuguese became dominant European sea power in the Indian Ocean
   - broke the Venetian monopoly
   - da Gama became personally wealthy

Context 5: "Tea and Freedom": The American Revolution, 1763-1783

1. The candidate compares the sources by referring to evidence such as:
   The sources fully agree

   Source A
   - many colonists regarded taxes as unfair as they were not represented in the British parliament
   - colonists were furious with the passing of the Stamp Act in 1765
   - killing of colonists by British soldiers in Boston reported as a brutal massacre

   Source B
   - colonists were unhappy about 'no taxation without representation'
   - the Stamp Act produced a furious storm of protest
   - the shooting of five protestors was portrayed as a terrible crime by the British

2. The candidate describes what happened at Lexington and Concord in 1775 by referring to evidence such as:
   - the British believed that the American militia had an arms store at Concord and set off to destroy it
   - spies had warned of the British Army's movement and counter-attack was launched at Concord
   - militia in Massachusetts had been training/preparing for war
   - British soldiers were confronted by a group of 'Minutemen' at Lexington
   - a number of Minutemen were killed
   - at Concord, the British did not find the weapons
   - the British were attacked by a larger force at Concord and many Redcoats were killed
   - the British soldiers were fired at all the way back to Boston

3. The candidate explains why some British people sympathised with America in the Wars of Independence by referring to evidence such as:

from the source:
- many people supported the view of Thomas Paine that Britain was abusing the rights of the American people
- Paine's ideas were very popular/150,000 copies were sold
- the King's rejection of the Olive Branch petition angered radicals in Britain
- the news that Britain was using mercenaries from Germany led some people in Britain to question the point of the war

from recall:
- radicals in Britain opposed the war and supported many of the Americans demands for reform
- radicals in Britain argued that British rule was hindering the economic development of the colonies
- Edmund Burke argued against taxing the Americans to raise money for Britain
- Edmund Burke argued force would never succeed in gaining authority over the American colonists
- William Pitt argued in Parliament that measures such as the Stamp Act were unfair on the colonists

Context 6: "This Accursed Trade": The British Slave Trade and its Abolition, 1770-1807

1. The candidate explains why the slave trade was important to many British cities by referring to evidence such as:

from the source:
- Liverpool profited directly from the transportation of human beings as slaves
- Glasgow had the largest share of the British tobacco trade and this helped the city's economic development
- profits from the tobacco trade also contributed to the development of industry in Glasgow
- Bristol merchants profited from the sugar trade

from recall:
- involvement in the slave trade provided employment in port cities
- the slave trade provided work for sailors
- involvement in the slave trade helped the population growth of cities
- the profits linked to the slave trade contributed to the wider economy and infrastructure of cities
- the products of the slave trade – cotton/tobacco/sugar – were in great demand

2. The candidate compares the sources by referring to evidence such as:
The sources fully agree

Source B
- armed raiders attacked African villages and seized as many men, women and children as possible
- the Africans left their villages and took to the forests to hide as soon as they saw the ship
- Europeans began to buy slaves from their African masters

Source C
- raiding and kidnapping spread terror deep into Africa
- frightened villagers, trying to escape the raiders, moved into remote areas
- the kings and chiefs of the African tribes became trading partners with European merchants and swapped their people for European goods

3. The candidate describes the ways in which slaves were prepared and sold in the West Indies by referring to evidence such as:
- slaves were prepared for sale by having oil rubbed into their body to improve the appearance of their skin
- tar was used to cover or disguise wounds
- hair was shaved to make the slaves look younger
- slaves were inspected by potential buyers/slaves were often inspected as though they are animals
- slaves were often paraded naked
- slaves were sold to the highest bidder
- sometimes the auction took the form of a scramble
- families were often split up during the auction process
- slaves were often branded by their new owner following the auction

Context 7: Citizens! The French Revolution, 1789-1794

1. The candidate describes the events of July 1789 which led to the attack on the Bastille by referring to evidence such as:
- riots broke out when Necker, a popular minister, was sacked by the king
- more riots broke out in Paris as food prices rose to an all-time high
- the soldiers refused to fire on the rioters/mob and joined them
- government weapons stores were attacked therefore many of the mob were armed
- rumours spread that the Bastille fortress held many political prisoners
- the Bastille garrison refused to give in and pointed cannon on working class areas of Paris
- the mob decided to capture the Bastille to take weapons stored there and release the prisoners

2. The candidate explains why many French people were unhappy with the results of the Revolution by 1792 by referring to evidence such as:

from the source:
- the Revolution benefited the middle class
- only the middle class had the right to vote for the Assembly
- only the wealthy could elect Assembly members
- it was easy for the nobles to buy Church lands

from recall:
- most working men and artisans were declared "passive citizens"/could not vote
- ordinary citizens could not join the National Guard
- nobility were to be compensated for loss of feudal rights
- workshops for the unemployed were closed
- many were unhappy with the treatment of the Catholic Church
- many still supported the monarchy

3. The candidate compares the sources by referring to evidence such as:
The sources agree

Source B
- to protect the gains of the Revolution
- trials and punishments are fair
- the members believe in perfect justice

Source C
- the great achievements of the Resolution are saved
- the Committee created the fairest system of justice ever known
- innocent citizens are protected from false accusations

Context 8: Cavour, Garibaldi and the Making of Italy, 1815-1870

1. The candidate compares the sources by referring to evidence such as:
    The sources agree

    Source A
    - each revolution had very different aims/revolutionaries failed to work together
    - Austria quickly defeated its own revolutions which was decisive in halting those in Italy
    - leadership of General Radetzky was superior to that of Charles Albert

    Source B
    - Italian revolutionaries failed to unite in a common aim/could not fully co-operate
    - Austria recovered quickly from its revolutions which allowed them to control the Italian revolutions
    - Austrian forces were better led

2. The candidate explains why Cavour was important to Italian unification by referring to evidence such as:

    from the source:
    - he developed Piedmont into a modern industrial state
    - Piedmont became the richest Italian state which eventually dominated the rest of Italy
    - he provoked Austria into starting the war of 1859
    - he secured an alliance with France to support the war with Austria

    from recall:
    - modernised the Piedmontese armed forces
    - encouraged the National Society in Sardinia to look to Piedmont for leadership
    - persuaded Victor Emmanuel to advance into the Papal States to prevent Garibaldi from taking Rome
    - expanded Piedmont in the North, central and Papal States

3. The candidate describes Garibaldi's contribution to Italian unification by referring to evidence such as:
    - he initially supported the aims of Mazzini's 'Young Italy' to unite states in a democratic republic
    - he defended Rome against the French in 1849
    - was a member of the nationalist society from 1857
    - led 'The Thousand' and sailed to Sicily in 1860
    - conceded his conquests to Victor Emmanuel at Teano in 1860
    - was a successful military leader who inspired the Red-shirts to victories, often against strong opposition
    - was hugely popular with the peasants
    - he used the peasant disturbances in Sicily to unite the north and south

Context 9: Iron and Blood? Bismarck and the Creation of the German Empire, 1815-1871

1. The candidate explains why the ideas of liberalism and nationalism failed to spread in Germany after 1815 by referring to evidence such as:

    from the source:
    - German Princes were allowed to hold on to their power which upset liberals and nationalists
    - ideas of liberalism and nationalism only appealed to a minority of educated people
    - Carlsbad Decrees outlawed the student movement
    - Carlsbad Decrees regulated universities so that liberal ideas could not spread

    from recall:
    - student unions were abolished in order to stop ideas spreading
    - newspapers and periodicals were censored to stop ideas spreading
    - students expelled from one university for spreading ideas could not go to another university
    - university teachers who encouraged liberalist and nationalist ideas were dismissed

2. The candidate describes the revolutions which began in Germany in 1848 by referring to evidence such as:
    - some demonstrators were killed when King Frederick William IV called troops in to disperse them
    - demonstrators built barricades
    - 300 demonstrators were killed after several days of fighting
    - King Frederick William changed his mind and agreed to give in to the demands of the demonstrators
    - King Frederick William agreed to call a National Assembly which would meet in Frankfurt in May 1848
    - Frankfurt Parliament took almost a year to decide on a constitution
    - Frankfurt Parliament failed to agree on what would be included in a united Germany (Grossdeutschland/Kleindeutschland argument)
    - King Frederick William refused to accept the invitation to become king
    - Frankfurt Parliament failed

3. The candidate compares the sources by referring to evidence such as:
    The sources agree

    Source B
    - gained a powerful hold over the king by force of his personality and powers of persuasion
    - Parliament annoyed at Bismarck's tactics of maintaining royal authority over Parliament
    - in 1863 Parliament declared that it could no longer work with Bismarck

    Source C
    - Bismarck gained influence over the king due to his strong personality
    - Parliament objected to Bismarck's methods of ensuring royal authority was upheld
    - in 1863 Parliament informed the king they were not willing to deal with Bismarck

Context 10: The Red Flag: Lenin and the Russian Revolution, 1894-1921

1. The candidate explains why the Orthodox Church was important in maintaining the Tsar's rule by referring to evidence such as:

    from the source:
    - the Church taught the people to be loyal to the Tsar
    - Tsar himself, as head of the Orthodox Church, appointed its chief bishops
    - the Holy Synod was a government department
    - the Church had influence, power and wealth

    from recall:
    - most people were religious so obeyed the Church
    - the Church taught that the Tsar was appointed by God/was their 'Little Father'
    - taught peasants that their poverty was the will of God/they should not complain/kept the peasants poor/quiet/helped keep the aristocracy in power
    - supported the policy of Russification

2. The candidate compares the sources by referring to evidence such as:
The sources mainly agree

Source B
- Duma was never intended to represent workers and peasants
- Tsar appointed Ministers
- Tsar could simply dismiss the Duma if it displeased him

Source C
- very few of the lower classes ever voted
- Tsar had chosen Stolypin as Prime Minister
- Tsar dissolved the first Duma after 10 weeks as it upset him

3. The candidate describes the weaknesses of the Whites in the Civil War by referring to evidence such as:
- White forces were split/never united their full strength
- White forces were fighting for different aims
- White forces could not communicate with each other
- White Generals did not co-ordinate their attacks/strategy
- Whites did not have enough men/too many officers
- Whites held peripheral areas/did not control the industrial centre
- Whites did not control rail networks
- Whites did not control factories
- Whites had difficulty getting food from peasants
- Whites were poor administrators
- many White officers were corrupt/decadent
- peasants thought Whites would take away the land they had gained
- areas such as the Baltic states and the Don resisted helping the Whites

Context 11: Free at Last? Race Relations in the USA, 1918-1968

1. The candidate compares the sources by referring to evidence such as:
The sources agree

Source A
- immigrants headed for the great cities
- few wanted to stay in the United States for long
- crime served as a ladder for upward mobility
- little formal education

Source B
- my family lived in Chicago
- Father wanted to return to Italy
- author committed crime with an older gang who were living a better life
- I started dodging school

2. The candidate describes the effects of the Jim Crow laws on Black Americans in the 1920s and 1930s by referring to evidence such as:
- created a segregated society/enforce segregation between Black and White people
- some states made relationships/marriage between races illegal
- separate schooling was enforced
- separate toilets and washrooms
- transport facilities were segregated
- Supreme Court decision in 1896 Plessey case fixed 'separate but equal' in law
- facilities made available to Blacks were of an inferior standard
- Black Americans were humiliated

3. The candidate explains why there was a split in the Civil Rights movement in the mid-1960s by referring to evidence such as:

from the source:
- some felt that the injury and loss of life did not justify the gains made by non-violent protest
- some were frustrated by the slow pace of change
- some were influenced by new leader/leaders who promised a better future for the northern ghettos
- some resented the way that Black people were bullied by the police

- **from recall:**
- some supported a more violent campaign/rejected non-violence
- some felt that the movement concentrated too much on Civil Rights in the South
- some rejected integration in favour of separatism
- some supported groups who offered new solutions to problems faced by Black people eg Nation of Islam/Black Panthers
- some felt that more had to be done to help Black people who faced poverty

Context 12: The Road to War, 1933-1939

1. The candidate compares the sources by referring to evidence such as:
The sources agree

Source A
- differences between the races was scientific fact
- Aryan people of northern Europe were superior in every way
- it was logical that people like this should control other races

Source B
- biological research had shown that there was a distinction between races
- Aryans of Germany and Scandinavia were the Master Race
- this gave them authority to rule over the other peoples of the world

2. The candidate describes Hitler's plans for Germany after 1933 by referring to evidence such as:
- to restore German power by breaking the treaty of Versailles
- to build up the German army
- to create a German air force
- to regain the lands given to Poland
- to remilitarise the Rhineland
- to unite all Germans and create a Greater Germany eg Austria/the Sudetenland
- to gain 'living space' in Eastern Europe for the German people
- to defeat Communism

3. The candidate explains why Britain followed a policy of Appeasement in the 1930s by referring to evidence such as:

from the source:
- many people felt that the Treaty had been unfair
- large sections of the population were against war
- there was fear of bombing from the air
- the Prime Minister thought Hitler could be persuaded to keep the peace

from recall:
- Chiefs of Staff warned the government that British forces were unprepared
- Britain had no reliable allies – Empire unwilling, France was not trusted and USA was isolationist
- the Great Depression meant there was no money for rearmament
- communist Russia was the real threat to peace

Context 13: In the Shadow of the Bomb: The Cold War, 1945-1985

1. The candidate compares the sources by referring to evidence such as:
    The sources fully agree

    Source A
    • as soon as the war ended a climate of suspicion developed
    • Soviet and American leaders held opposing ideological views
    • America's decision to use the atomic bomb against Japan placed further strain on relations

    Source B
    • the Soviet Union and the Americans developed open hostility towards each other
    • there were ideological divisions between both sides
    • tension was increased by America's use of the atomic bomb against Japan

2. The candidate describes the tactics used by the USA in the Vietnam War by referring to evidence such as:
    • the Americans rapidly increased troops on the ground
    • half a million US soldiers were in Vietnam by 1969
    • the US used conscripts on short tours of duty in Vietnam
    • the Americans used modern technology against their enemy – machine guns/long range bombers/helicopters/war ships
    • bombing raids were widely used against strategic targets in North Vietnam – factories/railways/bridges
    • the Americans tried to disrupt supply routes/the Ho Chi Minh Trail
    • the Americans used chemical weapons to destroy the forest/defoliation to allow them to see their enemy more clearly
    • the Americans used strategic hamlets to control the population of South Vietnam
    • tried to win hearts and minds

3. The candidate explains why relations between the superpowers improved in the 1970s by referring to evidence such as:

    from the source:
    • President Nixon began to withdraw troops from Vietnam/peace in Vietnam had a positive influence on superpower relations
    • President Nixon and Carter enjoyed the increased popularity they won as peace-makers
    • Brezhnev welcomed improved relations with America because he recognised the perils of all-out nuclear war
    • peace with America also left him free to concentrate on problems within the Soviet Union

    from recall:
    • Soviets and Americans had reached parity in the arms race and both had a surplus of weapons
    • both countries had economic difficulties and were keen to reduce spending on the military
    • President Nixon's visit to Moscow in 1974 helped to reduce tension
    • Soviets and Americans cooperated on a joint Soyuz – Apollo space mission in 1975
    • both sides were able to reach agreement to limit or reduce nuclear weapons
    • increased trade between both sides helped to improve relations